Resumes For Dummies,® 3rd Edition

W9-AVI-527

JOBHUNT ORGANIZER

GETTING READY

Write resumes & cover letters
Choose and research employers
Scout printed and online job ads
Mouse the Internet for job sites

GOING PLACES

Ace job interviews
Be visible at networking meetings
Visit libraries & career centers
Sleuth job fairs
Join job hunt support groups

TARGETING PEOPLE

Reach employers & recruiters
Contact your contacts
Network on the Internet
Call job services and hotlines
Stay in touch with references

FOLLOWING UP

E-mail or postal mail interview thank-you letters
E-mail or postal mail networking contact letters
Stay in touch with employers
Work out, chill out, cheer up
Repeat job hunting actions until employed

Ready! -- Do First ◆◆

Yesterday ❑ _____ ❑ _____
 ❑ _____ ❑ _____
 ❑ _____ ❑ _____
This Week ❑ _____ ❑ _____
 ❑ _____ ❑ _____

Aim! -- Grab the Phone, Surf the Net ◆◆◆◆◆◆◆◆◆◆◆◆◆◆◆◆◆◆◆◆◆◆◆◆◆◆◆

Yesterday ❑ _____ ❑ _____
 ❑ _____ ❑ _____
 ❑ _____ ❑ _____
This Week ❑ _____ ❑ _____
 ❑ _____ ❑ _____

Fire! -- Beat the Pavement ◆◆◆◆◆◆◆◆◆◆◆◆◆◆◆◆◆◆◆◆◆◆◆◆◆◆◆◆◆◆◆◆◆◆

Yesterday ❑ _____ ❑ _____
 ❑ _____ ❑ _____
 ❑ _____ ❑ _____
This Week ❑ _____ ❑ _____
 ❑ _____ ❑ _____

Sizzle! -- Keep It Hot ◆◆◆◆◆◆◆◆◆◆◆◆◆◆◆◆◆◆◆◆◆◆◆◆◆◆◆◆◆◆◆◆◆◆◆◆◆◆

Yesterday ❑ _____ ❑ _____
 ❑ _____ ❑ _____
 ❑ _____ ❑ _____
This Week ❑ _____ ❑ _____
 ❑ _____ ❑ _____

For Dummies™: Bestselling Book Series for Beginners

Resumes For Dummies, 3rd Edition

Resumes New Millennium Style

- ✔ Use print and online leads to source jobs. Work e-mail creatively into your job search.
- ✔ Discover useful online job sites: national, local, career field. See Chapter 14. Some addresses for national sites: www.joboptions.com; careerpath.com; monster.com; careerbuilder.com; careermosaic.com; headhunter.com; hotjobs.com; www.nationjob.com.
- ✔ Get a free e-mail address from Hotmail (www.hotmail.com) or Yahoo!Mail (www.yahoomail.com). The free Juno e-mail (www.juno.com) doesn't even require a Net connection, just a modem.
- ✔ Passive job-hunters can use smart-agent technology, sit back, and be e-mailed appropriate job openings.
- ✔ Use the right resume KeyWords to be picked from the crowd.
- ✔ Send most digital resumes in plain text (ASCII) inside the body of your e-mail. Forgo attachments.

Your Brisk Resume Review

Find the full, industrial strength FirstRate Resume Checklist in Chapter 27. As a quick check, ask yourself

- ✔ Have I selected the best format for my situation?
- ✔ Is my resume focused, with a theme backed up by examples of my qualifications?
- ✔ Does my resume illustrate to an employer the benefits of interviewing me — how I can handle the job, have positive work attitudes, get along well with others?
- ✔ Does my resume stress my accomplishments and skills?
- ✔ Does my resume contain negative information?
- ✔ Are all my claims believable, backed up by examples and measurable results?
- ✔ *Paper resumes:* Is mine inviting to read with good layout, adequate white space, professional-like word processing and laser printing? *Digital resumes*: Does mine have adequate KeyWords and wide margins?

Resume Do's

- ✔ Research, research, research — know what skills, education, and experience you need for the job.
- ✔ Include a Job Objective or Skills Summary targeted to the job you want.
- ✔ Use white paper, standard typefaces, and lots of white space to create a computer-friendly, searchable resume.
- ✔ Use the correct name, title, and address of your resume recipient.

IDG BOOKS WORLDWIDE

For Dummies™: Bestselling Book Series for Beginners

Praise, Praise, Praise for Joyce Lain Kennedy's For Dummies Books

"I just wanted to thank you for writing the wonderful book *Resumes For Dummies*. I am changing careers in the near future (as soon as I find a job) and this book is helping me out immensely in rewriting my resume. I have used numerous resources in identifying my resume needs and find this book to be the best — the most useful tool. Thanks again."

— Mohammed Fares, Rockville, Md.

"*Resumes For Dummies* is an all-purpose, content-filled resume book that has enough humor to focus your interest on what is a very serious matter: You as a marketable product. One chapter (Chapter 3) stood out for me. It clarifies the use of hooks — when to use an objective and when to use a skills summary, citing advantages and disadvantages of each. I also liked the detailed chart on updating your resume for scanning technology and for sending it online. A very timely read!"

— Patricia S. Pigg, Florissant, Mo.

"My sister Peggy recommended I read *Job Interviews For Dummies*. The night before my interview, I reread several chapters and also took it with me in the car and refreshed myself before the interview. The interview went great. One of the things that Ms. Kennedy mentions in her book that attracted my attention was "You have the determination, the willingness to work hard, and the quick-learning skills to make up for any lack of experience." I walked into that interview with my head held high — and got the job. I believe in Joyce Lain Kennedy's wisdom."

— Julie Beecroft, Portland, Ore.

"Joyce Lain Kennedy: I love your books. Because I used a cover letter that you suggested, I got my job. You mean a lot to my career."

— Pilar Mendiola Fernandez, Washington, D.C.

"Dear Joyce: I just finished your book *Cover Letters For Dummies*. It was terrific. I laughed and I cried when I saw some of my writing habits as the things not to do."

— Gretchen Nordby, Leesburg, Va.

"Joyce's book *Job Interviews For Dummies* is out and I think it's terrific! Joyce's job-interview directions should get you on an employer's Top Choice list every time."

— Jack Chapman, Wilmette, Ill.

"I borrowed a copy of *Job Interviews For Dummies* from the public library. After reading the book, I am now willing to invest in a personal copy for myself. It is an excellent book and I think you did such a fabulous job with presentations that now I actually look forward to job interviews."

— Sherry Akbar, Brampton, Ontario

"I never thought writing resumes could be fun and easy! *Resumes For Dummies* shows many magic formulas to create unbeatable resumes that get interviews! Highly recommended by the Professional Association of Resume writers, it is a must reference for all pro writers."

— Paul Chin, Papua, New Guinea

"Wow! *Resumes For Dummies* is a great resource. Since it has been 15 years since I wrote my last resume, I was at a definite loss as to where to begin — this book was the perfect resource for creating my resume. I really like the Web-oriented resume information. Now I need to get *Cover Letters For Dummies* and *Job Interviews For Dummies*."

— Tracy Pipkin, Houston, Tex.

"Thank you so much for *Resumes For Dummies*. Chapters 12 and 13 have become the two most valuable chapters of information in my life. I am currently relocating from Portland, Oregon to Tampa, Florida. I can not imagine trying to do this little feat without the help of the Internet. Your help in preparing a digital resume and your listing of job sites is invaluable. The resume that I've been posting looks great, the content is mine, but the display is a result of you! Again, thank you very much."

— Lisa Johnson, Tampa, Fla.

"I have read *Resumes For Dummies* with joy, laughter, and a deep sense of gratitude. What a godsend you are to those of us who are resuming a career. Thanks for you gifted advice."

— Carol Treadwell, San Diego, Calif.

"I'm an engineering/computer science college senior and have had several internships in college. For my last interview I prepared by reading Joyce's *Job Interviews For Dummies*. It is spectacular! I thought I knew how to interview but now I know how much I didn't know — from making a "commercial" about myself, gathering information on companies, telling about my strong points, and negotiating my salary. Thank you, thank you. This book is THE interviewing book!"

— Carole Beaudoin, Tottenham, Ontario

"Take it from an insurance guy: *Resumes For Dummies* Is the job insurance of the new millennium."

— Al Ferrari, St. Louis, Mo.

"I'm writing to show my appreciation to your book *Job Interviews For Dummies*. I had been working for a company for 5 years and being retrenched due to the bad economy condition in Asia countries.

Being through several job interviews but in vain, I was totally depressed and eager to know what was the problem. After finished reading your book, I realized that I had made several mistakes during job interviews. I decided to follow your guidance for my last job interview. And what happened, I got the job offer and the pay was (equivalent to) my last drawn salary."

Thank you for your book for giving me confidence and guidance."

— Lim Lie Ching, Singapore

"I love *Resumes For Dummies*! It's my job search bible."

— Bonnie J. Mclurg, Mayfield, Ohio

"I really did love *Job Interviews For Dummies*. It was the first book that actually taught me how to answer specific questions. It was VERY valuable in my job search process. I have a lot of experience, but was always lacking in interview skills. (I would get really nervous before and during the interview, and would bomb it because of this.) I can see why this book won the year's best career book award."

— Susan Postma, Burnaby, British Columbia

"After a disappointing job search I picked up *Job Interviews For Dummies*. In two days I read the first eight chapters, went to the interview and my answers flowed very smoothly — I showed confidence when meeting with three key people individually for three hours. The next day I had an offer for the pay I wanted plus stock options. I am overjoyed — your book was a tremendous help. Thanks for writing the book the way you did."

— Ali Khan, Fairfax, Va.

"I wish to thank Joyce Lain Kennedy for writing the books *Job Interviews For Dummies* and *Cover Letters For Dummies*. I relied solely on the two books in my attempt at a career move.

I have been driving a truck for eight years and just recently finished night school with a Magna Cum Laude BS degree in accounting. Every job interview and cover letter were tailored by Joyce.

I'm now a portfolio accountant with an investments company in Andover, Mass. I have begun my dream career thanks to you and your effective material.

[second letter]

Joyce's book saved me again. I had been interviewing for the past couple of months to take my career to the next level. After an interview that went awry, I dug out *Job Interviews For Dummies* and crammed all the pertinent chapters the night before the next big interview for a job I really wanted. The interview the next day with the director of human resources went PERFECTLY. For each forthcoming interview, I read this book again the night before interviews with the supervisor, manager and director of the department. I began working at my present great job a month ago, thanks to Joyce and her book.

I was so excited about the results that I let two co-workers at my previous employer borrow it before their interviews. They both received offers after those interviews. I'm touting the praises of Joyce's book all over Boston and it's having a great effect."

— Mark W. Emmith, Newburyport, Mass.

Resumes FOR DUMMIES® 3RD EDITION

by Joyce Lain Kennedy

IDG Books Worldwide, Inc.
An International Data Group Company

Foster City, CA ◆ Chicago, IL ◆ Indianapolis, IN ◆ New York, NY

Resumes For Dummies,® 3rd Edition

Published by
IDG Books Worldwide, Inc.
An International Data Group Company
919 E. Hillsdale Blvd.
Suite 400
Foster City, CA 94404
www.idgbooks.com (IDG Books Worldwide Web site)
www.dummies.com (Dummies Press Web site)

Library of Congress Catalog Card No.: 99-69713

ISBN: 0-7645-5226-0

Printed in the United States of America

10 9 8 7 6 5 4 3 2

3O/SR/QU/QQ/IN

Distributed in the United States by IDG Books Worldwide, Inc.

Distributed by CDG Books Canada Inc. for Canada; by Transworld Publishers Limited in the United Kingdom; by IDG Norge Books for Norway; by IDG Sweden Books for Sweden; by IDG Books Australia Publishing Corporation Pty. Ltd. for Australia and New Zealand; by TransQuest Publishers Pte Ltd. for Singapore, Malaysia, Thailand, Indonesia, and Hong Kong; by Gotop Information Inc. for Taiwan; by ICG Muse, Inc. for Japan; by Intersoft for South Africa; by Eyrolles for France; by International Thomson Publishing for Germany, Austria and Switzerland; by Distribuidora Cuspide for Argentina; by LR International for Brazil; by Galileo Libros for Chile; by Ediciones ZETA S.C.R. Ltda. for Peru; by WS Computer Publishing Corporation, Inc., for the Philippines; by Contemporanea de Ediciones for Venezuela; by Express Computer Distributors for the Caribbean and West Indies; by Micronesia Media Distributor, Inc. for Micronesia; by Chips Computadoras S.A. de C.V. for Mexico; by Editorial Norma de Panama S.A. for Panama; by American Bookshops for Finland.

For general information on IDG Books Worldwide's books in the U.S., please call our Consumer Customer Service department at 800-762-2974. For reseller information, including discounts and premium sales, please call our Reseller Customer Service department at 800-434-3422.

For information on where to purchase IDG Books Worldwide's books outside the U.S., please contact our International Sales department at 317-596-5530 or fax 317-572-4002.

For consumer information on foreign language translations, please contact our Customer Service department at 1-800-434-3422, fax 317-572-4002, or e-mail rights@idgbooks.com.

For information on licensing foreign or domestic rights, please phone +1-650-653-7098.

For sales inquiries and special prices for bulk quantities, please contact our Order Services department at 800-434-3422 or write to the address above.

For information on using IDG Books Worldwide's books in the classroom or for ordering examination copies, please contact our Educational Sales department at 800-434-2086 or fax 317-572-4005.

For press review copies, author interviews, or other publicity information, please contact our Public Relations department at 650-653-7000 or fax 650-653-7500.

For authorization to photocopy items for corporate, personal, or educational use, please contact Copyright Clearance Center, 222 Rosewood Drive, Danvers, MA 01923, or fax 978-750-4470.

About the Author

 **Joyce Lain Kennedy** is the author of the *Los Angeles Times* Syndicate's column **CAREERS**, now in its 32nd year and appearing in more than 100 newspapers.

Her twice-weekly column is carried in the *St. Louis Post-Dispatch, The L.A. Times,* the *Dallas Morning News,* the *Seattle Times,* the *Louisville Courier Journal, Tulsa World,* and more.

Recognized as America's favorite careers journalist, Kennedy has received more than three million reader letters. In her column, she has answered in excess of 4,200 queries from readers.

Kennedy's wise counsel about job and career development addresses universal problems experienced by most working people — problems ranging from dealing with demotion to celebrating or coping with defining career moments. First to report on many new technologies and trends, Kennedy advises job seekers to relearn many strategies and tactics to prosper in a distinctly new job market.

She is the author or co-author of eight books, including *Joyce Lain Kennedy's Career Book* (VGM Career Horizons) and *Electronic Job Search Revolution, Electronic Resume Revolution,* and *Hook Up, Get Hired! The Internet Job Search Revolution* (the last three published by John Wiley). The last three books are groundbreaking works for the new technology that's bringing people and jobs together. With Dr. Herm Davis, she wrote *College Financial Aid For Dummies.*

Resumes For Dummies is one of a trio of job market books by Kennedy published under the wildly popular *For Dummies* imprint: *Resumes For Dummies, Cover Letters For Dummies,* and *Job Interviews For Dummies.*

Writing from Carlsbad, California, a San Diego suburb, the dean of careers columnists is a graduate of Washington University in St. Louis. Her e-mail address is jlk@sunfeatures.com.

ABOUT IDG BOOKS WORLDWIDE

Welcome to the world of IDG Books Worldwide.

IDG Books Worldwide, Inc., is a subsidiary of International Data Group, the world's largest publisher of computer-related information and the leading global provider of information services on information technology. IDG was founded more than 30 years ago by Patrick J. McGovern and now employs more than 9,000 people worldwide. IDG publishes more than 290 computer publications in over 75 countries. More than 90 million people read one or more IDG publications each month.

Launched in 1990, IDG Books Worldwide is today the #1 publisher of best-selling computer books in the United States. We are proud to have received eight awards from the Computer Press Association in recognition of editorial excellence and three from Computer Currents' First Annual Readers' Choice Awards. Our best-selling *...For Dummies*® series has more than 50 million copies in print with translations in 31 languages. IDG Books Worldwide, through a joint venture with IDG's Hi-Tech Beijing, became the first U.S. publisher to publish a computer book in the People's Republic of China. In record time, IDG Books Worldwide has become the first choice for millions of readers around the world who want to learn how to better manage their businesses.

Our mission is simple: Every one of our books is designed to bring extra value and skill-building instructions to the reader. Our books are written by experts who understand and care about our readers. The knowledge base of our editorial staff comes from years of experience in publishing, education, and journalism — experience we use to produce books to carry us into the new millennium. In short, we care about books, so we attract the best people. We devote special attention to details such as audience, interior design, use of icons, and illustrations. And because we use an efficient process of authoring, editing, and desktop publishing our books electronically, we can spend more time ensuring superior content and less time on the technicalities of making books.

You can count on our commitment to deliver high-quality books at competitive prices on topics you want to read about. At IDG Books Worldwide, we continue in the IDG tradition of delivering quality for more than 30 years. You'll find no better book on a subject than one from IDG Books Worldwide.

John Kilcullen
Chairman and CEO
IDG Books Worldwide, Inc.

*Eighth Annual
Computer Press
Awards 1992*

*Ninth Annual
Computer Press
Awards 1993*

*Tenth Annual
Computer Press
Awards 1994*

*Eleventh Annual
Computer Press
Awards 1995*

IDG is the world's leading IT media, research and exposition company. Founded in 1964, IDG had 1997 revenues of $2.05 billion and has more than 9,000 employees worldwide. IDG offers the widest range of media options that reach IT buyers in 75 countries representing 95% of worldwide IT spending. IDG's diverse product and services portfolio spans six key areas including print publishing, online publishing, expositions and conferences, market research, education and training, and global marketing services. More than 90 million people read one or more of IDG's 290 magazines and newspapers, including IDG's leading global brands — Computerworld, PC World, Network World, Macworld and the Channel World family of publications. IDG Books Worldwide is one of the fastest-growing computer book publishers in the world, with more than 700 titles in 36 languages. The "...For Dummies®" series alone has more than 50 million copies in print. IDG offers online users the largest network of technology-specific Web sites around the world through IDG.net (http://www.idg.net), which comprises more than 225 targeted Web sites in 55 countries worldwide. International Data Corporation (IDC) is the world's largest provider of information technology data, analysis and consulting, with research centers in over 41 countries and more than 400 research analysts worldwide. IDG World Expo is a leading producer of more than 168 globally branded conferences and expositions in 35 countries including E3 (Electronic Entertainment Expo), Macworld Expo, ComNet, Windows World Expo, ICE (Internet Commerce Expo), Agenda, DEMO, and Spotlight. IDG's training subsidiary, ExecuTrain, is the world's largest computer training company, with more than 230 locations worldwide and 785 training courses. IDG Marketing Services helps industry-leading IT companies build international brand recognition by developing global integrated marketing programs via IDG's print, online and exposition products worldwide. Further information about the company can be found at www.idg.com. 1/26/00

Author's Acknowledgments

A million sunny smiles to

James M. Lemke, HR Staffing and Systems consultant, Redondo Beach, California (jmlemke@aol.com). Once again, Jim has proved himself to be the Number One "He who knows the answers."

Karen Hansen, IDGB acquisitions editor, Chicago, Illinois. Karen steps up the plate and hits one out of the park when challenges arise. Karen performed world-series work on this edition.

Linda Brandon, IDGB project editor, Indianapolis, Indiana. Thanks to Linda, who parachuted into a tight time race, grabbed the reins, and rode this book to the finish line. Winners Circle for you!

Lisa Roule, IDGB acquisitions coordinator, Chicago, Illinois. Lisa's production support couldn't be better. Cheers for Lisa!

Walter Tamulis, Sun Features Inc., Carlsbad, California, my technical associate. Wally knows weighty ways around the Web. Wally worked on this book at the same time that he was a student and a successful radio quiz show contestant.

Society for Human Resource Management (SHRM) in Alexandria, Virginia. Special thanks to *Allison Branick* and *Kathy Compton* for facilitating the SHRM survey in Chapter 1. Allison and Kathy, I appreciate you.

Gail E. Ross and **Howard Yoon**, Gail Ross Literary Agency. Where do I send the roses?

And very special thanks to

The Booksellers who've help make this book such a great success, allowing me to me help job seekers everywhere.

Publisher's Acknowledgments

We're proud of this book; please register your comments through our IDG Books Worldwide Online Registration Form located at http://my2cents.dummies.com.

Some of the people who helped bring this book to market include the following:

Acquisitions, Editorial, and Media Development

Project Editor: Linda Brandon

Previous Edition: Kathleen M. Cox

Acquisitions Editor: Karen Hansen

Acquisitions Coordinator: Lisa Roule

Technical Editor: James M. Lemke

Editorial Director: Kristin Cocks

Editorial Administrator: Michelle Hacker

Production

Project Coordinator: Emily Perkins

Layout and Graphics: Amy Adrian, Joe Bucki, Barry Offringa, Tracy K. Oliver, Brian Torwelle, Erin Zeltner

Proofreaders: Laura Albert, Vickie Broyles, Corey Bowen, John Greenough, Betty Kish

Indexer: Sherry Massey

Special Help
Kelly Ewing, Project Editor

General and Administrative

IDG Books Worldwide, Inc.: John Kilcullen, CEO

IDG Books Technology Publishing Group: Richard Swadley, Senior Vice President and Publisher; Walter R. Bruce III, Vice President and Publisher; Joseph Wikert, Vice President and Publisher; Mary Bednarek, Vice President and Director, Product Development; Andy Cummings, Publishing Director, General User Group; Mary C. Corder, Editorial Director; Barry Pruett, Publishing Director

IDG Books Consumer Publishing Group: IDG Books Consumer Publishing Group: Roland Elgey, Senior Vice President and Publisher; Kathleen A. Welton, Vice President and Publisher; Kevin Thornton, Acquisitions Manager; Kristin A. Cocks, Editorial Director

IDG Books Internet Publishing Group: IDG Books Internet Publishing Group: Brenda McLaughlin, Senior Vice President and Publisher; Sofia Marchant, Online Marketing Manager

IDG Books Production for Dummies Press: Debbie Stailey, Director of Production; Cindy L. Phipps, Manager of Project Coordination, Production Proofreading, and Indexing; Tony Augsburger, Manager of Prepress, Reprints, and Systems; Laura Carpenter, Production Control Manager; Shelley Lea, Supervisor of Graphics and Design; Debbie J. Gates, Production Systems Specialist; Robert Springer, Supervisor of Proofreading; Kathie Schutte, Production Supervisor

Dummies Packaging and Book Design: Patty Page, Manager, Promotions Marketing

◆

The publisher would like to give special thanks to Patrick J. McGovern, without whom this book would not have been possible.

◆

Contents at a Glance

Cartoons at a Glance

By Rich Tennant

page 27

page 237

page 91

page 123

page 193

page 279

page 7

Fax: 978-546-7747
E-mail: richtennant@the5thwave.com
World Wide Web: www.the5thwave.com

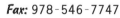

Table of Contents

Introduction

● ●

*W*e live in interesting times. Among recent clips from the nation's press:

- ✔ **Pay gap.** Have you ever heard of someone making more than $217 million an hour? That's the story of Michael Robertson, an Internet chieftain, who made $868 million in four hours the day his MP3.com music company went public.

  By contrast, school teachers usually get pay raises of 1 to 2 percent, or if taxpayers are generous, 3 percent.

- ✔ **Age and work.** U.S. Senator John Glenn handled space like a young man when he became the world's oldest astronaut at age 77. Scientists say Glenn showed there is no reason healthy older people can't fly in space.

  By contrast, age discrimination is shoving high numbers of America's brightest technical minds into underemployment — picture PhDs on computer help desks — or unemployment as professionals over 40 are replaced with cheaper, younger talent.

- ✔ **Talent demand.** MBAs are hot stuff in a booming economy with job offers pouring down like spring rain for top graduates. Many have turned away from the old gray favorite, Wall Street jobs, toward greener Internet start-up pastures where they hope stock options will make them rich. The climate is so good for executives that about 30 of them have signed up with a talent agent. From their hefty salaries, $90,000 to $450,000 annually, each month they pay an agent of corporate America to turbocharge their careers with "branding, marketing, and distributing" their products — themselves.

  By contrast, about 30 naturalized citizens of color, trained overseas as accountants, ask why a major bank has removed them from data entry (now done automatically by computer) and relegated them to opening envelopes eight hours a day.

A litany of change driven by technological revolution is showing up in unfamiliar ways as we plunge into the information-rich New Economy. About 200 million people worldwide now have Internet access, a figure that is expected to reach 1 billion over the next decade, according to research from International Data Corp. There's no doubt that Ford Motor Company and Delta Airlines get the message about this wired age — they recently decided to pass out computers with Internet access to every employee.

Interesting, but does all this mean that in the job market, the old way is a dead way? No way! It does mean "Think Transition."

The Art of the Resume Is in Transition

The American job market is in the middle of a shift from traditional to digital resume writing, distribution, and management. Even as we reach into the future, we still need to use time-honored methods of getting the word out to employers who can hire us. The current transitional status means you have to know two basic ways of marketing yourself — through familiar media and digital media. Unless you're in a high-tech field and have no reason to use a paper resume, or in a small, conservative business where paper still rules, the time has come to do the resume two-step.

In fact, the resume shift has become so deeply entrenched in our way of working that I offer a prediction: From now on until the transition is complete (no one knows when that will be), only job seekers who master the art of combining online resumes and other digital tools with classic job search resumes and strategies will rise to the top, reinventing the way they claim the best jobs.

In case you haven't looked for a job recently, an online resume is a plain text document that can be sent through e-mail or cut-and-pasted into online forms. It is done as an ASCII resume and has become wildly popular now that e-mail is a standard way of sending and receiving information. E-mail resumes and related digital tools, as well as classic resume strategies, are fully discussed in this new edition of a best-selling book. These pages will help you build a FirstRate resume.

What Is a FirstRate Resume?

A FirstRate resume is:

- ✔ Carefully constructed to compete, compel, and capture attention.
- ✔ Too skills-rich to overlook.
- ✔ Targeted to the job, showing you can and will do the work.

Because your resume holds your future in its grasp, take your time to zip it up with zest and pizzazz. This book shows you in detail how to add the punch and class you need.

How This Book Is Organized

To give you an idea of what's ahead, here's a breakdown of the seven parts in this guide. Each part covers a general topic. Each part's individual chapters dig into the details.

Part I: Resumes in the New Economy

A survey by the nation's largest human resource professional organization, the Society for Human Resource Management (SHRM) takes an across-industries pulse of what employers are looking for in resumes today. The survey report is followed by a periscope peek at how the 21st Century workplace is changing the way we think about work.

Part II: FirstRate Resumes Are Strong Sales Tools

This part shows you the basics of presenting yourself as a first-rate candidate; it explains formats, contents, words, and appearance.

Part III: Creating Your FirstRate Resume

Here you'll find the secrets of how to lay the personal groundwork that powers a FirstRate resume.

Part IV: Going Up and Cyber-Ways with Your Resume

Six chapters take you into the digital dimension of e-mail resumes and other digital tools, including an expanded listing of favorite Web destinations.

Part V: Answers to Specific Resume Stumpers

Few of us are perfect and this part has all the best solutions to specific problems in a resume, from ageism to newcomer to disability to career changing.

Part VI: Samples of FirstRate Resumes

This part presents examples of annotated FirstRate resumes, arranged by career fields. Special needs resumes are included.

Part VII: The Part of Tens

This part takes you on a tour of top-ten claim verifications, myths, tips, blunders, professional help, and a resume checklist.

Icons Used in This Book

When something in here is particularly noteworthy, I go out of my way to make sure it stands out. That's what these *Dummies* signature icons are for. They mark text that — for one reason or another — you *really* need to pay attention to. Here's a quick scan of the icons awaiting you in this book and what they mean.

This icon directs your undivided attention to resume techniques that make you reek of quality — first-class, grade A, top-of-the-line, second to none.

This icon highlights online information to make your resume soar into cyberspace and make a happy landing.

Have you been around the business block but need extra help to be seen as a prime candidate? This icon highlights tips for the seasoned pro.

Are you a new graduate or just new to the workplace? This icon signals tips that help you avoid coming across as a clueless beginner.

The dinosaur icon chomps away at job-killing goofs. Ignore these warnings and you may be eaten alive.

When you need to know the fundamentals of resume preparation and job scouting, this icon is your tipster.

This icon flags advice from pros in the job-finding business.

Differences of opinion are the very essence of recruiting and job searching. This icon lets you know there are varying views about the art of resume writing.

This icon zeros in on a snack-sized bit of information to help you think like a resume reader.

Your Resume: Write It Right

Whether you are a new graduate starting out, a person in the core working years, or a seasoned ace, this book shows you how to rank ahead of the competition with a top-of-the-line resume that says you're too superior a candidate to let get away.

Part I

Resumes in the New Economy

The 5th Wave   By Rich Tennant

"Your resume looks fine, I just don't think you're merry enough."

In this part . . .

A survey by the nation's largest human resource professional organization, the **Society for Human Resource Management (SHRM)**, takes an across-industries pulse of what employers are looking for in resumes today. The survey report is followed by a periscope peek at how the 21st Century workplace is altering how we find and do work.

Chapter 1

What Employers Are Telling Us

· ·

In This Chapter

▶ Finding the resume delivery method employers like best

▶ Understanding how employers treat unsolicited resumes

▶ Discovering the resume factors employers want most

· ·

*A*lthough the move to e-mailing resumes and to using the digital family of cybertools for job searches is clicking along, smaller firms continue to rely on manual methods. This chapter dissects a survey conducted by the **Society for Human Resource Management** (SHRM) and reveals many clues as to how employers view resumes today.

Getting Inside a Hiring Professional's Head

With more than 135,000 professional and student members throughout the world, SHRM is the leading voice of the human resource profession.

The SHRM Foundation, a nonprofit organization with multiple purposes, includes among its charges a mandate to support applied research aimed at helping its members stay current with the latest developments and trends.

A SHRM professional emphasis group, the Employment Management Association (EMA) — with more than 5,600 members — is the top professional association for employment management practitioners and service providers who are concerned with staffing issues and trends.

In late 1999, I had the pleasure of participating in the *SHRM Survey on Cover Letters and Resumes*. The survey was faxed to randomly selected members of the EMA; 582 human resource professionals responded. The SHRM resume survey data details were written by SHRM's Allison Branick and printed with permission from SHRM.

Demographics of the SHRM survey

Three-quarters of SHRM respondents work for companies of fewer than 1,000 employees, and nearly half of the respondents work for companies that employ 250 or fewer employees. Bear in mind that the majority of job openings in the United States occur in smaller companies. Here are the demographics for the companies that completed the survey:

Total number of employees

29% Fewer than 100 employees

19% 100 to 250 employees

15% 251 to 500 employees

12% 501 to 1,000 employees

11% 1,001 to 2,500 employees

4% 2,501 to 5,000 employees

4% More than 5,000 employees

5% No answer

Type of organization

23% Business and professional services

20% Manufacturing

13% Finance/Insurance/Real Estate

9% Nonprofit

6% Health services

5% Telecommunications

3% Retail

2% Education

2% Government

2% High Tech/computers

2% Publishing

2% Utilities

10% Other

2% No answer

Here are the highlights from the survey:

- ✔ Most resumes come via mail or fax, but e-mail is preferred.
- ✔ Unsolicited resumes tend to be kept on file.
- ✔ The majority of employers still screen resumes manually.
- ✔ Most resumes are screened in less than three minutes.
- ✔ Today's resumes are of good quality.
- ✔ HR professionals prefer certain resume characteristics.
- ✔ Employment dates and job histories are crucial to resumes.
- ✔ The majority of today's resumes are truthful.

Most resumes come via mail or fax . . .

Although technological advancements in recent years have opened the door for job applicants to submit their resumes to potential employers by e-mail and through Web sites, the majority of resumes continue to be delivered to potential employers through the mail or by fax, according to survey results. Respondents report that on average, 42 percent of the resumes they receive come through the mail, and an additional 30 percent of the resumes arrive by fax. E-mail delivery accounts for an average of 17 percent of resumes received by respondents' organizations. Respondents also report that 6 percent of the resumes they receive are hand delivered, and 5 percent arrive in a Web-based format.

. . . but e-mail is preferred

Although survey results show that fewer than one in five resumes are submitted via e-mail, 34 percent of human resource (HR) professionals prefer to receive them via e-mail, according to survey results (see Figure 1-1). Approximately three out of ten respondents (31 percent) choose regular mail as their delivery method of preference. Fax is favored by 25 percent of respondents, particularly those from smaller organizations; 7 percent favor Web-based delivery formats; and 2 percent like hand-delivered resumes.

Of the HR professionals who prefer to receive resumes sent via e-mail, nearly half (49 percent) report that they prefer the resume to be sent as an attachment. Twenty percent of respondents, however, prefer having the resume contents pasted within the body of an e-mail. Twenty-two percent of respondents say that they have no preference when it comes to e-mailed resumes.

Even though many resumes today are sent and received via e-mail, fax, and the World Wide Web, cover letters are still an important part of an applicant's package, according to HR professionals. Survey data show that even though applicants are using methods other than regular mail to send potential employers their resumes, applicants should not assume that cover letters are unnecessary when using these more technologically advanced delivery methods. Quite the contrary. More than eight out of ten survey respondents say that including cover letters with resumes that are sent via e-mail is either very important (28 percent), important (30 percent), or somewhat important (24 percent). Respondents from smaller organizations (32 percent) are more likely to say that including cover letters with e-mailed resumes is very important than are respondents from larger organizations (24 percent). Fewer than one in ten respondents (9 percent), particularly those from larger organizations, believe that including cover letters is not important at all. Seven percent of respondents' organizations do not currently accept resumes via e-mail.

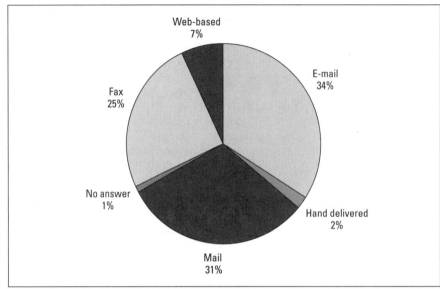

Web-based
7%

E-mail
34%

Fax
25%

No answer
1%

Hand delivered
2%

Mail
31%

Source: SHRM Survey on Cover Letters and Resumes

Figure 1-1:
Preferred
delivery
methods.

Although not all organizations currently accept resumes submitted via e-mail, electronic transmission of resumes will likely increase in the future. According to survey results, 84 percent of respondents believe that the number of resumes submitted electronically to their organizations will increase in the next year. Respondents from larger organizations are more likely to anticipate an increase than are respondents from smaller organizations. Six percent of respondents believe that the number will stay about the same, and 1 percent believe that the number of electronically submitted resumes will decrease. Two percent of respondents report that although they do not currently accept electronically submitted resumes, they plan to do so within the next year. Another 2 percent do not currently accept resumes electronically, nor do they have plans to begin.

More than four out of ten survey respondents (42 percent) report that their organizations' Web sites have mail-back features that enable applicants to post their resumes directly to the sites. Forty-eight percent of respondents, however, say that their Web sites do not have such features, and 8 percent say that their organizations do not have Web sites. Respondents from larger organizations are more likely to report having mail-back features on their organizational Web sites.

Unsolicited resumes tend to be kept on file

Not all resumes that organizations receive are requested. Frequently, applicants blindly send their resumes to organizations with the hope that they might be read and that their qualifications might fit with current openings. What becomes of these unsolicited resumes? Are they kept or simply discarded? Sixty percent of the responding HR professionals keep the unsolicited resumes they receive on file for future position openings (see Figure 1-2). Two out of three (66 percent) respondents from smaller organizations say that they keep the resumes on file, compared with slightly more than half (54 percent) of the respondents from larger organizations.

More than four out of ten respondents (45 percent) say that their HR departments respond to unsolicited resumes by sending written responses — either via letter, e-mail, or fax — to resume senders. Four percent of respondents report that their HR staff responds with some form of verbal communication, such as a phone call or an in-person meeting.

Not all unsolicited resumes are paid such attention, however. Twenty-two percent of participating HR professionals say that they supply no response to the unsolicited resumes they receive, and 14 percent discard such resumes.

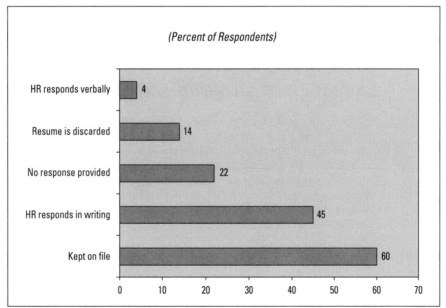

Figure 1-2: Handling unsolicited resumes.

(Percent of Respondents)

HR responds verbally	4
Resume is discarded	14
No response provided	22
HR responds in writing	45
Kept on file	60

Source: SHRM Survey on Cover Letters and Resumes

The majority of employers still screen resumes manually

Scanning and storing resumes received by job applicants in electronic databases is not currently a common practice, according to survey results. Three out of four (76 percent) survey respondents say that they do not scan and store the resumes they receive in electronic databases. However, approximately one out of four (24 percent) HR professionals report that they do scan resumes and use electronic databases for storage. Respondents from larger organizations are more likely to scan and electronically store resumes than are respondents from smaller organizations.

Given that only one out of four HR professionals scan and electronically store the resumes they receive, it is perhaps not terribly surprising that the majority of HR professionals screen resumes manually rather than electronically. Nearly nine out of ten survey respondents (88 percent) say that staff members manually screen the resumes their organizations receive, while 9 percent of respondents screen resumes electronically by using a database that searches for specific criteria. One percent of respondents use both methods for screening resumes, and 2 percent are unsure. Respondents from smaller organizations are slightly more likely to screen resumes manually, while HR professionals from larger organizations tend to do electronic screening more often, according to survey results.

Most resumes are screened in less than three minutes

Of the respondents who manually screen resumes, the majority scan one resume in less than three minutes (see Figure 1-3). More than half (54 percent) of the survey respondents report that on average, they or a member of their staff spends between one and three minutes screening a resume, while an additional 19 percent of respondents spend less than one minute on average. Respondents from larger organizations are more likely to report spending less than one minute screening a resume than are respondents from smaller organizations.

Nearly one out of five respondents (18 percent) who manually screen resumes spend an average of three to five minutes reviewing a resume, and 4 percent of respondents report spending six to ten minutes screening each resume. Reviewing a resume for more than ten minutes occurs infrequently, with only 2 percent of the respondents reporting that they spend that amount of time.

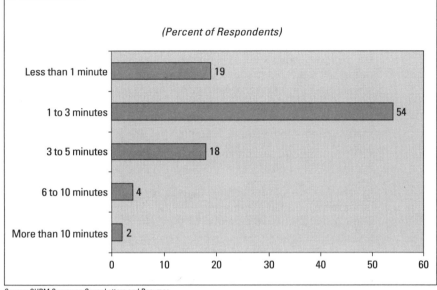

(Percent of Respondents)

Less than 1 minute	19
1 to 3 minutes	54
3 to 5 minutes	18
6 to 10 minutes	4
More than 10 minutes	2

Figure 1-3: Average time spent screening resumes.

Source: SHRM Survey on Cover Letters and Resumes

Today's resumes are of good quality

Two out of three HR professionals (66 percent) believe that the overall quality of the resumes their organizations receive today (the resumes themselves, not the quality of the applicant's qualifications) is good, and 2 percent find the resumes of excellent quality. Three out of ten respondents (30 percent) feel that resume quality today is fair, and only 1 percent find the quality poor.

Good resume quality has remained relatively constant in recent years, according to survey respondents. When asked if resume quality has changed over the past three years, nearly six out of ten respondents (57 percent) say the level of quality has remained the same, while nearly one out of five respondents (18 percent) report an improvement in resume quality. Thirteen percent of respondents note a decline in the quality of the resumes they have received in recent years, and the remaining 1 percent of respondents is unsure.

HR professionals prefer certain resume characteristics

Respondents who manually screen resumes were asked how they view certain resume characteristics. Well-organized, concise resumes tend to be the most favorable to HR professionals, according to the survey results (see Figure 1-4). For example, 74 percent of respondents positively view resume information presented in reverse chronological order where the most recent information is first. In addition, 55 percent of respondents view one-page resumes positively.

HR professionals view some resume characteristics negatively. Nearly nine out of ten respondents look negatively upon applicants that send only a cover letter (87 percent). Resumes that are more than two pages long are viewed negatively by more than six out of ten respondents (62 percent). Also, more than half of HR professionals dislike resumes that are presented in narrative format (55 percent), resumes that are one page but double-sided (53 percent), and resumes that present the pertinent information in chronological order with the most recent information last (52 percent).

In addition, respondents have neutral reactions to certain resume characteristics mentioned in the survey. Resumes printed on colored paper (63 percent) or with unusual designs (61 percent) are viewed neutrally by more than six out of 10 respondents. Resumes that are professionally done are viewed neutrally by 47 percent of respondents and viewed positively by a similar share (46 percent) of respondents, resulting in a mixed review. Resumes that are two pages but single-sided also receive mixed reviews, according to 47 percent of respondents who view such resumes neutrally and 44 percent who view them positively.

	(Percentage of Respondents)			
	Positive	*Neutral*	*Negative*	*No Answer*
Chronological order (most recent last)	28%	18%	52%	1%
Colored paper	6	63	30	1
Cover letter only	2	10	87	2
More than two pages	4	31	62	2
Narrative	8	34	55	2
One page	55	40	3	3
One page, double-sided	9	35	53	2
Professionally done	46	47	5	2
Reverse chronological order (most recent first)	74	11	14	1
Two pages, single-sided	44	47	7	2
Unusual design	13	61	24	2

Source: SHRM Survey on Cover Letters and Resumes

Figure 1-4: HR professionals' reactions to resume characteristics.

Employment dates and job histories are crucial to resumes

Specific employment dates and detailed job histories are two items that HR professionals deem very important to include in or along with resumes (see Figure 1-5). More than nine out of ten respondents say that including specific employment dates in a resume is either very important (69 percent) or important (22 percent). Nine out of ten respondents also feel that including detailed job histories in resumes is either very important (61 percent) or important (30 percent).

Other items presented to respondents are less important. For example, 51 percent of respondents say that including recommendation letters with a resume is not important at all. Forty percent of respondents do not think that including writing or work samples with resumes is important either; however, a slightly lower percentage of respondents (37 percent) feel that such samples are somewhat important.

Figure 1-5:
Important
resume
items.

	(Percentage of Respondents)				
	Very Important	Important	Somewhat Important	Not Important at All	No Answer
Specific employment dates	69%	22%	7%	1%	2%
Detailed job history	61	30	6	1	2
Cover letter	46	34	15	4	1
Professional certifications	41	38	17	2	2
Summary of experience	38	33	22	6	1
Salary requirements	24	42	26	6	1
Stated job objective/mission	24	38	27	10	1
Reason for leaving old jobs	11	25	36	26	2
Writing or work samples	6	15	37	40	2
Recommendation letters	3	10	34	51	2

Source: SHRM Survey on Cover Letters and Resumes

The majority of today's resumes are truthful

The majority of resumes submitted by applicants to potential employers are believed to be truthful, according to survey results. More than nine out of ten HR professionals report that the resumes of the candidates they interview are either very truthful (4 percent), truthful (64 percent), or somewhat truthful (28 percent). The remaining respondents are unsure.

Undergoing a Time of Transition

There you have it: a cross-section of current opinions about resume preferences from HR professionals. You may notice a few conflicts between their opinions and the suggestions offered in this book. What you just read is an X-ray into the minds of many talented professionals whose goals are to find the best candidates for their open jobs as quickly as possible. By contrast, your goals are to present your qualifications in the best light for the job you want. Understand that you and resume reviewers do not always share goal congruence. But it's always useful to know what they're thinking on the other side of the desk, don't you think?

You may have another question: Why do many HR professionals in this study report that they still deal with resumes manually? The answer may lie in the demographics: Nearly half of the respondents in the SHRM study represent employers with fewer than 250 employees. Smaller companies are moving more slowly toward the world of electronic recruiting than are larger organizations, but make no mistake — the digital domain is their destination.

As human resource professionals and consultants Gerry Crispin and Mark Mehler observe in their highly respected book *CareerXroads 2000,* what we are seeing now is "The end of an era and the beginning of a new millennium." The transition is on — and it's rolling along at a fast clip. With falling prices and improved electronic resume management systems, more companies of all sizes are finding automation to be an attractive option.

Expect Differences in Perspective

Human nature doesn't change very fast, but our tools do. The challenge for the 21st Century will be to gain comfort with faster and faster revolutions of technology.

Change is so embedded in our lives that there is no longer just one generally-agreed upon way to handle employment issues, either as job seeker or staffing professional. The lack of absolutes explains why various career advisers offer what may be conflicting advice, and why opinions expressed in this SHRM study may not always pair with the advice in these pages.

For instance, 76 percent of SHRM respondents say they do not scan and store resumes in electronic databases. But we know that respondents from larger organizations are more likely to scan and electronically store resumes than are respondents from smaller organizations; the demographics of this study show that half the companies responding employ fewer than 250 employees. Knowing of the diversity of recruiting practices, how shall you approach a job search?

This study clearly reveals that transition is the sign of the times. My tip: Take a bicentric approach and look in both directions before a job search — back toward paper and forward toward cyber-search. And most important, keep staffing expert Jim Lemke's point in mind, asking yourself:

> **The issue is not which media I use to communicate my availability but how do I organize my information to get a job interview?**

The solid, classic information in this book can be used as is with paper resumes, or adapted for e-mail and online resume distribution. Part IV specifically covers the cyber-resume knowledge you must know to compete in a new kind of job market that's closing in fast.

Chapter 2

The 21st Century Workplace

*T*oday it matters what part of the economy you work in. The Internet — changing the way we communicate, distributing both goods and services, and building "communities" — is bringing with it a new kind of prosperity gap.

The last big American boom in the 1960s jumped wages everywhere — schools, hospitals, banks, hotels, offices, factories. But in the swell of this sweet prosperity, the rising economic tide has not lifted everyone's boat.

The broad reason some people are being left behind as others move up is clear: They work in the Old Economy where earnings, after adjustment for inflation, have risen very little in the current good times. But people who work in the New Economy have seen their pay skyrocket since the mid-1990s — nearly four times the rate of earners in the Old Economy.

The Economy: What Once Was Old, Now Is New

The Old Economy has been with us for 300 years. It is

✔ An industrial economy based on hard resources — coal, steel, lumber, and oil — that provide tangible products/services.

✔ Composed of such sectors as construction, transportation, utilities, manufacturing, wholesaling, personal services, health, and education.

✔ The workplace for 91 million people.

The New Economy is dawning. It is

- ✔ Technology-driven, particularly by information technology because the main product/service is information.
- ✔ Composed of such sectors as high-tech equipment, software, computer services, consulting, financial services, media, and nonstore retailing.
- ✔ The workplace for 19 million people.

Netting a New Job: The Itch to Switch

People are noticing the disparity in wage growth between the old and the new. As many as half the people polled in various surveys say they're underpaid, and 40 percent declare they'll change jobs as soon as possible.

Many people have had an e-universe epiphany: With media headlines in full alert, the booming Net economy at the beginning of the new century is measured at more than $500 billion, blowing past such husky familiar sectors as energy at $223 billion and automobiles at $350 billion.

The Net is unlike anything we've ever known.

Sorting through Net job lingo

Here's a quick scan of some New Economy jobs:

- ✔ **New metrics analyst:** This employee works for a Web site firm. As the Web industry matures, individuals who in another life would market databases or analyze return on investments or contribute strategic planning are morphing into analyst jobs that pay $60,000 to $85,000, or $80,000 to $110,000 at the managerial level. This job is for people who love numbers and drawing conclusions from the data they manipulate.

- ✔ **Virtual organization leader:** Product cycles and crises move fast in the land of DotComs. Sometimes work efforts that have definable start and stop dates are handled by traditional project managers or staffing specialists, and sometimes by subject authorities, such as public relations specialists. Pay is in the $60,000 to $90,000 neighborhood for assembling quick-response teams of skilled and experienced contractors.

- ✔ **E-mail channel specialist:** This marketing job encourages customers to sign up for an e-mail service, such as a newsletter, which not only comes to you automatically on a regular basis, but also encourages you to visit the vendor's Web site. Monetary rewards can range from $95,000 to $180,000.

✔ **Chief Internet officer:** This executive, who may be paid in the $200,000 to $300,000 range, directs all online strategy and operations. A chief Internet officer is a fast-thinking business executive who may have moved over to e-commerce from traditional businesses, such as magazines or retail.

✔ **Content engineer (CE):** Workers in this occupation synthesize information technology, marketing, and suppliers to bring substance to Web sites. Not usually "engineers" in the classic use of the title, many CEs are subject authorities and may hold advanced degrees in life sciences. This is also an attractive field for liberal arts majors who are adept at technology operations. The pay range is $50,000 to $80,000.

✔ **Chief community strategist:** This job centers on operating a giant feedback process, making sure that what customers want translates to what management supplies. Customer retention is the name of the Web game. Political science or anthropology majors focus on this job, which can pay $125,000.

Hot spots of America's high-tech industry — the New Economy — are San Jose, Dallas, Los Angeles, Boston, and Seattle.

Taking the high-tech road

If you're debating "taking the plunge," here's a key to focus your search: Find a company that does online what you do offline. Your expertise is your leverage to make up for a lack of experience in DotCom companies.

Another pathway into DotCom land: Try the consulting route, choosing small companies that have a Net operation to learn from while you provide your marketing or other business talents.

Be prepared to encounter fanciful job titles in the Net world, such as

✔ Code connoisseur = programmer

✔ Minister of propaganda = publicist

✔ Virtual space planner = designer of interfaces

✔ Online liaison = one who responds to e-mail requests

✔ Web evangelist = enthusiastic consultant

✔ Vice president, online community = content specialist

Moving from bricks to clicks may not be as difficult as anything strange and new first appears, even if you don't know HTML from Adam's house cat, say Net employment specialists.

Realize that the Internet workplace is maturing, becoming structured and more like traditional corporate America than it was in the late 20th century.

- ✔ Stock options in lieu of salary are disappearing. Compensation is chiefly based on salary and bonuses, a mirror of conventional business.

- ✔ Nearly 20 percent more of today's entry-level talent has formal design education/training than a couple of years ago.

- ✔ The majority of executive-level positions are filled with business school graduates.

Despite the young Net industry's continuing penchant for whimsical job titles, career pathways in its workplace are being paved and curbed, taking on a mainstreet look and feel.

As to whether you can earn in the mid-six figures working on the Net fairly fast, how talented are you?

The New Economy is full of promise, but it's in no way a sure thing. Some of the smartest professionals I know — very Internet savvy — are still waiting for the big payday after five years.

During the same time, I know several others who have acquired major money in old favorites like real estate, stock investing, and broomsticks-and-billy-club manufacturing.

Going from Dog-Eat-Dog to Taking Your Dog to Work

Every decade or so, a movement turns up to liberalize the workplace. In the 1980s, for instance, the management approach was called "workstyle" and it sprang from Silicon Valley (where else?). Companies gave enormous bonuses, hosted white-water rafting trips to promote employee togetherness, paid for treks through the Rockies, sponsored sky-diving sports, encouraged employees to bring pets to work, and hosted Friday afternoon "unwinding parties" for the staff.

A liberalization trend is once again changing *some portions* of the 21st-century workplace for two main reasons:

✔ The majority of women of working age are holding paid jobs. Dual-career couples wanting quality-of-life benefits and young professionals wanting free time for personal pursuits have become a potent job market force. Now that many companies believe there's a shortage of the workers they want to hire that may force them to turn down the lights, they're more inclined to line up behind work-life balance programs than they were in recent years when they could find all the help they wanted. Contemporary benefits range from flexible work schedules to generous leave time.

✔ GenX workers (twentysomethings and thirtysomethings) are making their presence felt in the workplace, and they want signing bonuses, stock options, boisterous games at the office, casual dress, dentists who roll up in vans to the office, and concierges to shop and handle cleaning — autonomy and choices that previously were unheard of.

As you gear up for a campaign to change jobs — or write a resume because a headhunter called — research your socks off before accepting too little or demanding too much. Some online resources for checking up on what is and what isn't the norm for your industry are noted in Chapter 14.

Shaping Your Future: Seven Key Trends

As we make our way through the new century, keep your resume up-to-date in case you need to make a quick lane change. Among recognized big-picture factors are

✔ Technology that not only alters the kind of work we do but ignores where and when we do it

✔ Expansion of knowledge (expert) systems that take away white-collar jobs

✔ A virtual business world that, as long as you can connect by plug or wireless technology, allows you to work anywhere anytime

✔ A growing free agent workforce that companies hire as needed with no long-term promises

✔ Diversity in the workforce — women, people of different races, people with disabilities, people with alternative sexual orientations, people of all ages, people for whom English is a second language — that rewrites basic workplace rules

✔ Globalization of opportunity causing jobs to be impacted by trade policies, both import and export

✔ Privacy issues provoked by collection of data on the Internet that impact the way you handle e-mail resumes and submissions to resume databanks

Ladies and Gentlemen, Start Your Resumes

The chapters in Part I give you a pulse on today's job market. Think about preparing the marketing materials that will position you to advantage in that market. The time has come to begin your campaign in earnest.

Matthew thinks so, too. A reader of my newspaper column, *Careers,* he recently commented in an e-mail on my advice to a man thinking about changing jobs. Here's what Matthew said:

Dear Joyce, To that man who wrote to you I say: I think you should take time off your job and go to the other job where you want to be hired. Good luck! — Your friend, Matthew, 9 years old next month.

Don't laugh. In not too many years, Matthew might be writing this book. That's how fast things are changing in the 21st-century workplace.

Part II
FirstRate Resumes are Strong Sales Tools

The 5th Wave   By Rich Tennant

"I know it works on late night infomercials, but I still wouldn't separate paragraphs in my resume with, 'But wait, that's not all...', and, 'Act now, and I'll include this impressive list of high school trophies'!"

In this part . . .

Contents — that's the operative word for your
FirstRate resume — contents that say "Hire me fast!"
This part shows you what to put in the resume and how to
pull together its strands in a way that inspires managers
to book face-time with you ASAP.

Chapter 3

What Your Resume Reveals about You

- -

In This Chapter

▶ Using the FirstRate resume to get a better job

▶ Doing your homework to create FirstRate resumes

▶ Deciding how many resumes you need

- -

*Y*ou say you've been waiting for the right time to step out and find a terrific job? You say you're tired of selling off a piece of your life in return for forgettable pay in going-nowhere jobs? Or you're fed up with starving as a student? You say you want a job that speaks fluent money with an interesting accent? Sounds good. But that's not *all* you want, you say?

You want a job that puts jingle in your pocket and paper in your bank account. Yes. But you also want *meaningful* work.

I understand. What you want is a job that you love to get up in the morning to do and that pays major money, has first-class benefits, provides self-actualizing challenge, doesn't disappear overnight, and maybe sends you off on pleasant travels periodically. In Hollywoodspeak, what you want is one of those above-the-line jobs that star you in Purposeful Endeavor.

Okay, now is the right time to make your move to a better job.

The best jobs are going to people who, with FirstRate resumes and first-rate discipline, have found out how to outrun the crowd.

Now that the jobmarket is bubbling and unemployment is drop dead low, these are the years for solid career building — and to take risks. As Neil Simon says, "If no one ever took risks, Michelangelo could have painted the Sistine floor." If you don't move to capture the kind of job you want during these good times, you're leaving opportunity on the table. This chapter tells why you need a FirstRate resume to make the new workplace work for you.

What should you do when you want to change careers and you don't know exactly to what? Sorry, but you're not ready to write a FirstRate resume. First clarify your direction, whether through introspection or professional career counseling. For a jumpstart on mapping out your life's direction, see the sidebar in this chapter: *"Who am I? What do I want to do?"* When you've identified your new career, you can get tips for making a smooth transition in Chapter 19.

Really, Must You Have a Resume?

A resume used to be a simple, low-key sheet or two of paper outlining your experience and education, with a list of references at the end. That kind of resume is now a museum piece.

By contrast, your FirstRate resume is a specially prepared *sales presentation*. Created as a sales tool to persuade a potential employer that you are the best one to do the job you seek, your resume is a self-advertisement that showcases your skills. With a series of well-written statements that highlight your previous work experience, education, and other background information, your resume helps prove what you say about your achievements, accomplishments, and abilities. It tells an employer you have positive work attitudes and strong interpersonal skills.

As a sales presentation, your resume answers questions about you as a *product:*

- What skills do you bring to the organization?
- Why are you worth the money you hope to earn?
- How can you do the work better than other candidates?
- Can you solve company or industry problems?

In every statement, your resume strategically convinces employers that you can do the job, have positive work attitudes, and get along with others. Your resume — whether stored on paper or in the rapidly expanding electronic universe — helps employers see how they could benefit by interviewing you.

Periodically, job guide writers, with gunslinging self-assurance, assert that resumes are unnecessary baggage. These critics insist that the best way to find a job is to network and talk your way inside. Put wax in your ears on this one. The only people for whom the no-resume advice is okay are those who can leave talk-show hosts struggling to get a word in edgewise. Very few people are extroverted and glib enough to carry the entire weight of their employment marketing presentations without supporting materials.

More important, you need a resume because most employers say you need a resume. No one has spare minutes today. People are too busy to enjoy long lunch hours. Employers refuse to take oral histories when you call to "ask for a few minutes of time to discuss opportunities." Those days are gone.

Even if — as a corporate executive's child, pal, or hairdresser — you land on a payroll by fiat, somewhere along the way you'll need a resume. At some point, people who make hiring decisions insist on seeing a piece of paper or a computer screen that spells out your qualifications. Resumes are an important first step on the road to the perfect job.

Remember: Resumes open doors to job interviews; interviews open doors to jobs.

First impression — lasting impact

What does your resume reveal about you? Right off the bat, your resume reveals whether you're willing to take the time to discover what a prospective employer wants done that you are well qualified to do. It shows the health of your judgment and the depth of your commitment to work.

Whether you are an aspiring rookie, a veteran ace campaigner, or simply someone who seeks to leave miles of bad road to speed along the fast track to a super career, launch your resume-writing venture by putting yourself inside the employer's life form. The development of an inside perspective begins with both old- and new-fashioned research. Your overwhelming impulse may be to assume that you can write a resume out of your own head and history — that dogged, time-eating research makes a nice add-on, but is not essential. Don't listen. *At the core of a FirstRate resume is research, research, and more research.*

Research into your prospective company — in this usage, *company* means nonprofit organizations and government agencies as well as private companies — lets you glimpse how you might fit into the company and what you can offer it. Research gives you a sound basis for selecting those areas to include in your resume that demonstrate good judgment and commitment.

When you know what an employer is willing to employ someone to do, you can tell the employer why you should be the one employed. *In a tight job race, the candidate who knows most about the employer has the edge.*

When You Need More than One Resume

When do you need more than one version of your resume? Most of the time. Following the usual approach, you develop a core resume and then amend and slant it to fit specific positions, career fields, or industries.

The ultimate FirstRate resume, like a custom-made suit, is tailored to the job that you want. After researching the target company and position, you can make your resume fit the job description as closely as your work and education history allows.

What research do you need?

- ✔ At minimum, you should know the scope of the position and the skills that the company is looking for.

- ✔ For a more comprehensive approach, learn the company's history, growth and acquisition record, products and services, how recently and deeply it has downsized personnel, corporate philosophy on outsourcing, sales volume, annual budget, number of employees, division structure and types of people it hires, market share, profitability, and location of physical facilities.

- ✔ The section "Resources for Research" in this chapter, gives you more information about how to research your next job.

What should you do when a friend wishes to float your resume among clients and colleagues and you don't know where it will land? If you value the friendship and can't persuade your friend that you would appreciate an interview instead, create a general resume reflecting what you most want to do. Complete the worksheets in Part III and then write a resume based on what you'd most like to do, listing the qualifications that support your goal.

When One Resume Will Do — or Must Do

As I often say, nothing beats a perfect or near-perfect match. Suppose a company sports a job opening requiring A, B, and C experience or education; by designing your resume for the target position, you show that you are well endowed with A, B, and C experience or education — a very close match between their requirements and your qualifications. Welcome to the short list of preferred candidates.

The trouble with creating a custom-tailored resume for every job opening is that many busy and beleaguered people feel as though they can barely manage to get to the dentist for a checkup, buy groceries, pick up the dry cleaning, ship the kids off to school on time, run over to fix Mom's furnace, and generally get through the day — much less write more than one version of an irresistible resume.

It may come down to this: One great resume, or no great resume.

A single version of your resume will usually do when you (a) are a new graduate or (b) have a fairly well-defined career path and intend not to work outside the lines of your experience. Even when you allow yourself the luxury of fielding just one resume, you can't put your feet up, watch the sunset, and drink margaritas. With each resume that you distribute, you must attach a personalized cover letter that directly targets the specific job opening. If writing letters is not your strong suit, *Cover Letters For Dummies,* Second Edition (IDG Books Worldwide, Inc., by yours truly), tells you how.

Resources for Research

A global knowledge revolution, as far-reaching as the Industrial Revolution, is changing business, and business is changing the job market. No one is immune as lifetime jobs become a memory. The good news is that more resources to help us find new work connections have appeared during the past decade than in all of previous history.

By researching the company and industry to customize your resume and determine new job prospects, not only do you gain the firepower to create a FirstRate resume, but you also build an arsenal of data points to use later in interviews.

You won't use every scrap of research, of course. Some data will be useful only for impressing your future coworkers at the next office holiday party. The problem is knowing which data will be surplus; glean as much as time and your study habits permit. *In general, the higher the level of job you seek, the more research you need to do in order to be seen as the best candidate for the job.* Certainly, if you're writing a resume for an above-the-line job that you really want, pull out all the stops. (My book, *Job Interviews For Dummies,* Second Edition, contains a chapter on how to research companies.)

 ✔ Line up the usual suspects in printed form — directories, annual reports, newspapers, magazines and trade journals.

 ✔ Scout the Internet (see Chapter 14). If this suggestion is beyond your immediate reach, your new best friend should be a geek.

Entrepreneurs know that some people sell what they can make; others make what they can sell. Behind the simplicity of the statement is a profound concept. After you think about it for a few seconds, you'll realize that there's a corollary in resume writing. Don't be content with merely trying to sell what you can write. Find out what employers want when hiring for your field — find out what sells.

The FirstRate resume approach means that you write what you can sell. Research helps you find what you have that sells.

Write Until It's Right

Can you write a decent resume in nanoseconds? Several recent resume books sport titles insisting that you can do just about that. Bogus! A well-developed resume requires adequate curing time to form, mellow, and develop — as you recall, think, write, think some more, rewrite, proofread, get feedback, and rewrite.

All too many job hunters scatter hundreds of thrown-together resumes. Then they wait. Nothing happens. Why do you think nobody bothers to call with an interview offer? Does thrown-together too often get thrown out?

If you don't want to be left behind because of a thrown-together resume, write a FirstRate resume. It works. By now, you may be wondering which format to use. The fact is, any format can be molded into a FirstRate resume. Chapter 4 displays a selection of resume formats and suggests which ones may hold the most promise for you.

After tailoring your FirstRate resume, must you also customize a cover letter? Here's the wrong answer: No, just roll out the old I-saw-your-ad-and-I-am-enclosing-my-resume cliché. Here's the right answer:

Yes, a tailored cover letter is the perfect sales tool for a tailored resume.

But that's a topic for another book. (Check out *Cover Letters For Dummies,* Second Edition, for everything you need to know about cover letters and more.)

Who am I? What do I want to do?

Does your career make you feel as if you're stuck in traffic? Then here are a few free Web sites that can help you start moving again. They offer many tips on career decision-making and management:

The Career Key by Dr. Lawrence K. Jones and other academicians specializing in career development. Much of the work is based on legendary John Holland's six basic personality types. You're given a list of jobs which could be appropriate for analysis you devise. Directions: Go to www.ncsu.edu, click on Employment/career development, then University career center, then Explore careers, and Career key.

Bowling Green State University offers a series of non-scored tests to open your mind. Directions: www.bgsu.edu/offices/careers/process/process.html.

Online Personality Tests aren't scored but do focus on you as a person who works. Directions: Go to www.2h.com, click on Personality tests.

The Canadian University of Waterloo offers a vast collection of forms to help you think things out and create a career management plan. Directions: Go to www.uwaterloo.ca, click on Career services, then Career development manual.

The TrimaCareer Competency Questionnaire classifies personality traits and skills by five types. Directions: Go to psychometrics.com, click on Online Testing.

Kaplan Educational Centers provides 10 tests including the Kiersey Temperament Sorter, a kissing cousin to the Myers-Briggs and which results in a MBTI-like code. Directions: Go to www.kaptest.com, click on Mind games, then on Self quizzes, then on Test yourself.

Queendom's Best Tests for Career Hunters doesn't pretend to be scientific, but offers a collection of career-focused quizzes, ranging from personality to owning a business. Directions: Go to www.queendom.com, click on Tests, tests, tests.

TypeFocus is designed to help people find satisfying work by assessing personality type. The freebie self-test is short, perhaps taking eight minutes to complete. The full version is also available for a fee, find it at typefocus.com.

Chapter 4

Formats Mean a lot: Choose Wisely

* *

In This Chapter

▶ Selecting your best format

▶ Using handy templates

▶ Comparing format features

* *

*R*esume format refers not to the design or look of your resume but to how you organize and emphasize your information. *Different format styles flatter different histories.* This chapter helps you choose a format that headlines your strengths and hides your shortcomings.

If you've been in the job wars, resume formats focus your hard-news reporting of the forts you've captured, the flags you've flown, and the good-conduct medals you're entitled to wear. If you don't have a track record of achievements, accomplishments, and quantifiable results yet — if you just got out of school and haven't been to job boot camp — your resume's format impacts how long you will serve in the unemployed ranks. So pay attention!

An extensive lineup of resume formats follows. A template you can use for developing your own resume illustrates each. Reconnoiter the lot of them before deciding *which best tells your story.*

Resume Formats

The three basic resume styles are

✔ Reverse chronological

✔ Functional

✔ Hybrid (also called *combination*)

These basic styles have spawned a variety of other formats:

- Accomplishment
- Curriculum vitae, academic
- Curriculum vitae, international
- KeyWord
- Linear
- Portfolio
- Professional
- Targeted

Table 4-1 gives you a breakdown of which format to use when.

Table 4-1	Choosing Your Best Resume Format at a Glance
Your Situation	*Formats to Try*
Perfect career pattern	Reverse chronological, targeted
Rookie or ex-military	Functional, hybrid, accomplishment, targeted, linear
Seasoned ace	Functional, hybrid, accomplishment, KeyWord
Computer friendly	KeyWord
Business	Reverse chronological, accomplishment, targeted
Technical	KeyWord, targeted, accomplishment, reverse chronological
Professional	Professional, academic curriculum vitae, portfolio
Government	Reverse chronological, professional
Arts/teaching	Professional, portfolio, academic curriculum vitae
Job history gaps	Functional, hybrid, linear, targeted
Multitrack job history	Functional, hybrid, targeted, KeyWord
Career change	Functional, KeyWord, targeted
International job seeker	International curriculum vitae
Special issues	Functional, hybrid, targeted

REZREADER

Why the reverse chronological format is the heavy favorite

Recruiters and other RezReaders prefer the joy of a chronological job-by-job retelling of your experience because it's a fast read and permits them to spot flaws easily.

Screening *out* all but the very best candidates in a pool is the recruiter's job; screening yourself *into* the candidate pool is your job. If your story cannot best be told in a reverse chronological resume, don't roll over and use the chronological format just because recruiters favor the style.

You and the recruiter don't have the same goals on this issue. The recruiter wants to screen out quickly. But you want the recruiter to take a second look. Presenting your qualifications in the most flattering format best displays your experience and talents, possibly getting you into that *in* pool that the recruiter would otherwise have taken you out of.

At root, formats come in three family trees: The *reverse chronological* lists all employment and education, beginning with the most recent and working backward. The skills-based *functional* shouts what you can do instead of relaying what you've done and where you did it. The *hybrid* or *combination* is a marriage of both formats. Take a close look at each of these three progenitors before you examine their saplings.

Note: The narrative format is a chronological format starting with the oldest facts and working forward to the newest facts. It's old-fashioned. A pretentious variation of the narrative format is using the third person as though you were writing a biography.

Reverse Chronological Format

The reverse chronological (RC) format is straightforward: It cites your employments from the most recent back, showing dates as well as employers and educational institutions (college, vocational-technical schools, and career-oriented programs and courses). You accent a steady work history with a clear pattern of upward or lateral mobility.

Some famous, wise, and savvy resume gurus say reverse chronological and functional are the only two resume styles. They don't count hybrid styles. But what do they know?

Reverse chronological format

YOUR NAME
Home Address
City, State, Zip Code
(###) ###-#### (Telephone), (###) ###-#### (Fax)
###@###.### (E-mail)

Objective:
A position that uses your skills.

SUMMARY
- Number of years of work experience, paid and unpaid, relevant to target position
- Achievement that proves you can handle the target
- Another achievement that proves you can handle the target
- Skills, traits, characteristics — facts that further your ability to handle the target
- Education and training relating to the target (if unrelated, bury in resume body)

PROFESSIONAL EXPERIENCE AND ACCOMPLISHMENTS

20## - Present **Job Title** Employer, Employer's Location
A brief synopsis of your purpose in the company, detailing essential functions, products
and customer base you managed.
- An achievement in this position relevant to objective (do not repeat summary)
- A second achievement in this position relevant to current objective
- More accomplishments, i.e., awards, recognition, promotion, raise, praise, training

19## - 20## Job Title Employer, Employer's Location
Detailed as above.

19## - 19## Job Title Employer, Employer's Location
A briefer synopsis of your purpose in the company, overviewing functions, products,
customer base.
- An achievement made during this position relevant to current objective
- More accomplishments, i.e., awards, recognition, promotion, raise, praise, training

19## - 19## Job Title Employer, Employer's Location
An even briefer synopsis of your purpose in the company, overviewing functions,
products, customer base.
- An achievement made during this position that's relevant to current objective

EDUCATION AND PROFESSIONAL TRAINING

Degree(s), classes, seminars, educational awards and honors
Credentials, clearances, licenses

Strengths:

- ✔ This format is by far the most popular with employers and recruiters because it seems so, well, up-front.

- ✔ RC links employment dates, underscoring continuity. The weight of your experience confirms that you are a "social service," "technical," or other career specialist.

- ✔ RC positions you for the next upward career step.

- ✔ As the most traditional of formats, RC fits traditional industries (such as banking, education, and accounting).

Weaknesses:

- ✔ When previous job titles are at variance with the target position, this format does not support the objective. Without careful management, it reveals everything, including inconsequential jobs and negative factors.

- ✔ RC can spotlight periods of unemployment or brief job tenure.

- ✔ Without careful management, RC reveals your age.

- ✔ Without careful management, RC may suggest that you were plateaued in a job too long.

Who should use this format and who should think twice

Use the RC if you fall into any of these categories:

- ✔ You have a steady school and work record reflecting constant growth or lateral movement.

- ✔ Your most recent employer is a respected name in the industry, and the name may ease your entry into a new position.

- ✔ Your most recent job titles are impressive stepping-stones.

- ✔ You're a FirstRate-savvy writer who knows how to manage potential negative factors, such as inconsequential jobs, too few jobs, too many temporary jobs, too many years at the same job, or too many years of age.

Who says a reverse chronological resume can't be sexy?

Three tiny color logos seeded in an otherwise plain reverse chronological resume for a former-Marine-turned-new-college-graduate appealed mightily to a food-processing plant in Evansville, Indiana. The dime-sized logos were those of the Marine Corps, the University of Southern Indiana, and St. Mary's Medical Center, where the graduate worked while in school.

I usually discourage resume logos because the ones I've seen are about as tasteful as bumper stickers and, technologically speaking, accident prone (meltdown occurs when job computers meet resume graphics).

This logo-laden reverse chronological resume must have had star power, however, which proves that exceptions exist for every opinion. Former USI Career Services and Placement Assistant Director Tracy Powers says that not only was the new graduate tapped from an applicant pool of 2,000, but he was wooed with a top-dollar offer.

Here's who should think twice:

✔ Young people with anorexic employment histories may not do fabulously with this format. Listing a stray student job or two is not persuasive, even when you open with superb educational credentials that are even better with internships and co-op experiences. Rookies, with careful attention, you can do a credible job on an RC by extracting from your extracurricular activities every shred of skills, which you present as abilities to do work with extraordinary commitment and a head for quick learning.

✔ People with work history problems — gaps, demotions, stagnation in a single position, job hopping through four jobs in three years, reentering the workforce after a break to raise a family — must exercise very careful management to truthfully modify stark realities. Other formats may serve you better.

✔ This is not the format of choice for career changers or people who have significant work history problems — ex-inmates and people who have experienced mental disabilities, for example.

Instructions

The FirstRate way to create an RC is as follows:

▌ ✔ Focus on areas of specific relevance to your target position or career field.

✔ List all pertinent places worked, including for each the name of the employer and the city in which you worked, the years you were there, your title, your responsibilities, and your measurable achievements.

✔ The RC template included in this chapter is generic and does not show how to handle problems. You can group problems in a second work history section under a heading of *Other Experience,* or *Previous Experience,* or *Related Experience.*

Functional Format

The functional format is a resume of ability-focused topics — portable skills or functional areas. It ignores chronological order. In its purest form, the functional style omits dates, employers, and job titles. Employers do not like absence of particulars, which is why contemporary functional resumes list employers, job titles, and sometimes dates — but still downplay this information by briefly listing it at the bottom of the resume. The functional format is oriented toward what the job seeker can do for the employer instead of narrating history.

Strengths:

✔ A functional resume directs a RezReader's eyes to what you want noticed. It helps a reader visualize what you can do instead of locking into a rigid perspective of when and where you learned to do it. Functional resumes salute the future rather than embalm the past.

✔ The functional format — written after researching the target company — serves up the precise functions or skills that the employer wants. It's like saying, "You want budget control and turnaround skills — I have budget control and turnaround skills." The skills sell is a magnet to RezReader eyes!

✔ It uses unpaid and nonwork experience to your best advantage.

✔ It allows you to eliminate or subordinate work history that does not support your current objective.

Weaknesses:

✔ Because recruiters and employers are more accustomed to RC formats, departing from the norm may raise suspicion that you're not the cream of the crop of applicants. They may assume that you're trying to hide inadequate experience, educational deficits, or who knows what.

✔ Functional styles may leave unclear which skills grew from which jobs or experiences.

✔ A clear career path is not obvious.

✔ This format does not maximize recent coups in the job market.

Functional format

YOUR NAME
Address, City, State, Zip Code
(###) ###-#### (Telephone), (###) ###-#### (Fax)
###@###.### (E-mail)

Job Title You Desire

More than (# years paid and unpaid) work experience, in target area, contributing to an (achievement/result/high ranking in industry/top 5% of performance reviews). Add accomplishments, strengths, proficiencies, characteristics, education, brief testimonial — anything that supports your target job title.

PROFESSIONAL EXPERIENCE AND ACCOMPLISHMENTS

A TOP SKILL (Pertinent to objective)
- An achievement illustrating this skill, and the location/employer of this skill *
- A second achievement illustrating this skill, and the location/employer of this skill*

A SECOND TOP SKILL (Pertinent to objective)
- An achievement illustrating this skill, and the location/employer of this skill *
- A second achievement illustrating this skill, and the location/employer of this skill*

A THIRD TOP SKILL (Pertinent to objective)
- An achievement illustrating this skill, and the location/employer of this skill *
- A second achievement illustrating this skill, and the location/employer of this skill*

A FOURTH SKILL (Optional — must relate to objective)
- Detailed as above

A UNIQUE AREA OF PROFICIENCY (Pertinent to objective)
- An achievement testifying to this proficiency, including the location/employer *
- A list of equipment, processes, software, or terms you know that reflect your familiarity with this area of proficiency
- A list of training experiences that document your proficiency

EMPLOYMENT HISTORY

20## - Present	**Job Title**	Employer, Location
19## - 20##	**Job Title**	Employer, Location
19## - 19##	**Job Title**	Employer, Location
19## - 19##	**Job Title**	Employer, Location

PROFESSIONAL TRAINING AND EDUCATION
Degrees, credentials, clearances, licenses, classes, seminars, training

* Omit locations/employers if your work history is obviously lacking in lockstep upward mobility

Who should use this format and who should think twice

This resume is heaven-sent for career changers, new graduates, ex-military personnel, seasoned aces, and individuals with multitrack job histories, work history gaps, or special-issue problems.

Job seekers with blue-ribbon backgrounds and managers and professionals who are often tapped by executive recruiters should avoid this format.

Instructions

Choose areas of expertise that you have acquired during the course of your career, including education and unpaid activities. These areas become skill and functional headings, which vary by the target position or career field. Achievements are noted below each heading. A few examples of headings are: *Management, Sales, Budget Control, Cost Cutting, Project Implementation,* and *Turnaround Successes.*

List the headings in the order of importance. Use a series of short statements when grouping your skills. Turn your statements into power hitters with measurable achievements.

Hybrid Format

The hybrid, a combination of reverse chronological and functional formats, satisfies demands for timelines as well as showcases your marketable skills and impressive accomplishments. Many people find the hybrid — or one of its offspring — the most attractive of all formats.

Essentially, in a hybrid, a functional summary tops a reverse chronological presentation of dates, employers, and capsules of each position's duties.

The hybrid style is similar to the contemporary functional format — so much so that making a case for distinction is sometimes difficult.

Strength: A hybrid format combines the strengths of both the reverse chronological and functional formats.

Weakness: A hybrid style contains more "frills" than a very conservative RezReader may prefer.

Templates: Pro and con

Some resume advisers argue that people who use a model template reflect no ingenuity and independence, somehow forecasting future robotic behavior on the job. Lumping qualifications into a mold not parallel to the individual's background proves that the applicant is lazy, template critics say.

Other resume advisers diagnose the anti-template crowd as being out of their cotton-pickin' minds. Template advocates applaud predesigned formats. They appreciate applicants' abilities to use expert advice; these applicants show that they can follow by example but know how to channel their selling points. As one adviser says, "Everyone tweaks templates a bit. Why reinvent the wheel?"

Templates are guides, not handcuffs — you're not locked into anything.

Who should use this format and who should think twice

The hybrid is a wise choice for rookies, ex-military personnel, seasoned aces, those with job history gaps or a multitrack job history, and individuals with special-issue problems.

Career changers or job seekers needing more appropriate formats, such as functional or portfolio, should skip the hybrid.

Instructions

Build a functional format of ability-focused topics and add employment documentation — employers, locations, dates, and duties.

Accomplishment Format

Definitely not a boring read, an accomplishment format immediately moves your strongest marketing points to center stage, grabs the reader's interest, and doesn't let go. As a rapper might intone: Use flash and dash to go for cash.

A sapling to the hybrid resume, the accomplishment format banners both qualifications *and* accomplishments. This is the format of choice for many executives, particularly in traditionally mobile industries, such as advertising, communications, and publishing.

Hybrid format

YOUR NAME
Address, City, State, Zip Code
(###) ###-#### (Telephone), (###) ###-#### (Fax)
###@###.### (E-mail)

Objective: Position as_____using your___ (#) years of experience in skills key to target.

SUMMARY OF QUALIFICATIONS
Number of years in area of target position
Related education, training and accreditation
An achievement pertinent to objective
Traits that reinforce your candidacy for this position
Other accomplishments, characteristics, proficiencies

SUMMARY OF SKILLS
• Technical skills   • Processes   • Computer software

ACCOMPLISHMENTS AND EXPERIENCE

Job Title, Top Proficiencies Used   Employer, Location

A Top Skill (Pertinent to objective)
• Accomplishments made while in this position
• Several apt achievements from position, pertinent to this skill and the objective
Another Skill (Pertinent to objective)
• Several achievements pertinent to this skill and the objective
                                            20## - Present

Job Title, Top Proficiencies Used   Employer, Location

A Top Skill (Pertinent to objective)
• Accomplishments made while in this position, even more detailed
• Several apt achievements from this position, similar to above
Another Skill (Pertinent to objective)
• Several achievements pertinent to this skill and the objective
                                            19## - 20##

Job Title, Top Proficiencies Used   Employer, Location

A Top Skill (Pertinent to objective)
• Accomplishments made while in this position
• Several apt achievements from position, pertinent to this skill and the objective
Another Skill (Pertinent to objective)
• Several achievements pertinent to this skill and the objective
                                            19## - 19##

PROFESSIONAL TRAINING AND EDUCATION
Degrees, accreditations, licenses, clearances, courses

Strength: This format offers benefits similar to those of functional and hybrid styles noted earlier.

Weakness: Readers who prefer a reverse chronological style may view the accomplishment format as too jazzed up.

Who should use this format and who should think twice

Here's when to use the accomplishment format:

- ✔ The same people who consider functional and hybrid styles should look at this one: career changers, new graduates, ex-military personnel, seasoned aces, and individuals with multitrack job histories, work history gaps, or special-issue problems. The accomplishment presentation is especially effective for individuals whose work history may not have been smooth but was, at times, bright with great successes.

- ✔ Individuals returning to payroll status after a period of self-employment find this format effective.

People who have climbed career steps without a stumble should use a reverse chronological format instead of the accomplishment format.

Instructions

List accomplishments in order of importance, making chronology a secondary factor. Close with a summarized reverse chronological work history.

Formats to use when the executive recruiter calls

Executive recruiting is usually a response to an employer's known problem in a given business area. Accomplishment formats, along with reverse chronological and targeted styles, are well equipped to tell employers how you can solve their problems.

When an executive recruiter calls, ask for enough details about the position's problem areas to give you ammunition for whipping out a made-to-order resume. If you're a candidate, the recruiter may be happy to have as many as four *readable* pages about your background, as long as you grab attention on the first page. Remember that most executive decision makers favor reverse chronological presentations, so use conservative language in drawing attention to your accomplishments on this format. See Chapter 6 for more information about the language of resumes.

Accomplishment format

YOUR NAME

Address   Telephone Number: (###) ###-####
City, State, Zip Code   E-mail: #####@##.###
                                               Message and/or Fax Number(s): (###) ###-####

OBJECTIVE
Position as___using skills and experience accumulated over __(#) years.

QUALIFICATIONS
 • Number of years of experience that is pertinent to objective
 • Your record of improvement or reputation in the industry
 • Specific skills and training apt to objective
 • Areas of specialized proficiency
 • Work ethic traits demonstrating candidacy and constructiveness

SKILLS
 • Equipment familiarities   • Terminology familiarities
 • Procedural familiarities   • Technological
familiarities

ACCOMPLISHMENTS
In any order, list accomplishments (quantifying with numbers and percentages when
appropriate) that elaborate such achievements as

        -competitive skills, technological proficiency, professional aptness
        -improvements, innovations
        -revenue-saving strategies
        -promotions, raises
        -increasing responsibilities, management and troubleshooting functions
        -praise from employers and/or coworkers
        -training rendered, training received

PROFESSIONAL EXPERIENCE
 • **Job Title**   **Employer, Location**   **19## - 20##**
 • **Job Title**   **Employer, Location**   **19## - 19##**
 • **Job Title**   **Employer, Location**   **19## - 19##**
 • **Job Title**   **Employer, Location**   **19## - 19##**

EDUCATION
Academic and professional accreditation(s), major(s), minor(s), emphasis
Universities, schools, and courses attended or in progress

Targeted Format

A targeted format, tailored to a given job, is VIP (very important person) treatment. Targeting is persuasive because everyone likes to be given the VIP treatment.

The targeted style is written to match point-for-point a specific job that is offered by a specific employer.

The template in this chapter is but one way to build a targeted resume. You can equally benefit with other format options springing from the functional or hybrid branches of the resume family. You choose.

Strength: The targeted format shows the employer that you're a good match for the position.

Weakness: You may not be readily considered for other jobs.

Who should use this format and who should think twice

Pretty much everyone kicks butt with a targeted resume. Ex-military personnel can translate militaryspeak to civilianese, rookies can equate their non-paid experience to employer requirements, and seasoned aces can reach deep into their backgrounds to show, item for item, how they qualify. This format is a reasoned choice for people with strong work histories but a few zits here and there.

The targeted format is not a great idea for anyone who is lazy about doing research — the success of the targeted resume depends on your lining up data ducks in advance.

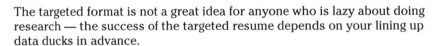

When resumes and research are beyond reach

You say you're not sure you want to do enough research on a position to write a targeted resume? Definitely not a FirstRate mind-set, but you're still ahead of an applicant who wrote the following query to the human resources department of a big company (I did not make this up):

Dear Sirs, I would very much like to send a resume to you, but I haven't the slightest idea how to fill out a resume, and I can't remember the dates or addresses for any of it anyway. So if that is going to keep me from being employed by your company, then to hell with it! Otherwise, call me in for an interview and a job.

Targeted format

YOUR NAME
Address, City, State, Zip Code
Telephone (###) ###-####, Fax (###) ###-####
E-mail ###@###.###

Objective: Position as_____(title of job employer offers) using your___ (#) years
of experience in skills essential and specialized to the position.

SUMMARY OF QUALIFICATIONS

- Number of years in area of target, explaining similarities to objective position/duties
- Related education, training, accreditation — specifically those employer appreciates
- An achievement directly related to target
- Traits reinforcing your candidacy for this position, specifically those employer wants
- Other accomplishments, characteristics, knowledge either rare or prized in the field

SUMMARY OF SKILLS

•Technical skills employer wants
•Processes employer uses
•Computer and software skills employer needs

ACCOMPLISHMENTS AND EXPERIENCE

Job Title   Employer, Location   20## - Present

A Top Skill (Pertinent to objective)

- Accomplishments made in this position targeting the employer's priorities or
customer base

- Several other apt achievements from position, pertinent to skill and objective

Another Top Skill (Pertinent to objective)

- Several apt achievements pertinent to this skill and the objective

Job Title   Employer, Location   19## - 20##
Details as above

Job Title   Employer, Location   19## - 19##
Details as above

PROFESSIONAL TRAINING AND EDUCATION
Degrees, accreditations, licenses, clearances, courses

Instructions

Find out what the position demands and — fact for fact — write how you offer exactly those goods. If you can meet better than 80 percent of the position's requirements, you've got a shot at an interview; if less than 80 percent, don't give up breathing while you wait for your telephone to ring.

Linear Format

A linear format (line by line — hence, *linear*) tells your story in the short spurts of benefits (achievements, winning moves) that you offer. An offspring of the reverse chronological format, the linear doesn't get into great detail; it sparks curiosity to meet you and find out more.

This spaced-out variation of the reverse chronological format lacks a job objective section and opens with a skills summary instead. Plenty of white space is the hallmark of this achievement-highlighted document.

Career advisers pin a blue ribbon on this format.

Strengths:

- ✔ Linear resumes are very easy to read quickly, particularly in a stack of resumes a foot high. Instant readability is increasingly important as harried RezReaders struggle with the clock and baby boomers become middle-aged RezReaders whose eyes do not enjoy poring over pages sagging with text.

- ✔ Because the format presents your starring events in a line-by-line visual presentation, your achievements are not likely to be overlooked as they would be if buried deep in a text paragraph.

Weakness: You can't pack as much information into a linear (remember the white space), but you can pack plenty of sell.

Who should use this format and who should think twice

This format works to showcase career progression — steady as you go. If that's you, use the linear.

Job seekers with gaps in employment, too many jobs, few advancements, or scant experience and those who have seen enough sunrises to be on the shady side of 50 should avoid the linear.

Linear format

YOUR NAME
Address, City, State, Zip Code
(###) ###-#### (Telephone), (###) ###-#### (Fax)
###@###.### (E-mail)

QUALIFICATIONS SUMMARY

- Number of years of work experience, paid and unpaid, pertinent to objective position
- Accomplishment(s) that prove your unique candidacy for this position
- Skills geared for the objective position or company
- Other things the employer will like to know — proficiencies, characteristics, achievements, training, credentials and education

PROFESSIONAL EXPERIENCE AND ACCOMPLISHMENTS

20## - Present   **Job Title**   Employer, Employer's Location

- An achievement made during this position that is pertinent to current objective, detailing job skills and responsibilities

- A second achievement made during this position also pertinent to current objective

- More accomplishments — that is, awards, recognition, promotion, raise, praise, training

* Divide description according to titles held with employer, listing titles as subheadings.

19## - 19##   **Job Title**   Employer, Employer's Location

Same details as above.

* Divide description according to titles held with employer, listing titles as subheadings.

19## - 19##   **Job Title**   Employer, Employer's Location

Same details as above.

* Divide description according to titles held with employer, listing titles as subheadings.

EDUCATION AND PROFESSIONAL TRAINING

Degree(s), university, year
Major
Top achievement

* Include other seminars, awards, honors, credentials, clearances, licenses.

COMMUNITY LEADERSHIP

Memberships and other offices in community organizations

Instructions

Write down your achievements and other necessary data, look at the big lumps of text, and then divide and conquer. Think white space.

Professional Format

A professional format, also called a professional vitae, is slightly long-winded (say, 3 to 5 pages) but factual. It emphasizes professional qualifications and activities. This format is essentially a shortened academic curriculum vitae.

Strength: The professional resume is mandatory for certain kinds of positions; your choice is whether to send this type or go all the way and send an academic curriculum vitae.

Weakness: Professional resumes are reviewed under a microscope; every deficiency stands out. Adding a portfolio that shows your experience-based work skills may compensate for missing chunks of formal requirements. Just be sure that any unsolicited samples you send are FirstRate quality and need no explanation.

Who should use this format and who should think twice

Professionals in medicine, science, and law should use this format. Also use it when common sense or convention makes it the logical choice.

For most nonprofessionals, especially managers, the professional format is tedious.

Instructions

Begin with education, professional training, and an objective. Follow with a summary of main points that you want the reader to absorb. Follow with details of your professional experience and accomplishments.

Follow the template in this chapter, paying attention to accomplishments. Just because you present yourself in a low-key, authoritative manner does not mean that you can forget to say how good you are.

Professional format

YOUR NAME
Address, City, State, Zip Code
(###) ###-#### (Telephone), (###) ###-#### (Fax)
###@###.### (E-mail)

EDUCATION AND PROFESSIONAL TRAINING

Degrees, credentials, awards, achievements, honors, seminars, clearances, licenses.

OBJECTIVE: A position that uses your talents, with an emphasis on your special skills.

SUMMARY

• Number of years of work experience, paid and unpaid, relevant to target

• Accomplishment(s) that prove your unique candidacy for this position

• Strengths geared for the objective position or company

• Other things the employer will like to know — proficiencies, characteristics, achievements, training, credentials and education

PROFESSIONAL EXPERIENCE AND ACCOMPLISHMENTS

20## - Present   **Job Title**   Employer, Employer's Location

A brief synopsis of your purpose in the company, detailing essential functions and products you managed, and your customer base.

   • An achievement made during position pertinent to target

   • A second achievement made during position also pertinent to target

   • More achievements — awards, recognition, promotion, raise, praise, training

19## - 20##   **Job Title**   Employer, Employer's Location

An even briefer synopsis of your purpose in the company, overviewing functions, products, customer base.

   • An achievement made during this position that is applicable to target

   • More achievements — awards, recognition, promotion, raise, praise, training

* *List three previous jobs with the same detail as above; divide jobs according to job title, not employer.*

KeyWord Format

Any resume can be a KeyWord resume, as described in Chapter 13. It becomes a KeyWord resume when you add a *profile of KeyWords* (nouns identifying your qualifications) anywhere on any type of format. I like front-loading a KeyWord preface at the top of the resume.

The template shown in this chapter is a format that works well for computer scanning. Support your KeyWords with facts but do not repeat the exact phrasing in a KeyWord profile and in other parts of your resume — vary your language. Repetition must be handled with thought.

Strength: Virtually everyone benefits from using a KeyWord profile — it functions like a skills summary. Job seekers sending resumes by e-mail or postings on the Internet should always include KeyWords.

Weakness: A minority of recruiters dislike a KeyWord preface. Their objection: "It appears to be a check-box–oriented approach to doing a resume." It's not a weakness that's likely to get you rejected out-of-hand, however. If the body of the resume supports your KeyWords (which it should if it's FirstRate quality), and you can do only one resume, it's worth the risk.

Who should use this format and who should think twice

Most job seekers should consider the KeyWord option. Resumes of technical people can't leave home without it.

However, top management executives (the $500,000-a-year-and-up kind) are unlikely to be recruited from resume databases. Executive recruiters do, however, construct their own in-house databases. In building these in-house databases, they may import from public-domain databases that input information from traditional resumes and other sources.

Instructions

As the KeyWord template shows, you begin with your contact information, followed by a KeyWord profile, followed by an objective, several strengths, and reverse chronological employment history.

You may choose not to use a front-loaded KeyWord profile but to use instead a one-paragraph qualifications summary or a skills section composed of brief (one- or two-line) statements. The more KeyWords (or skills) in your resume, the better your chances of being summoned for an interview.

KeyWord format

YOUR NAME
Address
City, State, Zip Code
(###) ###-#### (Telephone)
###@###.### (E-mail)

KeyWords: General nouns, phrases, and terminology known to be valued in the position and industry; specific KeyWords descriptive of duties and proficiencies necessary to position; specific terms known to be priority to employer/company you're applying to, including credentials, years of experience, areas of familiarity, and equipment involved

Objective: Title of opening, using the following highlights of your background:
• Number of years of work experience, paid and unpaid, relevant to target
• Accomplishment(s) that prove your unique candidacy for this position
• Strengths geared for the objective position or company, education, credentials and training

PROFESSIONAL EXPERIENCE AND ACCOMPLISHMENTS

20## - Present Employer, Employer's Location
Present Job Title
A brief synopsis of your purpose in the company, detailing essential functions and products you rendered, and customer base.
• An achievement made during position appropriate to current objective
• A second achievement made during position also apt to objective
• More achievements, awards, recognition, promotion, raise, praise
• Equipment used, processes, procedures, in noun form

19## - 19##   **Employer, Employer's Location**
Job Title
* Same details as above.

19## - 19##   **Employer, Employer's Location**
Job Title
A briefer synopsis of your purpose, similar to previous job.
• An achievement made during position pertinent to current objective
• A second achievement made during position that's a priority in current objective
• Equipment used, processes, procedures, in noun form

19## - 19##   **Employer, Employer's Location**
Job Title
An even briefer synopsis of position, overviewing functions, products, customer base.
• An achievement made during position pertinent to current objective
• Equipment used, processes, procedures, in noun form

EDUCATION AND PROFESSIONAL TRAINING
Degrees, classes, seminars, awards, achievements, honors, credentials, clearances, licenses

Look for the French flair

The French have a tasty twist on resumes: They have been known to put them on wine bottles. In a move to help young graduates find their places in the working society, some civic-minded winemakers a dozen years ago began the inspired custom of affixing a graduate's resume to the back of some of the year's best vintage reds and whites. *Bon emploi!*

Academic Curriculum Vitae (CV)

The academic CV is a comprehensive biographical statement, typically three to ten pages, emphasizing professional qualifications and activities. A CV of six to eight pages, ten at the most, is recommended for a veteran professional; two to four pages is appropriate for a young professional just starting out (see the professional format).

If your CV is more than four pages long, show mercy and save eyesight by attaching an *executive summary* page to the top. An executive summary gives a brief overview of your qualifications and experience.

Among various possible organizations, the template in this chapter (a sapling of the hybrid format but with exhaustive coverage) illustrates a lineup of your contact information, objective, qualifications summary, skills summary, and professional background.

Strength: A CV presents all the best of you.

Weakness: For people with aging eyes, a CV is reading-intensive. More important, weaknesses in any area of your professional credentials are relatively easy to spot.

Who should use this format and who should think twice

Anyone working in a Ph.D.-driven environment, such as higher education, think tanks, science, and elite research and development groups, needs to use this format.

Anyone who can avoid using it should do so.

Academic Curriculum Vitae format

YOUR NAME
Curriculum Vitae
Address, City, State, Zip Code
(###) ###-#### (Telephone), (###) ###-#### (Fax)
###@###.### (E-mail address)

Objective (optional): Position as_____(title of position employer offers) using ___ (#) years of experience in _____ (skills essential and specialized to the position).

SUMMARY OF QUALIFICATIONS

- A summary of your education, proficiencies, and career pertinent to target
- Number of years in objective area, explaining similarities to job and its responsibilities
- Related education, training, and accreditation, reflecting employer's goals/ priorities
- An achievement directly related to target
- Traits reinforcing your candidacy for this position, specifically those asked for by the employer and those generally in demand in the field
- Other accomplishments, characteristics, knowledge either rare or prized in the field

SUMMARY OF SKILLS

•Topics of specialty or innovation within field •Areas of particular familiarity
•Software equipment •Processes •Terminology relevant to target •Languages

PROFESSIONAL BACKGROUND

EDUCATION
Degrees:
   Ph.D., institution, date of degree (or anticipated date), specialization
   M.A./M.S., institution, date of degree, major, minor, emphasis, concentration
   B.A./B.S., institution, date of degree, major, minor
Courses: Those taken, honors, seminars, number of units, G.P.A. (if a recent graduate)
Other Accreditations: Licenses, clearances
Academic Achievements: Appointments, nominations, leaderships, scholarships, grants, awards, praise, scores, recognitions, accomplishments
Affiliations: Societies, associations, clubs, fraternities, sororities, leagues, memberships

PH.D. DISSERTATION
   Title, advisor, director
   Abstract summary (4-5 sentences) discussing content and methodology

HONORS, AWARDS, AND ACHIEVEMENTS
Appointments, nominations, leaderships, awards, praise, scores, recognitions, accomplishments, high scores, grades, G.P.A.s, fellowships, scholarships, grants, (including B.A./B.S.)

TEACHING EXPERIENCE

Job Title, Top Proficiencies Used   Employer, Location   **20## - Present**

A Top Responsibility (Relevant to objective)
• Accomplishments made in this position targeting the employer's priorities/mission
• Several other achievements from this position, pertinent to objective
Another Skill (Appropriate to objective)
• Several achievements from this position, pertinent to objective

* *Repeat above pattern for each position.*

RESEARCH EXPERIENCE
Positions, locations, dates, descriptions of research in pertinence to target position

TEACHING INTERESTS
Discipline, certification

RESEARCH INTERESTS
Areas of inquiry

PUBLICATIONS
* List all those you are willing to show the search committee
* Include work in progress or pending
* Cite works as follows:

•**"Title of work,"** Name of publication/publisher (*Newsletter, Newspaper, Magazine, Journal, Book*), location of publisher (state & city or major city), date of publication, volume number (v.##), issue number (#.#), series number (#.#.#), page numbers (# - #) (type quotes around the title of your article).

PRESENTATIONS AND PUBLIC APPEARANCES
* Include conference papers and research reports
* List as follows:

•**"Title of presentation,"** location of presentation (City, State), Date (20## - 20##); optional synopsis of content and/or purpose of presentation, audience, results, etc.

 PROFESSIONAL AFFILIATIONS
A society, association, league, or club with which you associate, position held, 19## - 20##
A society, association, league, or club with which you associate, position held, 19## - 20##
A society, association, league, or club with which you associate, position held, 19## - 20##

RECOMMENDATIONS
Names and contact information of 3-4 references willing to write recommendation letters

CREDENTIALS
Address where the recipient can access your career/placement file

Instructions

Create a comprehensive summary of your professional employment and accomplishments: education, positions, affiliations, honors, memberships, credentials, dissertation title, fields in which comprehensive examinations were passed, full citations of publications and presentations, awards, discoveries, inventions, patents, seminar leadership, foreign languages, courses taught — whatever is valued in your field.

FirstRaters, I recommend that you read a book or two on writing CVs because even these stereotypically somber documents can be brightened. I like the second edition of the *Academic Job Search Handbook* by Mary Morris Heiberger (University of Pennsylvania Press, Philadelphia; telephone 800-445-9880) and the second edition of *The Curriculum Vitae Handbook* by Rebecca Anthony and Gerald Roe (Rudi Publishing, San Francisco; telephone 800-999-6901).

International Curriculum Vitae Format

The international CV is not the same document as an academic CV. Think of an international CV as a six-to-eight-page excruciatingly-detailed resume. Although it solicits private information such as your health status that is outlawed in the U.S., the international CV is favored in some nations as a kind of global ticket to employment.

The international CV is usually a reverse chronological format that includes your contact information, qualifications summary, professional background, education, and personal information. Some European countries prefer the chronological format, which lists education and work experience from the furthest back to the present.

Americans should remember that when working overseas for a native employer, they are not protected by Equal Employment Opportunity laws.

Strength: International employment experts say that if you don't use this format, foreign recruiters may think you're hiding something.

Weakness: The international CV format intrudes into private areas of your life.

Who should use this format and who should think twice

Use this format if you're seeking an overseas job and do not object to revealing information that may subject you to discriminatory hiring practices.

Individuals who feel strongly about invasions of privacy or who are not willing to be rejected out of hand because of gender, religion, race, age, or marital status should avoid this format.

Of course, if you want an overseas job and you don't use this format, you may be out of luck unless you're working through an American recruiter. The recruiter can interpret your concerns and negotiate for a bare minimum of personal information. Nationals of countries other than the U.S. can also use this technique.

Instructions

Formality prevails with the international CV. In Japan, for example, job hunters still fill out standard forms, available at Japanese book shops. England has a suggested CV form, which is more like the American resume than not.

- ✔ If you're applying in a non-English-speaking country, have your CV translated into the appropriate foreign language. Send both the English and the native-language version.

- ✔ Unless it's untrue, mention in the personal section that you have excellent health.

- ✔ Suggest by appropriate hobbies and personal interests that you'll easily adapt to an overseas environment.

- ✔ Handwrite the cover letter that goes with your CV — Europeans use hand-writing analysis as a screening device. If your handwriting is iffy, enclose a word-processed version as well.

In addition, make sure that your cover letter shows a sincere desire to be in the country of choice.

Portfolio Format

Samples of your work, gathered in a portfolio, have long been valuable to fields such as design, graphics, photography, architecture, advertising, public relations, and education. Often the portfolios are delivered as part of the job interview, but some highly motivated job seekers include a brief portfolio when sending their resumes.

Even though recruiters say that they prefer less paper, the portfolio format is beginning to gain acceptance over the traditional resume format in other fields as well. The reason is jungle warfare in the job market: Portfolios are a way to prove by the quality of your work that you're right for a specific position.

International Curriculum Vitae format

YOUR NAME
Curriculum Vitae
Home Address, City, State, Country, Province, Zip Code
Include international codes:
(###) ###-#### (Telephone) (###) ###-#### (Fax)
###@###.### (E-mail address)
Objective (optional): Position as_____(title of position employer offers) using
your___ (#) years of experience in _____ (skills essential and specialized to the position).

SUMMARY OF QUALIFICATIONS

• A summary of your education, proficiencies, and career pertinent to target
• Number of years in area of objective, explaining similarities to it/its responsibilities
• Related education, training, and accreditation, reflecting employer's goals/priorities
• An achievement directly related to target, that the employer needs
• Traits reinforcing your candidacy for this position, specifically those asked for by the
  employer and those generally in demand in the field
• Other accomplishments, characteristics, knowledge either rare or prized in the field
• Traveling in field, countries visited, improvements made, distinctions, and so forth

SUMMARY OF SKILLS
• Topics of specialty or innovation within field   • Areas of particular familiarity
• Software equipment   • Processes   • Terminology relevant to target   • Languages

PROFESSIONAL BACKGROUND

EMPLOYMENT

Job Title   Employer, Location   **20## -**
Present
A Top Responsibility (Relevant to objective)
     • Accomplishments made in this position targeting the employer's
       priorities/mission
     • Several other achievements from this position, pertinent to objective
Another Skill (Appropriate to objective)
     • Several achievements from this position, pertinent to objective

     * *Repeat above pattern for all jobs.*

PROFESSIONAL HONORS
All honorary positions, awards, recognitions, or titles, with locations, 19## - 20##

PUBLICATIONS
•**"Title of work,"** Name of publication/publisher (*Newsletter, Newspaper, Magazine,
     Journal*), location of publisher (country, languages, state & city or major city), date of
     publication, volume number (v.##), issue number (#.#), series number (#.#.#), page
     numbers (# - #)

     * *Repeat above citation for all publications.*

PRESENTATIONS AND PUBLIC APPEARANCES
•**"Title of presentation,"** location of presentation (Country, City, State, Province, Language), Date (19## - 20##); optional synopsis of content and/or purpose of presentation, audience, results, etc.

> * *Repeat above citation for all presentations.*

PROFESSIONAL AFFILIATIONS
> All societies, associations, leagues, or clubs, positions held, locations, 19## - 20##

EDUCATION

Degrees: Ph.D., institution, date of degree (or anticipated date), specialization
M.A./M.S., institution, date of degree, major, minor, concentration
B.A./B.S., institution, date of degree, major, minor
> * *Give equivalents of these degrees in other countries*

Courses: Those taken, honors, seminars, number of units, G.P.A. (if a recent graduate)
Other Accreditations: Licenses, clearances
Academic Achievements: Appointments, nominations, leaderships, scholarships, grants, awards, praise, scores, recognitions, accomplishments
Affiliations: Societies, associations, clubs, fraternities, sororities, leagues, memberships

DOCTORAL DISSERTATION
Title, advisor, director
Abstract summary (4-5 sentences) discussing content and methodology

HONORS, AWARDS AND ACHIEVEMENTS
Appointments, nominations, leaderships, awards, praise, scores, recognitions, accomplishments, high scores, grades, G.P.A.s, fellowships, scholarships, grants, (including B.A./B.S/equivalents)

PERSONAL INFORMATION
• A sentence or so that describes personal attributes pertinent to employer's interests. Think positively, omit negatives, and highlight goal-oriented, functional characteristics that promise of a good worker-employer relationship and reliably good work product. Present specific work-related examples of these personality highlights and explain how they are significant to the employer. Without exaggerating, accentuate the positive, and include all favorable quotes from employers and co-workers, members of the clergy, and public service, volunteer organization, nonprofit organization and political officials
• Age, Marital Status (Single, Engaged, Married)
• Hobbies and leisure activities (travel, clubs, sports, athletics, collections, subscriptions)
• Volunteer service, public service

In designing your portfolio, when you summarize your key points for your resume, include samples that demonstrate each: printed material listing you as the leader of seminars and workshops, performance reviews, easily understandable examples of problem solving and competencies, and work samples. Include praise from employers, people who reported to you, and customers. Make at least two copies of your portfolio in case potential employers decide to hold on to your samples or fail to return them.

Your portfolio should document the skills that you want to apply on the job, so begin by identifying those skills; then determine what would prove your claims. The best book on the subject is Martin Kimmeldorf's *Portfolio Power* (Peterson's). A personal Web site contains many of Kimmeldorf's materials (`amby.com/kimeldorf`).

Choosing What Works for You

The big closing question to ask yourself when you have settled on a format is **Does this format maximize my qualifications for the job I want?**

If the format you've chosen doesn't promote your top qualifications, take another look at the choices in this chapter and select a format where you can shine.

Chapter 5

Contents Make the FirstRate Difference

● ●

In This Chapter

▶ Understanding the parts of your resume

▶ Making each part dazzle

● ●

*D*eciding what information to put into your resume isn't difficult if you remember the basic purpose: You must show that you can and will provide benefits to an employer. A small lad whom author Robert Fulghum met understood that principle very well. Fulghum wrote about him in *All I Really Need to Know I Learned in Kindergarten.* The boy rapped on Fulghum's door and handed him this note: *My name is Donnie. I will rake your leaves. $1 a yard. I am deaf. You can write to me. I read. I rake good.*

Regardless of how many sophisticated bells and whistles you add, the content of your resume must tell employers just how well you will rake their leaves.

The Parts of Your Resume

To make your contents easy to access, you organize the facts about you into various categories. Essential parts that make up a resume are

- ✔ Contact information
- ✔ Objective or summary statement
- ✔ Education and training
- ✔ Experience
- ✔ Skills
- ✔ Activities
- ✔ Organizations
- ✔ Honors and awards

Other sections that may be included on a resume are

- ✔ Licenses, work samples
- ✔ Testimonials

To increase the likelihood that your resume will position you for an interview, take the time to understand the purpose of the different resume parts.

Contact Information

No matter which format you choose, place your name first on your resume, followed by contact information.

- ✔ **Name:** If your name is not first, a job computer may mistake *Excellent Sales Representative* for your name and file you away as Mr. Representative. Often a name is displayed in slightly larger type and in boldface.

- ✔ **Mailing address:** Give a street name with the unit number, city, state, and zip code. If you're a college student or member of the military who will be returning home, give both addresses — *Current Address* and *Permanent Address.*

- ✔ **Valid telephone number:** Use a personal number, including the area code, where you can be reached or where the RezReader can leave a message. Do not allow children to answer this line. Do not record a clever message — play it straight. If you must share a telephone with kids, emphasize the need for them to answer the phone professionally and keep their calls short.

- ✔ **Other contact media:** Use any or all of the following if available to you: e-mail address, pager number, telephone answering service number, Web page address, and fax number.

What about using company resources? Should you ever use your employer's fax number, e-mail address, or letterhead? Many employers see an employee's use of company resources to find another job as small-time theft. In certain situations, however, you can use your company's help.

For example, when a company is downsizing, it is expected to provide resource support for outplacement. Contract employment is another exception: When you are ending the project for which you were hired, your employer may encourage you to use company resources. Indicate permission to use them in your resume's cover letter — *The project for which I was hired is finishing ahead of schedule; my grateful employer is cooperating in my new search.*

Is it okay to list your work telephone number on your resume? In a decade when employers have been tossing workers out without remorse, it's a tough world and you need speedy communications. The practical answer is yes, list your work number — if you have a direct line and voice mail or a pager. To show that you are an ethical person, limit calls to a couple of minutes — just long enough to arrange a meeting or an evening callback. Avoid the issue by packing your own cell phone.

Hooks: Objective or Summary?

Your FirstRate resume needs a hook to grab the RezReader's attention. The hook follows your name and contact information and is expressed as a job objective or as a skills summary — or some combination of the two.

A job objective can look like this:

Objective: Assistant to Executive

A skills summary can look like this:

> *Summary:* Over 14 years of progressively responsible office support experience, including superior computer skills, with an earned reputation for priority-setting and teamwork.

Or a job objective can be linked to a skills summary:

> *Objective:* Assistant to Executive, to keep operations under firmer control, using computer skills, contemporary office procedures, and pleasant manner with people.

However fashioned, the hook tells the RezReader what you want to do and/or what you are qualified to do.

Debate rages among career pros over the topic of objective versus summary.

- ✔ Objective backers say RezReaders don't want to slog through a document, trying to guess the type of position you want and how you'd fit into the organization — a serious consideration when they have to hand-sort big stacks of resumes.

- ✔ Summary advocates argue that a thumbnail sketch of your skills allows you to be evaluated for jobs you haven't identified in your job objective — a serious consideration in this new age of computerized resume database searches.

A quick guideline taken from a sampling of six recruiters, as reported in *Job Choices* magazine, is this: "Objective statement is essential for recent graduates, summary statement for seasoned professionals."

On balance, I agree with the six recruiters: An objective may be a self-defeating force for seasoned aces with well-established career paths, whose insistence on a particular job objective may be seen as rigid, and for those whose resumes will be stored in electronic databases. But an objective is nearly essential for job seekers who are short on experience or do not have a clear idea of what they'd like to do, but know the general direction.

What you really need on your resume is *focus,* whether you style it as a job objective or as a summary.

The following sections highlight specific points for each type of resume opener.

The job objective statement

Weigh these considerations when deciding how to help readers visualize what you could do in the future for them.

When to use an objective

Use a job objective when

> ✔ You are a new graduate, or a career changer exiting the military, the clergy, teaching, or full-time homemaking. A job objective says what you are looking for.
>
> ✔ You have a greatly diversified background that may perplex some employers.
>
> ✔ You know the job being offered; make that job title your job objective.

Advantages of an objective

Most studies show that employers prefer objectives for quick identification purposes. They like to see the name of their job openings and/or companies at the top of a resume. Because you cite those achievements that support your objective and forget random experiences, the finished product (when done well) shows that you and the desired job are a well-matched pair.

Disadvantages of an objective

Do you have the time to write a resume for each position (or career field) to which you apply? A narrow job objective may keep you from being considered by the same employer for other positions. And if the objective is too broadly focused, it becomes a meaningless statement.

The skills summary

A summary statement (see Chapter 9) announces who you are and identifies your strengths. Take a look at the sections that follow for tips on when a summary statement is best.

When to use a summary

Use a summary statement when

> ✔ You are a person with widely applicable skills. Recruiters especially like a skills summary atop a reverse chronological resume because it lets them creatively consider you for countless jobs that you may not know exist. The skills summary gives recruiters greater latitude to consider you for more than one position.

> ✔ You are in a career field with pathways to multiple occupations or industries (an administrative assistant, for example).

> ✔ You know that your resume is headed to an electronic database — or, more likely, you do not know whether humans or computers will screen your resume — and you want to be considered for multiple jobs.

Advantages of a summary

A summary can be more appropriate to status — senior executives, in particular, can let their records speak for them. Recruiters believe that what you're prepared to do next should be pretty evident from what you've already done. Another argument is premised on psychology: Employers are not known for being overly concerned with what you want *from* them until they are sure of what you can do *for* them.

Disadvantages of a summary

A summary does not explicitly say what you want and why the employer would want you. The technique of specifying a job objective in a cover letter attached to a skills-summary resume is common; the problems arise when the cover letter is inadvertently separated from the resume or the resume is passed out alone, as at a job fair. Furthermore, the fact that a skills summary resume leaves many doors open is a two-edged sword: Your accomplishments do not thrust you toward a specific target, so you may be abandoning a success strategy that has been proven again and again.

> ## What's first — education or experience?
>
> The general rule in resume writing is to lead with your most qualifying factor.
>
> With certain exceptions (such as law, where your choice of alma mater can dog you throughout life), lead off with experience when you've been in the workforce for at least three years. When you're loaded with experience but low on credentials, list your school days at the end — and perhaps even omit them entirely if you didn't graduate.
>
> Young people just out of school usually start with education, but if you've worked throughout school or have relevant prior work history, start with experience. Remember, begin with your most qualifying factor for the job you want.
>
> Young readers, if your research shows that a prospective employer wants education and experience, provide a summary linking them together as interdependent. For example, explain how your education was part of your professional experience, or how your experience was an education itself. Following this consolidation, create a heading under which you can merge both sections — such as *Professional Preparation* or *Education, Training, and Employment.*

A summary can be stated in paragraph form or in four to six bulleted quick-hits, such as:

- Recruited and trained more than 300 people

- Installed robotics, standardizing product, reducing retraining cost by 16%

- Slashed initial training costs from $800,000 to $650,000 within one year

- Created dynamic training culture to support the introduction of a new product

Education

List your highest degree first — type of degree, major, college name, and date awarded.

- ✔ New graduates give far more detail on course work than do seasoned aces who've held at least one job for one year or more.
- ✔ Omit high school or prep school if you have a college degree.

✔ If you have a vocational-technical school certificate or diploma that required less than a year to obtain, list your high school as well.

✔ Note continuing education, including seminars related to your work.

Experience

Describe — with quantified achievements — your present and previous positions in reverse chronological order. Include dates of employment, company names and locations, and specific job titles. Show progression and promotions within an organization, especially if you have been with one employer for eons.

Consider using more than one Experience heading. Try headings such as "Accounting and Finance-Related Experience," "General Business Experience," and "Healthcare and Administration Experience." This is yet one more way of reinforcing your suitability for the job you seek.

Some resume formats use a more rigid approach than others, allowing little leeway as you fill in the blanks. Most formats, however, leave all kinds of room for stacking your blocks to do you the most good.

Skills

Skills today are the heart and soul of job-finding and, as such, encompass a variety of experiences. These are skills:

> Collaborating, editing, fund-raising, interviewing, managing, navigating (Internet), researching, systematizing, teaching

And these are skills:

> Administering social programs, analyzing insurance facts, advising homeless people, allocating forestry resources, desktop publishing, coordinating association events, designing home furnishing ads, marine expedition problem-solving, writing police reports

And these are also skills:

> Dependable, sense of humor, commitment, leadership, persistence, crisis-resilient, adaptable, quick, results-driven

And these are still more skills:

> Brochures, UNIX, five years, 100% quota, telemarketing, senior management, spreadsheet, MBA, major accounting firms

Naming skills as a basic element of resumes may surprise you. I include them here because they have taken on new importance and the skills concept has changed in the past decade. Once, we thought of skills in the classic meaning of general and industry-specific abilities. That notion has expanded to include personal characteristics, as well as past employers, special knowledge, achievements, and products.

As the term is used in job searching today, skill is any identifiable ability or fact that employers value and will pay for. That means that "five years" is a skill, the same as word processing — employers pay for experience.

Where do skills belong on your resume? Everywhere. Season every statement with skills, if you can. Skills are indispensable. Whether you use a traditional paper resume or a digital resume, you must name your skills or be left behind.

What's the best way to name your skills? An excellent book with a comprehensive skills treatment aimed at adults is *Five Steps to Career Success: The Essential Guide for Students, Job Seekers and Lifelong Learners* by Urban Whitaker, $12.50 plus $2 postage, from West Coast Print Center, P.O. Box 10973, Oakland, CA 94610; (510) 663-7061; books@westcoastprintcenter.com.

Another skills defining resource is a popular card-sorting exercise, Motivated Skills Card Sort Kit, available for $12 from Career Research & Testing in San Jose, CA; (408) 559-4945.

Or if you're up for software, the best two programs to help you uncover all your skills are Jumpstart and SkillsUP, each of which is available for less than $80 from Up Software in San Francisco, CA; (800) 959-8208.

Activities

Activities can be anything from hobbies and sports to campus extracurricular participation. *The trick is to analyze how each activity is relevant to the target job, discussing skills or knowledge developed and listing all achievements.* Make sure that this section doesn't become meaningless filler.

In addition, don't note potentially controversial activities: Stating that you're a moose hunter will not endear you to RezReading animal lovers. If you've been able to research the RezReader and have found that you two have a common interest, however, that interest is worth listing on the resume so it can become an icebreaker topic in an interview.

Organizations

Give yourself even more credentials with professional and civic affiliations. Mention all important offices held. Relate these affiliations to your reader in terms of marketable skills, knowledge, and achievements. A high profile in the community is particularly important for sales jobs.

Just as you should be careful about which activities you identify, so too should you be sensitive to booby traps in organization memberships.

- ✔ Listing too many organizations may make the RezReader wonder when you'd have time to do the job.

- ✔ Noting that you belong to one minority group organization may work in your favor, but reporting your membership in five minority group organizations may raise red flags. The RezReader may worry that you're a trouble-making activist who's willing to exhibit poor work performance and unacceptable behavior in order to create a public issue if you're due to get fired.

- ✔ And, of course, you know better than to list your membership in religious or political organizations (unless you're applying for a job that requires such membership). They don't apply to your ability to do the job, and some RezReaders may use them to keep you out of the hunt.

Honors and Awards

List most of the achievements for which you were recognized. If the achievement had zero to do with work or does not show you in a professional light, don't take up white space with it; you probably would not, for example, list a Chili Cook-Off Winner award (unless applying for a job as a chef).

Testimonials

After you've cited an achievement, you can follow up with a short, flattering quote from your boss or a client:

- ✔ (From an information systems technician): Bob Boss said he was "ecstatic" that I cut Internet access costs by 50 percent.

- ✔ (From a sales rep at a supercopy shop): Expanded the SoapSuds account by 15 percent. How? By contacting not the office manager but the chief financial officer and offering to remove signature authority of 250 terminated employees. "Jennifer Robertson's resourcefulness in getting inside SoapSuds after others had tried for months is truly impressive," said Barbara Boss, my direct supervisor.

Testimonials work, or advertisers wouldn't use them. Be sure to check with your source before adding the quote to your resume, however. That way, there'll be no surprises.

Licenses and Samples of Your Work

If you are in the legal, certified accounting, engineering, or medical profession, you need to add to your resume the appropriate license, certifications, and other identifications required for the position. For a professional resume or CV, you may also need to list descriptions or titles of specific work you have done, or include samples of your work along with your resume. If asked to include samples of your work, be selective about what you send. Make sure your samples have no obvious flaws or errors.

Start Fresh, Win Big

To capture the best jobs, you know you can't simply add the latest job description and recirculate the same old resume with updated data. Like the small lad at the beginning of this chapter, you've got to convince employers that you will rake their leaves extremely well.

Focus on your best content and present it forcefully. Because you have very few words to work with, choose precisely the correct words; the next chapter takes you to the word desk. Don't rush the construction of your resume: If you build it (right), the interviews will come.

Chapter 6

Score Big: It's All in the Words

In This Chapter

▶ GoodWords: Action verbs that sell you

▶ Resume grammar: Simple rules that sell you

*W*ords: How powerful they are. It doesn't take many to change the world: The Lord's prayer has 66 words; Lincoln's Gettysburg address numbers just 286 words; and the U.S. Declaration of Independence contains but 1,322 words.

Winston Churchill needed only two words to bind Russia to the *Iron Curtain*. A brief four words memorialized Martin Luther King's vision: *I have a dream*. And in a single sentence, John F. Kennedy set the challenge for a generation: *Ask not what your country can do for you, but what you can do for your country*.

Words are powerful — big words, like *motherland* and *environmentalism*, and small words, like *peace* and *war*, or *dawn, family, hope, love*, and *home*.

Words are pegs to hang your qualifications on. Words are the power that lifts you above the faceless crowd and sets you in Good Fortune's way. The right words can change your life.

Now begin your hunt for the right words to build a FirstRate resume. This chapter shows you how to use *GoodWords*, or action verbs, plus resume grammar made simple.

GoodWords — used on paper resumes — are action verbs describing your strengths: *improve, upgrade, schedule*. **KeyWords** — used on electronic resumes — are usually nouns demonstrating essential skills: *technology transfers, Ph.D. organic chemistry, multinational marketing*. (See Chapters 12 and 13 for more on KeyWords.) A smattering of both can make your resume stand up and sing.

GoodWords Can Bring Good News

Resume advisers always urge you to use power-play verbs to communicate your abilities and accomplishments. The action verbs work great on paper resumes, although they're not so great on digital resumes which tend to scan for nouns. On paper, a punch-zip delivery keeps these achievement-oriented verbs campaigning for you. Try not to use the same word twice on your resume — the thesaurus in a word-processing program can give you more possibilities. The important thing is to choose words of substance and power that zero in on your abilities and achievements.

Take a look at the GoodWords that follow and see which work for you:

GoodWords for administration and management

advised	initiated	prioritized
approved	inspired	processed
authorized	installed	promoted
chaired	instituted	recommended
consolidated	instructed	redirected
counseled	integrated	referred
delegated	launched	reorganized
determined	lectured	represented
developed	listened	responded
diagnosed	managed	reviewed
directed	mediated	routed
disseminated	mentored	sponsored
enforced	moderated	streamlined
ensured	monitored	strengthened
examined	motivated	supervised
explained	negotiated	taught
governed	originated	trained
guided	oversaw	validated
headed	pioneered	
influenced	presided	

GoodWords for communications and creativity

acted	edited	proofread
addressed	enabled	publicized
arranged	facilitated	published
assessed	fashioned	realized
authored	formulated	reconciled
briefed	influenced	recruited
built	initiated	rectified
clarified	interpreted	remodeled
composed	interviewed	reported
conducted	introduced	revitalized
constructed	invented	scheduled
corresponded	launched	screened
costumed	lectured	shaped
created	modernized	stimulated
critiqued	performed	summarized
demonstrated	planned	taught
designed	presented	trained
developed	produced	translated
directed	projected	wrote

GoodWords for sales and persuasion

arbitrated	established	influenced
catalogued	expedited	inspired
centralized	familiarized	installed
consulted	identified	integrated
dissuaded	implemented	interpreted
documented	improved	investigated
educated	increased	judged

launched	planned	restored
lectured	processed	reviewed
led	produced	routed
liaised	promoted	saved
maintained	proposed	served
manipulated	publicized	set goals
marketed	purchased	sold
mediated	realized	solved
moderated	recruited	stimulated
negotiated	reduced	summarized
obtained	reported	surveyed
ordered	researched	translated
performed	resolved	

GoodWords for technical ability

analyzed	drafted	inspected
broadened	edited	installed
charted	educated	instituted
classified	eliminated	integrated
communicated	excelled	interfaced
compiled	expanded	launched
computed	expedited	lectured
conceived	fabricated	maintained
conducted	facilitated	marketed
coordinated	forecast	mastered
designed	formed	modified
detected	generated	molded
developed	improved	operated
devised	increased	packaged

pioneered

prepared

processed

programmed

published

reconstructed

reduced

researched

restored

revamped

streamlined

supplemented

surveyed

systematized

trained

upgraded

wrote

GoodWords for office support

adhered

administered

allocated

applied

appropriated

assisted

assured

attained

awarded

balanced

budgeted

built

charted

completed

contributed

coordinated

cut

defined

determined

dispensed

distributed

documented

drafted

enacted

enlarged

evaluated

examined

executed

followed up

formalized

formulated

hired

identified

implemented

improved

installed

instituted

justified

liaised

maintained

managed

operated

ordered

organized

packaged

planned

prepared

prescribed

processed

provided

recorded

repaired

reshaped

resolved

scheduled

screened

secured

solved

started

GoodWords for teaching

acquainted	designed	influenced
adapted	developed	informed
advised	directed	initiated
answered	dispensed	innovated
apprised	distributed	installed
augmented	educated	instituted
briefed	effected	instructed
built	empowered	integrated
certified	enabled	lectured
chaired	enacted	listened
charted	enlarged	originated
clarified	expanded	persuaded
coached	facilitated	presented
collaborated	fomented	responded
communicated	formulated	revolutionized
conducted	generated	set goals
coordinated	grouped	stimulated
delegated	guided	summarized
delivered	harmonized	trained
demonstrated	implemented	translated

GoodWords for research and analysis

administered	augmented	composed
amplified	balanced	concentrated
analyzed	calculated	conducted
applied	charted	constructed
articulated	collected	consulted
assessed	compared	critiqued
audited	compiled	detected

determined	found	pinpointed
discovered	generated	planned
documented	grouped	prepared
drafted	identified	processed
edited	integrated	proofread
evaluated	interpreted	researched
examined	interviewed	reviewed
exhibited	invented	riveted
experimented	investigated	screened
explored	located	summarized
extracted	measured	surveyed
focused	obtained	systematized
forecast	organized	unearthed

GoodWords for helping and caregiving

advanced	consulted	mentored
advised	contributed	ministered
aided	counseled	negotiated
arbitrated	demonstrated	nourished
assisted	diagnosed	nursed
attended	encouraged	nurtured
augmented	expedited	obliged
backed	facilitated	optimized
balanced	familiarized	promoted
boosted	fostered	provided
braced	furthered	reassured
clarified	guided	reclaimed
collaborated	helped	rectified
comforted	instilled	redeemed
consoled	liaised	reeducated

referred	served	streamlined
reformed	settled	translated
rehabilitated	supplied	treated
repaired	supported	tutored
represented	stabilized	unified

GoodWords for financial management

adjusted	economized	reported
administered	eliminated	researched
allocated	exceeded	reshaped
analyzed	financed	retailed
appraised	forecast	saved
audited	funded	shopped
balanced	gained	secured
bought	generated	sold
budgeted	increased	solicited
calculated	invested	sourced
computed	maintained	specified
conciliated	managed	supplemented
cut	marketed	systematized
decreased	merchandised	tested
developed	planned	tripled
disbursed	projected	underwrote
dispensed	purchased	upgraded
distributed	quadrupled	upsized
doubled	reconciled	vended
downsized	reduced	

GoodWords for many skills

accomplished	evaluated	overhauled
achieved	executed	performed
adapted	facilitated	prioritized
adhered	forecast	promoted
allocated	founded	proposed
appraised	governed	reconciled
arbitrated	guided	rectified
arranged	illustrated	remodeled
articulated	improved	repaired
assured	increased	reshaped
augmented	initiated	retrieved
collected	integrated	solved
communicated	interpreted	stimulated
composed	invented	streamlined
conceptualized	launched	strengthened
conserved	led	trained
contributed	navigated	upgraded
coordinated	optimized	validated
demonstrated	organized	won
dispensed	originated	

The last word on GoodWords: Little words never devalued a big idea.

Get a Grip on Grammar

Resume language differs from normal speech in several ways described here. In general, keep the language tight and the tone professional.

✔ **First-person pronouns (I, we):** Your name is at the top of each resume page, so the RezReader knows it's about *you*. Eliminate first-person pronouns. Also, don't use third-person pronouns (he, she) when referring to yourself — the narrative technique makes you seem pompous.

✔ **Articles (the, a, an):** Articles crowd sentences and don't clarify meaning. Substitute *retrained staff* for *retrained the staff*.

✔ **Helping verbs (have, had, may, might):** Helping verbs weaken claims and credibility — implying that your time has passed and portraying you as a job-hunting weakling. Say *managed* instead of *have managed*.

✔ **"Being" verbs (am, is, are, was, were):** Being verbs suggest a state of existence rather than a state of motion. Try *monitored requisitions* instead of *requisitions were monitored*. The active voice gives a stronger, more confident delivery.

✔ **Shifts in tense:** Don't switch back and forth between tenses. Another big mistake: Dating a job as though you are still employed (2000 – Present) and then describing it in the past tense.

✔ **Complex sentences:** Keep your sentences lean and clean — RezReaders won't take time to decipher them. Process this mind-stumper:

Reduced hospital costs by 67% by creating a patient-independence program, where they make their own beds, and as noted by hospital finance department, costs of nails and wood totaled $300 less per patient than work hours of maintenance staff.

Complex sentences can be eliminated by dividing ideas into sentences of their own and getting rid of extraneous details:

Reduced hospital costs by 67%. Originated patient independence program that decreased per-patient expense by $300 each.

✔ **Overwriting:** Use your own voice; don't say *expeditious* when you want to say *swift*.

✔ **Abbreviations:** Abbreviations are informal and not universal — even when they are career-specific. Use *Internet* instead of *Net*. The exception is industry jargon — use it, especially in digital resumes. It adds to your credibility to be able to correctly and casually use terms common to the industry in which you're seeking employment.

Here's a trick that writers of television commercials use to be sure they give the most information in the fewest words: Set yourself an arbitrary limit of words to express a unit of information. For example, allow yourself 25 words to explain one of your former jobs. The 25-word limit almost guarantees that you'll write with robust language.

Remember, when your words speak for you, it's important to use words that everyone can understand and that relate to the job at hand.

Chapter 7

Deadweight Must Go!

● ●

In This Chapter

▶ Dumping dangerous or useless information

▶ Knowing exceptions to the rules

● ●

Make every resume fact pack a wallop — if it doesn't, kick that excess baggage right off your pages! Just as you would toss out chipped drinking glasses that might cut your lips, dispose of potentially dangerous admissions. Useless statements have to go, too. Save your precious space for the details that sell you.

Getting Down to Fighting Weight

Here are suggestions on unloading spare facts that weaken your claim to target jobs.

Exceptions exist for almost every guideline. When in doubt about whether to include or omit an item, use this litmus test: *If the fact supports your qualifications for the job you want, include it. If it doesn't, snip, snip, snip.*

Salary needs

Slide aside your salary wishes for now. This blooper undercuts your salary negotiating position. Handle money talk in person after your FirstRate resume helps land you a job interview. If a salary history is requested in a recruitment advertisement, you may want to address it in your cover letter as negotiable. (See *Cover Letters For Dummies,* Second Edition, by yours truly for an entire chapter devoted to the salary issue.) Don't include salary figures on your resume — period. Never!

Reasons for leaving other jobs

Because good-bye explanations raise negative questions, the resume is the wrong place to explain why you left. *Exception:* You were terminated in a downsizing debacle — which means you weren't at fault. See Chapter 17.

Date available for employment

Drop dates related to when you are available for employment, such as "Available June 2, 2004." If you're still looking on April 4, 2005, the RezReader will wonder why no one hired you. *Exception:* If you're a graduating senior or leaving military service, it's okay to list the date you'll be available to start work.

References

Don't include references. Print them on a separate sheet of paper matching your resume to hand out only when requested. References are valuable allies and should not be contacted more than is absolutely necessary. Don't add "References available upon request." That's a given.

Unnecessary headings

Omit extraneous headings such as *Resume;* they're deadweight. White space leaves your resume leaner and is a relief to bloodshot eyes, which is what RezReaders get after plowing through 100 or so resumes.

Unexplained time gaps

A Texas recruiter describes gaps in work histories as "black holes of uncertainty." These black holes raise questions in a RezReader's mind: "Why is there a gap — did you serve time for an act of workplace violence? Do you have a serious illness that will skyrocket insurance rates? What?" See Chapter 18 for suggestions about managing gaps.

Marital status

If a job involves travel, will the RezReader be more inclined to hire a single person? If a woman is young and married, will the RezReader worry that she'll bail out soon to start a family? Snip this status report.

Weakening qualifiers

After making a strong statement, don't cut it off at the knees. In an education section, for example, do not say, "Dean's List, one year." Say, "Dean's List," period.

Leave personal info for the Personals section of your daily newspaper.

Age

Age references plant you in the vulnerable zone. Let RezReaders do the figuring based on other listed dates. Make them work for it! See Chapter 17 for help on ways to combat ageism.

Parents' occupations

Rarely should you reveal how Mom and Dad earn a living (especially if you're over 25!). The data isn't dangerous, but it's certainly useless.

Exception: You may want to note it when a parent's occupation explains a puzzling fact on your resume. Suppose that you want a global traveling position and your resume shows that you're unusually well traveled. You may want to note that your parents were in the Foreign Service, if that's the case. It can also be argued, however, that a little mystery doesn't hurt a job seeker. If a RezReader wants to know why you're so cosmopolitan, you can be invited to an interview where you will resolve the mystery.

Children's names and ages

Wait until the company picnic to break out the family tree. If you're a single parent, the RezReader may anticipate absences due to sick kids.

Ethnicity or national origin

If you run into a prejudiced RezReader, statements of ethnicity or national origin may hinder your chances for an interview. Discriminating on the basis of ethnicity or national origin went out the door when the Civil Rights Act of 1964 was adopted; these issues have no relevance to your suitability for a job. Don't make an issue of them on your resume.

Physical description or photograph

Concerned about charges of discrimination, smart companies don't want to see what you look like. Give your honey the picture. *Exception:* If you're a model or an actor, you need to include a photo.

Health

The Americans with Disabilities Act of 1990 directs employers to snip the health question. Even if you're in excellent health, the information is meaningless — no one ever writes "sickly health." *Exception:* If you're applying for a job in another country, you should include your excellent health status. See Chapter 4 for more on international resume etiquette.

Leisure activities

Some — but certainly not all — RezReaders make the argument that reporting leisure activities amplifies a candidate's profile and that they want to see "what kind of person you are." Maybe so, but as a general rule, don't waste resume space on hobbies.

Exception: Note leisure activities that qualify you for the target position. Or, even when your paid experience qualifies you, you may believe that your leisure activities gild the lily. Does the activity have an inferred relationship to the job you want? Playing chess, for example, is a good hobby for a management consultant where strategizing is important. Green-thumb expertise is magic when applying for a job at a plant nursery.

New FirstRate Resume Maxims

Blue pencil in hand, strike out any bits of jetsam and flotsam gunking up your resume. Get in the mood for major resume surgery by glancing at these office guides:

- ✔ It's not only what you write, it's how fast the RezReader can find it.
- ✔ Avoiding a problem in your history takes less space on your resume than trying to explain it.
- ✔ You don't get job interviews from unfocused resumes.

Part III
Creating Your FirstRate Resume

The 5th Wave   By Rich Tennant

"Your resume won me over. Not many people can list looting and pillaging as a transferable skill."

In this part . . .

How do you start to build your FirstRate resume? You start by identifying your selling points. The worksheets that follow can help. Scribble away on them, and you'll have the material you need to create a ferociously strong resume that nobody backs into a corner.

Chapter 8

Pumping Resume Iron with Worksheets

In This Chapter

▶ Focusing on what you want and do not want

▶ Sizing up your education and training

▶ Examining your paid skills

▶ Reviewing your unpaid work skills

▶ Translating your hobbies/activities to skills

▶ Assessing your employability skills

Referring to low unemployment, an employer recently told me that the labor pool is so shallow that his company hires any breathing body, so long as the applicant doesn't currently possess a large caliber weapon.

That's stretching it a bit, but years when the number of positions needing to be filled exceed the number of applicants qualified to fill them are the time to jump for the jobs that you really want and leave behind the jobs that plunge you into clinical depression. The worksheets in this chapter are meant to help you defend against a recurrence of the horrific episodes in your work history that you never want to visit again, and to bring into sharp focus those experiences that revealed to you what working happiness is.

Getting the Job You Want

The subjects accentuated include positive reasons why you left previous jobs, beneficial lessons learned in previous jobs, the components that you really want in a job, the skills and responsibilities that you enjoy using well, and those that you would like to use and improve in future jobs.

This worksheet offers the opportunity to identify factors you wish to avoid in a job and lets you examine which of your transferable skills from leisure activities puts roses in your bouquet of fulfilling activities. Doing this will help you identify prospective jobs that are likely to pay off well for you and your employer — jobs that you can really sell yourself for in your resume.

Make copies of this worksheet for each job that you want to review. Take a step toward losing a desperate I-need-any-job panic — find that pencil the cat hid under the sofa and sharpen it. Go to work on the worksheet that follows.

How to avoid working for a jerk

When researching prospective employers, be alert to any clues about the manager to whom you would report.

Here's a letter from a reader of my weekly column, *Careers,* and my response:

Dear Joyce: I've been with my company for 26 years but feel that long-service employees are not valued here. Why is that? What can I do about it? Should I change jobs? — K.L.

Dear K.L.: I discussed your question (much abbreviated here) with career coach Temple Porter, a partner of the Raleigh Consulting Group, Inc., in Raleigh, N.C. (raleighconsulting.com). Temple has 20 years of major-league experience in outplacement, employee selection, career crisis, and executive effectiveness coaching.

Some organizations recognize and appreciate their employees while others couldn't care less, Temple says. "As the nation enters the information age in a big way, the unappreciative organizations face devastation as employees pick and choose their employers."

Temple says your issue of appreciation is paramount for your productivity. "The best job in the world can be made torture by working for a jerk."

You need to know how your boss handles expectations, goals, disagreements, priorities, risks, mistakes (including his own), decisions, negotiations, satisfaction, anger, and conflict. Once you know the prospective boss's style, compare that with your style — are you compatible?"

How do you find that out? "After you receive a job offer, ask questions that supply clues," he explains. "Make notes of the answers — you may need to refer to them at some point." Temple identifies pertinent topics for questions:

What is your number one priority in the next six months? What specific results do you expect of me over the next six months? How would you define a top performer? How would you plan to measure my productivity? How will I know if my performance displeases you? How receptive are you to productivity innovations (finding ways to do things faster or cheaper)? What level of decisions would you expect me to make in money, resources, and authority? What should I do if I think you are making a mistake?

How will I know what your decisions are? What is your negotiation period after you make a decision — how should I approach you in negotiating a decision change?

How can I tell whether something is important to you? How often would you want to see me for updates and information? How do you express satisfaction? How do you handle conflict? What should I do if you become angry?

Do you have any idiosyncrasies that I should know about? What are the ground rules for calling you at home? Do you have strong feelings about any moral or ethical issues? What should I do if I feel that my work puts me in an ethical bind? Do you accept rough drafts, or should everything be in final form?

Do you expect written status reports? How much do you want to know about a problem? What period of the day do you prefer to get information? How much social interaction do you want me to have with you? How should I address you?

Thanks to Temple Porter. Clip this list and tailor it to your needs.

New Job Worksheet

Reasons for Leaving Job

Employer: _____ From:_____(Year) To:_____(Year)

What did you most like about your job here and why did you apply for it in

the first place? _____

_____

_____

_____

What did you most dislike about your job here? _____

_____

_____

_____

Why did you choose to leave (pay? title? no promotion? unfulfilling?): ____

_____

_____

Areas of Highest Performance

Of the skills you used here, which gave you the most satisfaction (give

example)? Why?_____

_____

_____

_____

Of the duties, which made you feel your best? Why? _____

_____

_____

Which skills and responsibilities would you like to use in your next job? ___

_____

_____

_____

What You Never Want in a Job

Of the skills you used here, which were the least fulfilling?

_____

_____

_____

Which tasks did you dread most? Why? _____

_____

_____

_____

Your Most Attractive Attributes

In your leisure activities, which skills have you used that can transfer to your

next job? _____

_____

_____

_____

Note: Don't bother writing a summary of this exercise; its message will be indelible in your mind.

Knowing What You Have to Offer

You can't present the best of yourself until you have a handle on the goods. Harold W. Ross, founding editor of the urbane and wildly successful *New Yorker* magazine, got that gem of wisdom dead straight when he drolly assessed who he was in the scheme of things.

Ross, a high school dropout and a Colorado miner's son who blew out of the Silver West nearly a century ago to become a famous figure in American journalism and letters, once advised a staff member of the magazine:

"I am not God," he reportedly said. "The realization of this came slowly and hard some years ago, but I have swallowed it by now. I am merely an angel in the Lord's vineyard."

On these pages, you get a chance to show why you, too, are an angel. I assume that you already have labored in the vineyards of career determination and have a fair idea of the kind of job or career field that you want to lay siege to. If not, back up and pursue the issue of career choice with a career counselor. See the sidebar in Chapter 3: *Who am I? What do I want to do?*

As you flip pages and anticipate the task ahead, I don't want to hear one word of protest about too much rigmarole. The assessment exercises in this and the following chapter give you the design tools you need to craft resumes too good to be ignored. Throw your shoulder into them whether you are a raw rookie or a seasoned professional, executive, manager, or other pooh-bah. After you finish the evaluations, what a job dealmeister you'll be!

Working the Worksheets

Collectively, these worksheets lead to the creation of a personal inventory. My strategy for building a personal inventory is for you to first collect and document your job-qualifying skills. Don't waste time by starting off with an effort to photograph your inner self with words — "I'm intuitive," "I'm sensitive," "I'm insightful." Get to the meat of the matter right away. Too many RezWriters are convinced that they have no marketable skills, no relevant experience, no desirable attributes, and no hirable traits. Discouraged, they give up and just throw a bare outline on paper. Big mistake. Think a lot! Write a lot!

The worksheets that follow are the front-runners of a powerful summary of summaries described in the next chapter. Each worksheet looks at your life in a wide-angle, rear-view mirror and then narrows the focus by suggesting that you target the most useful and vital accomplishments.

Many people lose the resume derby because they merely report where they have worked and enumerate the duties they were assigned. That information alone won't karate the competition.

- ✔ What did you accomplish?
- ✔ What value did you bring to a specific position?
- ✔ What did it matter that you showed up at the office most days?
- ✔ How have you put your degree to work?
- ✔ What good has your education done anyone?

It's the *identification* and *measurement* of *results, outcomes,* and *achievements* that make recruiters book you for interviews.

If you still have the pencil that the cat dragged off, begin your inventory of education, paid work skills, unpaid work skills, hobbies and activities translated to skills, and employability skills.

Harried career? Use worksheets to rethink your direction

Do you find yourself working too many hours a week and neglecting other parts of your life — friends, family, hobbies, community, and spiritual activities?

Women are especially prone to burnout from the work-go-round grind of rising early, struggling through the day, falling asleep wondering how you'll get it all done, and then getting up again the next morning and starting all over.

Do you really want a career change?

If you're overwhelmed and overworked, these worksheets can help you with more than resume preparation. You may be ripe for a career change, or a flexible work schedule, or telecommuting, or starting your own business.

Use worksheets as a diary for discovery

Use these worksheets to fuel an introspective look at who you are and where you've been. Think of them as a kind of worklife diary to identify the experiences you most enjoyed and did well at, as well as those you never want to repeat.

The personal inventory you create in these worksheets can take you a long way toward identifying solutions to a work/life dilemma that's eating away at your happiness. You may realize that you really don't want a career that's all-consuming but one with more balance. The personal inventory you create for resumes also serves as a straightforward tool to guide you toward a more fulfilling future.

Education and Training Worksheet

Name of institution/program _____

Address_____Telephone _____

Year(s) attended or graduated _____Degree/diploma/certificate _____

Overall GPA _____Major GPA _____Class rank (if known) _____

Work-relevant study

(Photocopy and complete one worksheet for each relevant course)

Course_____

Knowledge acquired_____

_____

_____

Skills acquired _____

_____

Accomplishments (with concrete examples) _____

_____

Relevant projects/papers; honors_____

_____

KeyWords/GoodWords_____

Quotable remarks by others (names, contact data) _____

_____

_____

Paid Work Worksheet

(Photocopy and complete one worksheet for each job)

Name of employer   _____

Postal address, e-mail address, telephone, fax   _____

_____

_____

_____

_____

Type of business/career field _____

Job title   _____

Dates   _____

Direct supervisor's name, contact information (if good reference; otherwise, note coworkers or sources of good references)_____

_____

_____

Major accomplishments (Promotion? Awards? Business achievements? — "increased sales by 30 percent" or "saved company 12 percent on office purchases?" What credit can you claim for creating, implementing, revamping, designing, saving? Jog your memory by recalling problems faced and action taken.) _____

_____

_____

_____

Problems faced _____

_____

_____

_____

Action taken _____

_____

_____

_____

_____

Skills acquired _____

_____

_____

_____

Job responsibilities _____

_____

_____

_____

KeyWords/GoodWords_____

_____

_____

_____

_____

Quotable remarks by others (names, contact data) _____

_____

_____

_____

_____

Unpaid Work Worksheet

(Photocopy and complete one worksheet for each relevant unpaid job)

Name of Employer _____

Type of organization _____

Volunteer job title _____

Dates _____

Direct supervisor's name, contact information _____

_____

Major accomplishments (What credit can you claim for creating, implementing, revamping, designing, saving? Jog your memory by recalling problems
faced and action taken.) _____

_____

_____

_____

Problems faced _____

Action taken _____

Skills acquired _____

KeyWords/GoodWords_____

Quotable remarks by others (names, contact data) _____

_____

_____

_____

_____

Hobbies/Activities-to-Skills Worksheet

*(Photocopy and complete one worksheet for each relevant **work-related** activity)*

Name of hobby, organization, club (location) _____

_____

Dates _____

Title/position (officer/member) _____Elected (yes/no)

Accomplishments_____

_____

_____

_____

_____

Work-related skills acquired _____

_____

_____

Knowledge acquired_____

_____

_____

_____

KeyWords/GoodWords_____

_____

_____

Quotable remarks by others (names, contact data) _____

_____

_____

_____

Employability Skills Worksheet

(Photocopy and complete one worksheet for each relevant position)

Name of company/supervisor _____

Aspects of your work ethic that the employer appreciated _____
_____

Example _____

Facets of your personality that the employer valued _____
_____

Example _____

Name of coworker/client/industry contact _____

Aspects of your work ethic that the person appreciated_____
_____
_____

Example _____
_____

Facets of your personality that the person valued _____
_____

Example _____

KeyWords/GoodWords_____
_____

The Business of You

Having completed your worksheets, you've brought research on your product (that's you) up to combat-ready status. You're moving ahead rapidly.

Chapter 9

Draft Asset Statements That Sparkle

*Y*ou say you've filled out forms until your pen's run dry? You say *nuts* to this whole paper parade?

Understandable. I'm just like those other how-to authors who stick you with a ton of forms to fill out. Those other guys may be indulging in overkill, but I'm not. My forms are trail-markers to the best jobs.

The forms I ask you to complete not only add steel to your resume, but they are a workout for interviews. When you're asked to describe yourself, you'll be prepared to deliver the message as smoothly as a network news anchor.

This chapter shows you how to write great summary statements that attract initial attention to your abilities. Like polishing a house's "curb appeal" when you put it on the market, summary statements are an invitation to look into your interior and see what's there.

The message to master is clear. Whether you're writing resumes and marketing yourself in boom years when you want a better job or in slump years when you just want to stay employed, you need all the help you can give yourself.

Become very good at *packaging and presenting* what you have to sell. Start with power summaries.

No more grumbling about being buried in a paper avalanche, okay? Sit up straight and continue your form-filled, genuine, career moment. After you compile the data from Chapter 8, sift through it and go back over everything you've done, circling the items that relate most closely to the job you want.

Hone in on the power-packed information summaries that your resume needs to lift you out of the masses of unemployed, underemployed, mis-employed, and future nonemployed people.

Why You Need Power Summaries

Power summaries get you to create a muscle statement of *position-related* skills, achievements, education, and other special qualifications to use primarily for the opening of your resume. But power summaries provide several other benefits as well. A quick overview:

- **Opening statement:** Despite various nuances, a power summary is basically a skills summary. It is also called a highlights statement, profile section, marketing summary, objective/summary, KeyWord summary, KeyWord profile, professional history capsule, and qualifications summary.

  The summary contains the three to five best skills (sales points) that support your job aspiration. The exception to this definition of the summary is in KeyWord resumes (see Chapter 4) — use all relevant skills when you characterize yourself rather than full sentences. *Important: The data need not be proven with examples in this section; it can stand alone for now.* You are saying, "Here's who I am, and here's what I can do for you." The tease is to read on for proof of what the opening says.

- **Summary page:** A power summary can be expanded to an entire summary page, which you place atop a reverse chronological resume (in effect turning your reverse chronological resume into a hybrid resume format, as discussed in Chapter 4).

- **Old successes:** A power summary can revive a fading job achievement. Suppose you have an achievement that took place four or five years ago and is now needed to qualify you for a job. By amplifying the old achievement in a summary statement (and perhaps choosing a functional format for your resume), you don't bury it in a bazaar of your past jobs. When crystallized in a focused power summary, the golden oldie achievement still works for you.

- **Basis for achievement statements:** Power summaries provide the raw material for achievement sections (paragraphs) and brief (one- or two-line) high-voltage statements that you use later in your resume. *Important: Data in achievement statements must be proven by examples, the best of which are quantified. Measure, measure, measure!*

What's the difference between an opening statement and the achievement statements that are used later in your resume? The difference is where you incorporate documentation, or "storytelling," to authenticate what you're saying. *Opening statements are credible without examples or results.*

So do FirstRaters ever give examples or results in an opening statement? You can bet your booties they do. And those examples may add to the sell, provided that they aren't merely repeated later on. *Reinforcing themes by revisiting related issues is good,* but rehashing the very same thing on a resume looks like you attended copycat school.

What do power summaries look like? Read on!

A Sampling of Power Summaries

To lend a helping hand, I give you a few examples of power summaries suitable for opening statements.

Human resources manager

Well-rounded experience in all human resource functions. Focus: Benefits and Labor Relations. Managed an HR staff of 200,000-population, unionized city. Reputation for progressive programs attractive to both city and employees.

Marketing account executive

Award-winning marketer with impressive performance record in Internet merchandising. Proficient in international conventions and customs. Attentive to details while focusing on the big picture. Excellent at organizing, tracking, and managing projects. Relate well to both customers and coworkers.

Construction manager

General construction-manager experience covers all areas: start-up and financing, site selection, building design, and construction. Hire and train. Properties never litigated. Work ahead of schedules. Rehired several times by same developers.

Junior accountant

Seek opportunity to demonstrate superior accounting skills developed at top-rated Midwestern university where ranked in top 5% of class. GPA 3.8. Dean's List. Class officer. Computer software: Peachtree Accounting, QuickBooks Pro, MYOB Accounting, Windows 95, Word, WordPerfect. Enthusiastic, eager learner. Single. Happy to travel, relocate.

Note: The personal information included in the junior accountant's combination objective/summary statement is provided as an additional plus. Normally, except in international C.V. resumes, you want to avoid listing personal information, and employers in the U.S. cannot require that you include it. "Single. Happy to travel, relocate" is a good addition for jobs not in your city of residence or for jobs that may require frequent travel.

Technical support manager

Well-qualified senior manager with more than 15 years' experience in software industry, 8 of the last 10 with Microsoft. Professional history proves I can cost-effectively manage support systems and supply consulting services for field, regional, and national areas. Directed staff of 12 managers, 40 analysts, overseeing seven-figure profit center.

Communications graduate

Entry opportunity in print or broadcast news. Completing rigorous communications degree, with minor in English. Interned as editorial associate in newspaper columnist's office, achieved top performance review; editor of college newspaper; instructor of adult students at writing lab.

Hospitality manager

Superior comprehensive management record. Check me out on profit and cash flow, cost controls, financial reporting of operating figures, food and beverage for restaurant rooms, catering, entertainment booking, golf course, and clubhouse. Developing convention business is my specialty. Use all current accounting software.

Note: The "check me out" phrase that this candidate uses matches the strong sell the candidate is trying to convey. A glad-hander is good for the hospitality industry, and she's showing she has what it takes.

Contract specialist

Six years' experience in contract negotiation, promoted from *assistant* to *processor* to *contract administrator* in first two years. Streamlined strategies for JIT contract delivery, beating schedule requirements by two days. Familiar with relevant aspects of finance and law, including budgeting, contract estimation, and contract litigation and legality.

Sifting through Your Data

Turn to each of your worksheets (if you don't have any worksheets, check out Chapter 8) and concentrate on the data that most clearly show how well you qualify for the job — or jobs — that you want.

Use the following forms to transfer data that explain why you are qualified for the position you seek.

Note in the left column of the PreSummary Worksheet what the employer wants in the target job or career field. Get this information from recruitment ads, job descriptions, and occupational literature.

In the right column, drawing the information from your worksheets, jot down how you meet each requirement with a qualification.

When the job calls for specific skills, the employer doesn't necessarily care how or where you obtained the requisite skills in the summary — so the headings in the left column merely say *Skills Required.*

By contrast, the headings in the right column correspond to the worksheets in Chapter 8; they are noted here as yet another reminder to include your skills from any source — paid or unpaid.

Prepare a Power Worksheet for each target job or career field.

More paperwork! Why aren't you surprised? Move the best material from the PreSummary Worksheet onto your Power Summary worksheet.

Yes, you can write a summary based on your Chapter 8 worksheets and skip the middle step of making a PreSummary worksheet. And maybe you want to do it that way. Others find it easier to use an additional transfer step and also find the PreSummary worksheet a reinforcing action to focus on targeting, targeting, targeting.

The more you can tailor your resume to target a specific job, the more opportunity you'll hit.

PreSummary Worksheet

The Employer Wants ➡ **You Have**

Education and Training Required	Education and Training Skills Including Achievements
1)	
2)	
3)	
4)	
5)	
6)	
7)	
8)	
9)	
10)	

Skills Required	Paid Skills Including Achievements
1)	
2)	
3)	
4)	
5)	
6)	
7)	
8)	
9)	
10)	

(1 of 2)

PreSummary Worksheet

The Employer Wants ➡ **You Have**

Skills Required	Unpaid Skills Including Achievements
1)	
2)	
3)	
4)	
5)	
Skills Required	Hobby/Activity Skills Including Achievements
1)	
2)	
3)	
4)	
5)	
Skills Required	Employability Skills Including Achievements
1)	
2)	
3)	
4)	
5)	

(2 of 2)

Power Summary Worksheet

The Employer Wants	You Have
Employer 1)	Summary 1)
Employer 2)	Summary 2)

E-Z Asset Statements

Remember, you don't have to prove what you say right there in the opening statement or summary — but you do have to prove it later in your resume, in achievement statements. Here's a collection of write-in forms to start you off. Just fill in the blanks.

✔ After _____ (number of years, provided the number is not too high) years in _____ (your occupation), seek opportunity to use extensive experience and _____ (your favorite skills) as a (your target position).

✔ Knowledge of _____ (your expertise) and familiarity with _____ (type of product, industry, or clientele). Seek position as _____ (job title) using intensive experience as a _____ (occupation).

✔ Developed new _____ which resulted in increased _____; maintained an aggressive _____ program that increased employer's revenues by ___%. Seeking a position as a _____ (your objective) in an organization needing expertise in _____ (your top skills).

✔ A position as a _____ (a job slightly higher in rank than your top employment), specializing in _____ (a skill unique to you).

✔ A _____ (type of) position that needs _____ (list skills and accomplishments). Demonstrated by _____ (list of paid and volunteer responsibilities and successes). Will _____ (an improvement that your prospective employer appreciates).

✔ Offering _____ (your field) skills in _____ (related industry), with ability to solve _____ (one or more problems common in the field), including _____ (your top skills).

✔ Encyclopedic knowledge of _____ (your top skills in technical aspects of position), familiarity with _____ (qualifying duties of position), and effective management of _____ (your lesser job-related skills).

Aim for Powerful but True Statements

Review your finished summaries the next day. Did you get carried away with fantasy writing? Ask yourself, "Can I live up to this advance billing?" If not, tone it down to reality — that is, your *best reality*. Unfortunately — you smooth writer, you — when you land a job based on hype that you can't back up, you should be ready to renew your job search.

Chapter 10

Nailing Down the FirstRate Look

In This Chapter

▶ Creating great-looking paper resumes

▶ Incorporating graphic elements that sell you

*P*aper resumes continue to thrive, even in a cyberspace campaign. Take five copies of your resume when you go for an interview. Offer one copy to your interviewer, reserving the other copies for unexpected interviews with other managers.

In other job searches, you can't know where your resume will land. But you do know that your resume had better look better than good.

It's not logical, but it's true: A paper resume that looks superb is assumed to be superb and will trigger far more readership than will a visually inferior document with stronger content.

As the competition for good jobs grows fiercer by the year, you can't afford a resume that a RezReader perceives as second-rate and doesn't read further. This chapter offers an overview of do's and don'ts. Check out the sample resumes in Chapters 20 and 21 to see examples of how your resume can look.

Paper Resumes That Keep On Kicking

Although the market is moving away from paper resumes toward digital resumes, trees-and-ink remain the dominant resume technology for most people. Here's how to look outstanding on paper and make the first cut in the employment screening process.

Word processing

You need a computer equipped with word-processing software to produce your resume. Typewritten copies are still acceptable, but most people don't type well enough to produce crisp, clean, sparkling copies. If word processing is not yet one of your skills, scout out a word-processing class — you'll need this ability in nearly any job you take. In the meantime, find a friend who will key in your resume. If you have the skill but not the tools, can you use a friend's computer? Rent a computer by the hour at supercopy shops? Use a computer at a school's computer lab or career center, or try your local public library? If none of this is possible, take your handwritten resume to a professional office support firm and hire someone to do the production work.

Unemployed people can use computers for free at Private Industry Council (PIC) offices nationwide; ask for PIC locations at public job service offices.

Printing

Producing your resume on a laser or inkjet printer is today's standard. The old-fashioned dot matrix printers lack the firepower to print resumes that compete in today's jobmarket. If you photocopy a core resume — rather than custom-tailor each resume to the job at hand — make sure that the copies look first-rate. No blurring, stray marks, streaks, or faint letters.

Paper

How good must your paper be? For professional, technical, managerial, and executive jobs, the stock for a paper resume should be quality paper with rag content, perhaps 25 percent, and a watermark (a faint image ingrained in the paper). Small printing firms and specialty-paper mail-order catalogs offer a wide range of choices. Restrict the color of your paper to white or off-white, eggshell, or very pale gray. Print on one side of the sheet only.

The ink on a FirstRate resume is evenly distributed across each page, which is best achieved with a smooth paper stock. The image evoked by a high-quality paper is diminished when it looks as though the ink just didn't flow consistently — the print looks alternately dark or faded, and there may be smears or streaks. Linen (textured) paper is impressive, but the ink from a laser printer or photocopier may not move smoothly across a sheet, making your resume hard to read. Try before you buy. If there's the slightest doubt about readability, switch to laid (smooth) paper.

The quality of paper is immaterial when your resume is to be scanned into job computers or spun across the Internet. (See Chapters 12 and 13 for more information.) Hiring managers never see it.

Open spaces

Which style of reading do you prefer: a paper so packed with text that your eyes need a spa treatment before tackling it, or a paper so generous with white space that you *want* to read it? You'd be surprised how many people, hearing that they must not exceed one page, try to cram too much information in too little space.

A ratio of about one-quarter white space to text is about right. Line spacing between items is vital. Do not justify the right side of the page — that is, do not try to have the type align down the right side of the page — leave it ragged. Right justification creates awkward white spaces. An overcrowded page almost guarantees that it will not be read by younger RezReaders who grew up in an age of television and *USA Today* – style newspapers. And older RezReaders? Their eyes won't take the wear and tear of too many words crashing in too small a space. White space is the master graphic attention-getter.

Typefaces and fonts

A typeface is a family of characters — letters, numbers, and symbols. A font is a specific size of typeface, which is generally measured in points (each point is 1/72 of an inch). Helvetica is a typeface; Helvetica 10-point bold, Helvetica 12-point bold, and Helvetica 14-point bold are three different fonts. The two basic classes of typefaces are *serif* and *sans serif* (see Figure 10-1). Serif typefaces such as Times Roman have cross-lines at the ends of character strokes and tend to look curved and elegant. *Sans* means *without* in French. Sans-serif typefaces like Helvetica do not have cross-lines and are simple and clean.

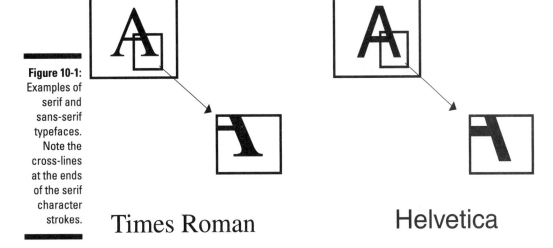

Figure 10-1: Examples of serif and sans-serif typefaces. Note the cross-lines at the ends of the serif character strokes.

Times Roman

Helvetica

Typefaces and their fonts are tricky. Your computer can print a variety of typefaces and fonts — book, italics, bold lettering — and other graphic elements, once available only at printers' shops. Whipping out a fancy-looking piece of paper has become so easy that some resumes, overweight with a jumble of excess typefaces and fonts, tip over and sink to the bottom of the applicant pile. Showing an enormous lack of judgment by their writers, these design-happy resumes are the paper equivalent of resorting to shouting when your argument is weak. RezReaders go nuts trying to read the stuff.

Here's a technique that advertising pros use to avoid going overboard on design: Tape versions of your resume on a wall and decide which one looks classy and attractive.

Tips on typefaces

Times Roman is a popular serif typeface. Examples:

- 10-pt. Times Roman book
- **10-pt. Times Roman bold**
- *10-pt. Times Roman italics*
- 12-pt. Times Roman book
- **12-pt. Times Roman bold**
- *12-pt. Times Roman italics*
- 14-pt. Times Roman book
- **14-pt. Times Roman bold**
- *14-pt. Times Roman italics*

Helvetica is a popular sans-serif typeface. Examples:

- 10-pt. Helvetica (basic)
- **10-pt. Helvetica bold**
- *10-pt. Helvetica italics*
- 12-pt. Helvetica book
- **12-pt. Helvetica bold**
- *12-pt. Helvetica italics*
- 14-pt. Helvetica book
- **14-pt. Helvetica bold**
- *14-pt. Helvetica italics*

No more than two typefaces should appear on one resume; if you don't have an eye for what looks good, stick to one typeface. Either Times Roman or Helvetica used alone is a fine choice for your resume. But if you want to mix the two typefaces, choose Helvetica for the headings and Times Roman for the text and lesser headings. Why? A serif typeface is considered more readable in blocks of copy, which is why most newspapers and this book use a serif typeface for the text. Look at the sample resumes in Chapter 20 for ideas on how to mix and match various typefaces.

Many typefaces are akin to each other and not easily distinguishable to the graphics nonprofessional. If you don't have Times Roman, similar typefaces are equally pleasing, such as a proportionally spaced Courier, CG Omega, Garamond, and New Century Schoolbook.

If you don't have Helvetica, comparable typefaces include Futura, Letter Gothic, Optima, and Univers.

Font sizes

Type is measured in points, with 72 points equaling one inch. A standard font size is usually 10 points with the same amount of *leading* (space) between the lines. *Kerning* is the space between characters; employ it to condense or spread a heading or line of text. Most word-processing programs let you adjust the kerning of individual letters. If you don't know how, accept the program's default kerning.

Paying attention to the spacing of your resume contributes much to its readability. Printing the RezWriter's name in small capital letters can be pleasing. Using larger type for headings (12 or 14 pt.) or bold face can give necessary prominence. Use italics sparingly — you don't want to overdo emphasis, and italicized words lose readability in blocks of text. Most job computers cannot read italics.

Design structure

Your name and contact information can be flush left, centered, or flush right. Look at examples in Chapter 20.

Some RezReaders suggest that you type your name flush-right because they thumb through the right-hand corner of resume stacks.

Aim for a tasteful amount of capitalization and bold lettering for emphasis. Unless you're willing to risk a train wreck of blurred text, omit underlining. On names, for example, **Fred Figler** may become **Ered Eigler**.

Important information jumps in the RezReader's face when set off by bullets, asterisks, and dashes.

Typos and spelling errors are unacceptable. They are seen as carelessness or lack of professionalism. It is far better that I have a spelling mistake in this book than you have one in your resume. In the tens of thousands of resumes mistakenly sent to me for review as a columnist (a service I do not offer), spelling has at times been creative. One man claimed to be *precedent* of his company. Do you think he was a good one? Use your computer's spell-checker and read your finished resume carefully.

Do not staple together a two- or three-page resume or put it in a folder or plastic insert. The resume may be photocopied and distributed, or it may be scanned into a database. To minimize the risk of a page becoming an orphan, put a simple header atop each page after the first: your name and page number. In a multiple page resume, it's a good idea to indicate how many pages there are, as in page 1 of 2, in case the pages get separated. You can also put the page number at the bottom.

Your FirstRate Resume Is Moving Right Along

Take the time to make sure your resume is as strong as it can be to attract the employer who has the right job for you. The resume samples later in this book can give you a good idea of the variety of clean-cut, appealing resume designs you can adopt.

Part IV
Going Up and Cyber-Ways with Your Resume

The 5th Wave   By Rich Tennant

WHY YOU SHOULD CHECK FIRST BEFORE FAXING RESUMES

In this part . . .

*W*hat's the hottest resume trend right now?
Cyberspace. Vast numbers of companies are listing
their jobs online and vast numbers of job seekers are
posting their resumes online. Digital resumes, also called
electronic resumes — computer-friendly, searchable, and
retrievable — are everywhere. This part explains what
you must know to make the new technology work for you.

Chapter 11

Learning E-Resumes' New ABCs

· ·

In This Chapter

▶ Why you urgently need an e-resume

▶ How employers are using digital resumes

▶ Who's who in the family of resumes

· ·

*H*aving survived its adolescence, the Internet recruiting industry is growing up. A major U.S. Eastern research company, Forrester Research, reports there are more than 2.5 million resumes and nearly 30,000 job posting Web sites on the Internet as the 21st Century begins.

Companies say they're swamped with digital resumes — one Fortune 500 corporation reportedly gets 20,000 to 30,000 a year. By necessity, companies are turning to electronic resume management systems (also called automated applicant tracking systems) to deal with them efficiently.

Companies call their digital frenzy "E-cruiting." Statistics are a moving target in the Internet era, but it seems as though everybody is jumping into the cyberpool. Net-based employment activity is the second most popular way of finding a job next to using the newspaper.

If you haven't found your way into the DotCom culture, now is the hour. The chapters in Part IV lead you painlessly through the electronic maze of e-mail resumes.

Taking It from the Top

First, if you're not yet comfortable with the computer culture, you need to get used to a few terms:

✔ I use the terms *digital* and *electronic* interchangeably here to encompass both the scannable and e-mail resumes discussed later in this chapter.

✔ *Scannable* refers to a resume that can be "read" by a computer's optical character recognition (OCR) software.

✔ *E-mail* or *Online* refers to sending a resume through a computer that is connected to a computer network; the *Internet* is the world's biggest computer network. The *Web* (World Wide Web) is a graphical overlay on the Internet that makes possible sound, film, video, and various special effects as well as text.

As you know, change is inevitable (except from a vending machine). The resume business is no exception, and the change within it is irreversible. Take note of main trends that are changing the face of resumes as they have been known for a half century:

✔ During the past decade an amazing acceleration of knowledge-based computer software has reinvented many of the elements we once accepted as fixed in the way we *prepare and submit* our resumes, and in the way others *read and manage* them.

✔ During the same past ten years, the Internet — the greatest communications coup ever seen on Earth — has connected the globe's computers, altering forever the way resumes *are sent* from one place to another.

Taken together, these trends have sparked the birth and growth of the digital resume — a document made for electronic handling.

Digital Resumes: Don't Leave Home without One

Here are a handful of reasons why from this moment on you can't ignore digital resumes and should add them right now to your employment arsenal.

✔ **Career management technique.** You can simplify your life by using new career management techniques. With a minimum of effort, employed people are positioning themselves to trade up jobs by parking their resumes in carefully chosen resume banks, preferably those with personal agents (see Chapter 15), sitting back in their ergonomic chairs, and waiting for better offers to flash on their computer screens.

(Don't try this at home if you're jobless; rather than sitting and waiting for a call from the blue, be proactive in many directions. You can't afford to wait.)

Working on the theory that workers who have been hired by someone must be desirable candidates, these passive job hunters are the big game headhunters try to capture.

✔ **Fewer resume readers.** The downsizings of the past 20 or so years have taken their toll on human resource departments; if yesteryear's large-sized HR staffs were lost in a sea of paper resumes, the leaner staffs are drowning in them. Fewer and fewer internal and external recruiters who source (find) candidates use paper.

✔ **Ever-changing workforce.** Flexible employees — temporary, part-time, contract, and self-employed — need efficient connections for quick job changes. Computer-assisted technology, including digital resumes, shortens job search and response time. Although the true number is elusive, some studies assert that three out of ten U.S. employees are in the flexible workforce.

✔ **More knowledge jobs.** Computer and high-tech jobs are the fastest growing employment sector. Millions of new jobs will be created within the next decade for the Internet and intranets (company internal networks). Computer-based job hunting, using digital resumes, is the method of choice for knowledge workers.

✔ **Tight employer budgets.** Employers say online recruiting costs less than most other kinds of recruiting and that's why they intend to use more of it. Online recruiting typically calls for digital resumes.

✔ **Requests for online response.** Help-wanted newspaper ads instruct you to send your resume to something like `screener@moderncompany.com` (not a real name). You need a digital resume ready to go.

✔ **Modernizing recruitment.** Virtually all third-party recruiters (headhunters) use digital databases to manage their resume volume.

In fact, the headhunter/candidate Net traffic has grown so there's a very helpful new book out telling you exactly how to deal with recruiters via e-mail. *Headhunters Revealed! Career Secrets for Choosing and Using Professional Recruiters* by Darrell W. Gurney, C.P.C., can be ordered through Hunter Arts Publishing's Web site `www.hunterarts.com`.

Although the digital resume means more work for you because you have to prepare several versions of your resume, additional electronic efforts are never a waste of time and can pay big dividends.

Digital resumes bring a number of advantages, including the ones listed in the following sections.

Faster response time

Waiting to hear back from someone whom you have contacted about your future can be maddening. I wish I had a dollar for every reader who has complained to me that employers must be subhuman because, after the readers send resumes, employers never write, never call. Or if they do, the response comes weeks later. It's Waiting-to-Hear-about-Hiring Torture.

Because online mail is a lot faster than postal mail, digital resumes have the technical potential to speed up the hiring process. Moreover, resume management systems that keep track of incoming resumes have built-in response features, which means that you may actually get a postcard or e-mail back within a week confirming that your resume arrived and is resting safely in the employer's database.

Clarity-check: Computerization applies only to the *screening* portion of the hiring process, not to the *selection* portion. Selection is made by humans, usually line managers, who may drag out the decision of whom to hire for any number of reasons.

No lost resumes

You're powerless to do anything about the loss if a clerk misplaces your paper resume in the back of a filing cabinet or the wrong folder. This happens. You may not find out that you were never up for consideration.

By contrast, you hold the power when you construct a digital resume that computers can read because your resume will slide into a database. From your viewpoint, that accomplishes the first step in the hiring process. To use a sports analogy, when a digital resume lands in a database, it's like a baseball player sliding into first base. Much more must happen before the player crosses home plate, but at least the player didn't strike out and is still in the game.

Continual matching to new jobs

Unlike paper resumes, which are often disposed of after a position is filled, your digital resume can hang around for a long time in a database, and your name will come up each time your qualifications meet the job's requirements.

Bias bashing

Computers look at skills, not race, ethnic background, gender, or age. This means that everyone at least gets into the game on a level playing field — even if humans discriminate later.

A Foursome of Resume Types

Chapter 4 of this book divides resumes by formats that are based on their organization and emphasis of material.

This chapter divides resumes by their appearance. The four main types of resumes are formatted, scannable, plain text, and Web. The formatted resume is the traditional paper; the scannable resume starts as paper but becomes digital after being scanned into a database; the plain text resume is sent online as e-mail; the Web resume lives online.

The following sections explain each type. Samples of each are at the end of this chapter.

Formatted resume: The old stand-by

The formatted resume (described in Chapter 4) is the traditional paper resume laid out with aesthetics that humans appreciate. Graphic elements used include underlining, indentations, bold type, italics, both solid and hollow bullets, vertical lines, shading, boxes, and design elements.

Action verbs abound ("accelerated," and "capitalized on," and "built"). A formatted resume looks best on quality paper. Formatted resumes are sent by postal mail, fax, delivery service, or hand delivered before or after job interviews.

Scannable resume: From paper to database

The scannable resume (described in detail in Chapter 12) is a formatted resume without the graphic elements that make it toxic to computers. Designed to be entered into a computerized database for future search and retrieval, the electronically scannable resume has few bells and whistles but can handle solid bullets, bolding, and indenting. KeyWords are its essence, consisting chiefly of nouns (such as "engineer," "fluid dynamics," and "marketing"). Scannable resumes can be hand delivered or sent by postal mail or fax.

Jim Lemke, the staffing authority par excellence and technical reviewer for this book, irreverently calls the scannable resume a "medieval art form" that will be around for a few more years as transitional technology. But Jim thinks maybe we should start referring to scannables as "computer-friendly" resumes because that term covers both scannable and e-mail resumes. Maybe we should. The trend is definitely toward e-mail resumes and away from scanning paper resumes into databases.

Plain text resume: For e-mail delivery

The plain text resume (described in Chapter 13) is an online document constructed without formatting in plain text file format (ASCII, which stands for American Standard Code for Information Interchange, a generic file format that is commonspeak for all computers). Frequently called a "text" resume, it is most often sent by e-mail.

The main characteristic about this resume is its looks (or lack of same): It's so ugly only a computer could love it.

Web resume: Adding bells and whistles and wings

The Web resume (described in Chapter 13), also called an HTML resume, is sent on the World Wide Web. When sound, video, or film is added, it becomes a multimedia resume. The Web resume can be a detailed lengthy document with hotlinks to your work, or a simple page or two. The Web resume can also be formatted, scannable, or plain text.

A Transition to the Age of the Digital Resume

The birth of the digital resume is a harbinger of what lies ahead, placing us squarely in the midst of transition from paper to electronic resumes.

How long will we be in a state of transition? When will paper resumes disappear from view? Maybe in 10 years. Maybe in 25 years. Maybe never — some observers say paper resumes will not go away, and they may be right.

My guess is that younger job applicants who grew up in a digital generation and those in technical jobs are migrating almost exclusively to digital resumes. Older workers (whose applications would get a fresh coat of paint by showing e-mail addresses and using digital resumes) and those seeking work in small businesses (where large numbers of applicants aren't overwhelming) are likely to continue to use paper.

Highly creative people who once would have used only a glorious collage of paper to strut their stuff now turn to (digital) multimedia resumes if they're showcasing their skills with film, video or sound. But they use paper resumes and portfolios to illustrate their talents in the print industries.

Even if you decide to shop your prospects using only a digital resume, consider keeping a FirstRate paper resume on tap to leave at job interviews as something to remember you by.

As e-mail resumes take the field, who shouldn't touch the electrons with a 10-foot joy stick? Among those whose interests are best served by paper resumes are individuals whose skills are not in high demand, or who depend on personality, characteristics, and charm to find employment. Computers don't search for "Work well with all levels of society."

Anyone who has used a word-processing program understands the technique of naming KeyWords to search and retrieve information. If your skills can't be captured by searchable KeyWords, stick with paper and personal networking in your quest for employment.

For most people, I recommend a dual-resume track — paper and digital. The content of your resume versions will be alike, more or less. Their presentations will differ. Which version should you do first, paper or electronic? The argument is close and I'm not sure that it matters. Start with the version with which you feel more comfortable and then branch out to the other.

Four Styles of the Same Resume

To fix in your mind the differences between the main types of resumes, the following samples display a resume for Della Hutchings in each type: formatted, scannable, plain text, and Web. (The Web resume is represented in static screen shots, while in its electronic environment it might show film, video, animation, and interactivity.) Note the graphic changes in each variation.

Check out the sidebar for tips on keeping your resume away from unauthorized viewers.

Resumes: How to keep your identity private

Boss avoidance on your cyberroad can be accomplished by keeping these tips handy as a checklist when you are not using a confidential resume bank (see Chapter 15):

✔ **Current employer.** Omit the name of your current employer, simply describing the company as "vendor to automotive industry" or "manufacturer of plastic automotive parts." Use your job title unless it's an odd and identifiable one like "Head Geek."

✔ **Prior employers.** Continue to camouflage yourself with the use of generic terms for the past 10 years. Instead of "Five years with Jackson Plastics as a research design engineer," substitute "respected plastics company" for Jackson Plastics.

Listing previous employers by name, title, and dates of employment — such as research design engineer, 1992-1997, Jackson Plastics — can strip you of stealth options. A suspicious boss can check personnel files for your old resume.

✔ **Education.** Use either your degree and institution (Ch.E, RensselaerPolytechnic Institute) or your degree and date (Ch.E, 1987). Using all three makes you identifiable through alumni associations. A determined, suspicious manager can also track you down if you use both your undergraduate and advanced degrees by cross-checking lists of alumni.

If one or both of your degrees is from a prestigious institution, ride on those coattails, leaving off dates. Or just list your advanced degree and decide whether the school or a recent graduation date is most important in qualifying you.

The age factor as a potential discriminator plays a role in deciding which identifiers to include; if you're over 40, consider sticking to institutions and degrees. On the other hand, if you're under 40 and using your youth as a marketing tool, include dates.

✔ **Accomplishments.** Veil defining accomplishments with generic language. No to: "Lead design engineer on development of DayNight onboard navigation component — headed a team of eight design engineers with a project budget of $10 million." Yes to: "Led a large task force in a multi-million dollar automotive technology launch."

✔ **Certifications and licenses.** Showing national or local certification isn't high risk, but virtually all professional associations sell their member lists, and state governments open their licensing rosters to inspection. That's why you generally should not list the date or state certifying your professional designation or granting your license. Exception: When state recognition (like a lawyer admitted to the New York bar) would be a job requirement in that state.

✔ **Memberships.** Be careful which organizations you include. The Carlsbad (Calif.) Chamber of Commerce has few if any design engineers specializing in plastics. But the Society of Plastics Engineers has 37,000 members and you can hide in a crowd.

✔ **On balance.** If you deposit your resume in an open (think public access) resume database, or even a password-protected database that allows you to black-out a list of employers, flukes happen. Your boss's friend could spot you and say, "Did you know Ted is moving on?"

You can also play the stealth game by paying to use a privacy-focused resume distribution service, such as Resume Courier (www.resumecourier.com). See the site for details.

Formatted Resume

Della Hutchings

890 Spruce Ave., Las Vegas, NV 22222

945-804-5829 E-mail: dellah@aol.com

Job Objective: ADMINISTRATIVE ASSISTANT

Profile: Four years' experience taking care of business in academic and nonprofit lean/mean environments where everyone does two jobs. Proficient with Word, WordPerfect, Lotus, Excel, PageMaker, and QuickBooks. Am complimented for bilingual (Spanish) fluency. Skills include time management, budgeting, and organizing.

Experience and Accomplishments

University of Upper Carolina   June 1999-Present
Church Knoll, NC
Assistant to Director of Academic Technology
- Use, support, collaborate on wide variety of computer applications
- Work with and know latest hardware for both Macintosh and IBM computers
- Communicate with and mentor clients in South America
- Apply troubleshooting and problem solving skills
- Maintain complex scheduling for employer, staff, self
- Responsible for dept. budget administration;100% balanced

Awards: Administrative Assistant of the Month four times — 3/99, 8/99, 3/00, 9/01
Recognized for productivity, organization, attention to detail, and interpersonal skills.

Mothers for Wildlife Inc.   1998-1999
Rockville, MD
Administrative Assistant
- Edited/wrote newsletter (employer praised as "best ever")
- Organized rallies and letter-writing campaigns
- Assisted Director in growing membership by 800 in one year
- Upgraded mailing lists
- Saved organization $1,200 changing hardware

Education   **References prove**

University of Central Carolina at Church Knoll, NC   Highly motivated
BA with honors in International Studies, 1996   - Enjoy teamwork
- Won Gil award for best honors thesis on Latin America   - Can work with diversity
- GPA in Major: 3.8

Affiliations   **Hobbies**

- Carolina Hispanic Students Association   - Like details: writing and
- Amnesty International   Web design
- Concept of Colors (Multicultural group)

Scannable Resume

Della Hutchings
890 Spruce Ave., Las Vegas, NV 22222

945-804-5829   E-mail: dellah@aol.com

Administrative Assistant - 4 yrs exp in fast-paced, achieving office

SOFTWARE: Word. WordPerfect. Lotus. Excel. PageMaker. QuickBooks
COMMUNICATIONS: Bilingual: English and Spanish; editing, writing
OFFICE SKILLS: Time management. Budgeting. Organizing
INTERNATIONAL: Customer service for South American clients

Experience and Accomplishments

University of Upper Carolina, Church Knoll, NC   June 1999-Present
  Assistant to Director of Academic Technology
Use, support, collaborate on wide variety of computer applications
Work with and know latest hardware for Macintosh and IBM computers
Communicate with and mentor clients in South America
Apply troubleshooting and problem solving skills
Maintain complex scheduling for employer, staff, self
Responsible for dept. budget administration; 100% balanced
Awarded Assistant of the Month four times — 3/99, 8/99, 3/00, 9/01
    Recognized for productivity, organization, attention to detail.

Mothers for Wildlife Inc., Rockville, MD   1998-1999
    Administrative Assistant
Edited/wrote newsletter (employer praised as "best ever")
Organized rallies and letter-writing campaigns
Assisted director in growing membership by 800 in one year
Upgraded mailing lists
Saved organization $1,200 changing hardware

Education
University of Central Carolina at Church Knoll, NC
BA with honors in International Studies, 1996
Won Gil award for best honors thesis on Latin America
GPA in Major: 3.8/4.0

Affiliations
Carolina Hispanic Students Association
Amnesty International
Concept of Colors (Multicultural modeling group)

Hobbies
Like details: Writing and Web design

Plain Text Resume

```
Della Hutchings
890 Spruce Ave.
Las Vegas, NV 22222
945-804-5829
    E-mail: dellah@aol.com
Admin Assist,4 yrs exp, 6 software pgms, time mgt skills


SUMMARY
============================================================
Word. WordPerfect. Lotus. Excel. PageMaker. QuickBooks
Bilingual: Spanish. Time management. Budgeting. Organizational
skills.


EMPLOYMENT
============================================================
University of Upper Carolina            1999-Present
Church Knoll, NC


ASSISTANT TO DIRECTOR OF ACADEMIC TECHNOLOGY
Use and support a wide variety of computer applications
Work with both Macintosh and IBM computers
Communicate with clients in South America
Apply troubleshooting and problem solving skills
Maintain complex scheduling for employer, staff, self
Responsible for dept. budget administration; 100% balanced


Mothers for Wildlife Inc.                  1998-1999
ADMINISTRATIVE ASSISTANT


Edited/wrote newsletter
Organized rallies and letter-writing campaigns
Maintained mailing lists
Saved organization $1,200 changing equipment


EDUCATION
============================================================
University of Upper Carolina at Chapel Hill, NC
BA with honors in International Studies, May 1996


Won Gil award for best honors thesis on Latin America
GPA in Major: 3.8/4.0


AFFILIATIONS
============================================================
Carolina Hispanic Students Association
Amnesty International
Concept of Colors (Multicultural modeling group)


HOBBIES
============================================================
Like details: Writing and Web design


AWARDS
============================================================
On present job: Administrative Assistant of the Month four times
-- 3/99, 8/99, 3/00, 9/01
Recognized for productivity, organization, attention to detail
and interpersonal skills.
```

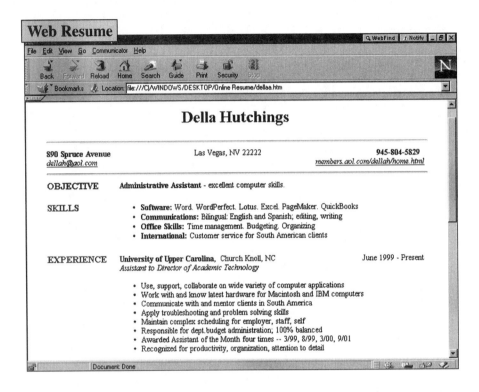

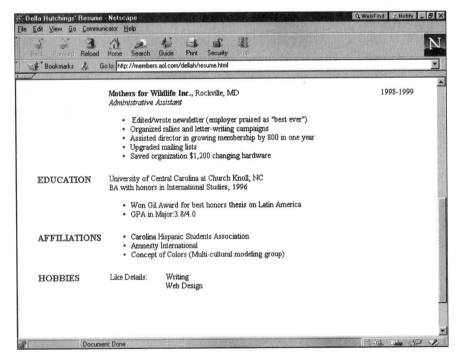

Chapter 12

Your Resume's Scanner Planner

* *

In This Chapter

▶ Planning for scannable resumes

▶ Putting KeyWords to work for you

▶ Tips to maximize scannability

▶ Tips to maximize FirstRate results

▶ Several scannable resume samples

* *

A *scannable* resume is a paper resume scanned into a computer as an image. It can be postal mailed, hand delivered, faxed on a fax machine, or faxed from your computer to the employer, printed on paper, and then scanned into a computer.

A scanner is a machine akin to a photocopier. Once a scanner gets your resume in its sights, optical character recognition (OCR) software examines your resume's image to distinguish every letter and number. The letter "m" must be distinguished from two letter "n"s, "F" from "E", "1" from "7" — and so forth.

When the OCR software has looked over every nook and cranny of your resume's image, the software creates a text file from which it can pull out important information about you.

What's important? Your name, address, telephone number, skills, work history, years of experience, and education.

After extraction of such information, the data enters the silicon darkness of an electronic storage system where it is either categorized by qualifications or kept as a searchable plain text document. Nothing further happens until a recruiter searches for the qualifications you offer and summons your resume into the light of a computer screen.

During a search for the best qualified candidates for a particular job opening, applicant tracking software picks through the electronic storage system to find candidates whose resumes match the requirements of the job opening (described in the KeyWords section later in this chapter). The system ranks candidates, from the most qualified to the least qualified. Figure 12-1 illustrates the evolution of paper into electronic resumes.

The OCR systems are fallible. You've probably experienced checking out in a supermarket when a scanner misreads a bar code on a product and you are overcharged. Although you can see and correct the goof at the supermarket, when OCR software misreads your resume you can't correct the error because you won't know that your resume never made it into the appropriate areas of electronic storage where it can be *searched for* and *retrieved* when the right job comes along.

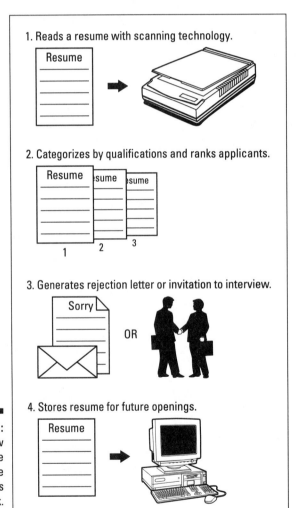

Figure 12-1:
How scannable resume searches work.

Once is enough

It's no longer a good idea to send two versions of your resume to the same employer — although you should bring a formatted (paper) copy with you at a job interview.

Scannable resumes — although now considered a transitional technology, which is giving way to e-mail resumes that travel online and go straight into an electronic resume management database — are still very much in use. Now that millions of job hunters know about scannable resumes, the paperwork created by a double-helping of self-marketing materials is overwhelming for those who receive them.

Here's what one staffing manager in New Jersey candidly says about twofers:

"A lot of job seekers miss the boat because they don't understand what's happening on the other side of the desk, which is where I sit. The typical human resource department is understaffed, underbudgeted, and overworked. My staff, which is me and an assistant, will process 10,000 resumes this year.

"If each of 10,000 resumes consists of a cover page and two pages, that amounts to 30,000 sheets of paper. If each sends an attractive resume along with a scannable version, that means one cover sheet and two to four pages, or 50,000 pieces of paper. I ask you: 'Exactly how many trees do you want to kill? What am I supposed to do with 50,000 pieces of paper?'

"Since I use a scanner, I'll toss the pretty one away and the hiring manager won't ever get to see it. Data I've seen says there are 1.4 billion resumes floating around this country each year (not people looking for jobs, but multiple copies from each job seeker). Industry has to have ways to deal with that paper and now uses technology to help.

"I advise job seekers to assume that the company to which you're sending your resume may very well have some sort of scanning system, even smaller companies, recruitment firms and several state employment service departments."

When your resume goes AWOL in a database, your name just never comes up for the right jobs, or maybe any jobs. Fortunately, you can take steps to prevent scanning errors from putting you on the sidelines.

Your mission: Take the correct steps to make your scannable resume *searchable* and *retrievable*.

You will approach this type of digital resume with scannability in mind, making sure that scanning technologies can distinguish the letters, and that your KeyWords are spelled correctly so the computer can find them. This chapter turns you into a RezWriter with a terrific scan plan.

KeyWords Open Doors to Interviews

Just as action verbs, also called power verbs (Managed, Organized, Developed), work well on formatted paper resumes, nouns and short noun phrases (Total Quality Management, CAM) called "key words" work magic on digital resumes because they make the resumes searchable.

Key words (or KeyWords, as I consider them) are the magnets that draw non-human eyes to your talents.

"Key words are what employers search for when trying to fill a position: the essential hard skills and knowledge needed to do the job," is how automated staffing consultant James M. Lemke classifies the words that describe your bundle of qualifications.

Rather than focusing on action verbs, connect your achievements. You managed *what?* You organized *what?* You developed *what?* Job computers look for the *whats* and the whats are usually nouns.

Having said that, never say never. Employers scanning for management and administrative positions may search for verbs and adjectives that define soft skills — "assisted general manager," "outgoing personality," "self-motivated." But job computers normally prefer a hard skills diet.

How can you find KeyWords for your occupation or career field? Use a high-lighter to pluck KeyWords from these resources.

- ✔ Printed and online help-wanted ads.

- ✔ Job descriptions. Ask employers for them, check at libraries for books or software with job descriptions, or search online. To find them online, just enter the term "job descriptions" on a search engine such as Alta Vista (av.com).

- ✔ *The Occupational Outlook Handbook* and *Dictionary of Occupational Titles* (both published by the U.S. Department of Labor). Both books are at schools and libraries; the Handbook is online at stats.bls.gov/ocohome.htm.

- ✔ Your core resume.

- ✔ Trade magazine news stories.

Just as you should keep your resume up to date, ready to move in a flash if you must, it's a good idea to keep a running log of KeyWords that can help you reconnect on a moment's notice.

Is your KeyWord resume scannable?

A question: Is a KeyWord resume the same thing as a scannable resume? No.

A scannable resume can meet all the technical requirements described in this chapter and be heavy on action verbs and light on KeyWords. It may scan like a dream but be lifeless in electronic storage during a KeyWord search of the database.

By contrast, KeyWords, the lifeblood of electronic search and retrieval, may liberally appear on a resume that won't scan because the text is degraded or for another reason described in this chapter.

The value of dosing your resume with FirstRate KeyWords goes well beyond resumes that are scanned; they are used in online (e-mail and Web-based) resumes as well, which I describe in Chapter 13.

One more definition: KeyWord resume can also mean a resume which begins with a KeyWord profile.

In summary:

✔ *Scanned resumes* eliminate toxic graphic elements that prevent computers from processing them.

✔ *KeyWord resumes* empower computers to search databases for desired skills and points of background.

Always use KeyWords with your scannable resume, so your resume will be scanned into the right databases for your skills.

KeyWords are to your labor as savings programs are to your capital: extremely valuable. The more KeyWords you can claim, the better. But be warned: You can't just throw KeyWords on your resume indiscriminately. You can't add "P.E." behind your name if you aren't a professional engineer. Nor can you write "Lack MBA" merely to get MBA on your resume so it will pull up in a search. Somewhere in your resume you must legitimize any KeyWord you use by showing it in context.

Internet job search authority Michael R. Forrest makes another valuable point about the indiscriminate use of KeyWords:

"Job seekers should be careful not to laundry-list all of their skills, but to select those that relate to the type of job being sought. An executive, for example, could easily list Microsoft Office, HTML, Java, Lotus Notes, C, and C++, but these key words ordinarily would not be useful to screen the executive into high-level management positions."

See Chapter 13 for a further discussion of KeyWords.

Plan Your Scan, Work Your Plan

Making a scanner-compatible version of your resume is fairly easy to do if you read the guidelines and follow them. I'm going to tell you more than you may want to know to cover all the questions that I've been asked since I wrote the first book on the topic (*Electronic Resume Revolution,* Wiley, 1994).

Tips to charm computer eyes

By following these tips, your resume technically will survive 99.9 percent of all types of OCR software in resume databases.

"But," asks the technically astute reader, "can't the newer software handle more sophisticated treatments such as italics?"

Yes, the newer stuff can handle all sorts of typographical flourishes. But the problem is you can't be certain whether old fud or young hip scanner software is looking you over.

That's why I endorse the *LCD rule* (for Lowest Common Denominator): **Assume every scanning technology that scouts your resume is a museum piece.**

You may miss a few artistic opportunities but you'll know that your resume wasn't trashed by default at a place where you would dearly love to work because the employer's prehistoric scanner/OCR software couldn't read it. The LCD rule will pass into history within a few years, but for now, stick with it.

YES, DO THIS	NO, DON'T DO THIS
Do use white 8.5" x 11" paper.	Don't use colored paper, including paper that has a background pattern of any type: marble, speckles, lacy or abstract designs. The OCR software tries to read the designs and gets very mixed up. Avoid odd-sized paper. Especially don't use 11" x 17" paper and fold it over like a presentation folder (the fold-over has to be cut apart and painstakingly fed through the scanner's automatic document feeder on the front side and then again on the back side). Paper that is too dark (or type that is too light) is a risky read for computers.
Do print on one side of the paper.	Don't print on two sides of the paper.

YES, DO THIS	NO, DON'T DO THIS
Do provide a laser-printed original that has good definition between the type and the paper. Your resume needs all the help it can get if it is faxed from one location to another: each successive generation of copying degrades the quality of the reproduction.	Don't send a typewritten original (it makes you look like an old fud), a photocopy (unless you are certain its reproduction quality is tops), and dot matrix printouts. Ink jet printers can be okay but with the wrong paper, slightly-smeared ink can cause the letters to bump into each other.
Do use standard typefaces such as Helvetica, Futura, Optima, Univers, Times, Courier, New Century Schoolbook, and Palatino.	Don't use a condensed typeface; white space separates letters, no space smushes them together. Letters must be distinctively clear with crisp, unbroken edges. Don't use arty, decorative typefaces.
Do make sure that none of the letters touch together; in some typefaces, the letter "r" touches the following letter and looks like an "n." Computers relate to correctly spelled words and so a "misspelled" word will not be read.	Don't try to crowd too much on one page by using 8-point or 9-point fonts. (Technically, some 9-point fonts are computer readable but older human eyes may hate squinting to read your prose packed tightly with petite type.)
Do use, for the body of the resume, a font size of between 10 and 12 points (but avoid 10 point in Times).	Don't worry about using 12-point fonts for your section headings and name if that's what you prefer. The OCR software will convert everything into the same size font no matter what's on the image, and you may need the space taken up by larger fonts to add a skill point.
Do feel free to use larger fonts for section headings and your name: 14 to 16 points is good. Larger headings look better on the electronic image of your resume when humans read it (which they don't always do, instead they read merely the text version). Personally, I like the body of resumes in 12 point, the section headings in 14 point, and the name in 16 point.	Don't use any of these bad-scan elements: • italics or script • underlining • reverse printing (white letters on a black field) shadows or shading • hollow bullets (reads like the letter "o") • number (#) signs for bullets (as computer may try to read as a phone number) • boxes (computers try to read like letters) • two-column formats or designs that look like newspapers • symbols (such as a logo) • vertical lines (computers read them like the letter "l") • vertical dates (use horizontal dates: 2000-2004)

(continued)

YES, DO THIS	NO, DON'T DO THIS
Do use boldface and/or all capital letters for section headings.	Don't overdo the use of special characters when alternatives are available. Rather than write telephone/fax number, write telephone-fax number.
Do keep your scannable resume simple in design and straightforward — what recruiters call "plain vanilla." Do use white space to define sections.	Don't overdo the use of horizontal lines and leave plenty of white space, about 1/4 inch, around each one.
Do place your name on the top line. If your resume runs more than one page, put your name as the first text on the other pages. Use a standard address layout below your name. List each telephone number on its own line; list your e-mail address on its own line; list your Web address on its own line. If you combine contact information — such as your telephone and e-mail address on the same line — put 6 spaces of white space between them.	Don't use unusual placements of your name and contact information.
Do send your resume without staples. Paper clips are okay but it is better to put your name at the top of every page.	Don't use staples (can cause processing of two pages as one).
Do send your resume flat in a 9" x 12" envelope; don't forget to add extra postage.	Don't fold or crease your resume. Laser print and copier toner may flake off when your resume is folded, or the software may just look at the fold and shrug in defeat.

Tips to charm human eyes

After you examine the mechanics of scanner-savvy resumes, consider the content.

YES, DO THIS	NO, DON'T DO THIS
Do include a one-page cover letter — or online cover note — to all employers and recruiters, or when special instructions are needed. Use KeyWords in your cover letter.	Don't bother to send a cover letter if you are sending your resume to a resume bank where its insertion into the bank is understood.

YES, DO THIS	NO, DON'T DO THIS
Do realize that multiple page resumes are not discouraged. Computers can easily handle multiple-page resumes, allowing you to give more information than you might for a formatted (paper) resume. Once the computer begins to search and retrieve for skills and other points of background, it laps up information to determine whether your qualifications match available positions. Generalized guidelines: • New graduates, one page (two with heavy facts) • Most job seekers, one to two pages • Senior executives, two to three pages • CV users, three to six pages	Don't cram-jam so much data onto a single page that it looks like the fine print on an insurance policy. Be concise, but use the pages you need to effectively sell your abilities.
Do consider putting a KeyWord profile (see Chapter 4) or approximately 20 to 30 words at the beginning of your resume. It's an attention grabber and a jiffy picture of the essence of your qualifications. Although a KeyWord profile isn't technically necessary — computers can extract your skills anywhere on your resume — leading off with a KeyWord preface assures that human RezReaders see your strengths on the first screen, enticing them to scroll down and see in what context your skills are offered. If you fail to grab the RezReader's interest on the first screen, it's too easy to click to the next resume. And, creating a KeyWord profile forces you to specifically think of the KeyWords you need to use.	Don't be redundant by layering summary upon summary. If you use a KeyWord summary, don't follow up immediately with a qualifications summary.
Do be generous with your KeyWords to define your skills, experience, education, professional affiliations, and other marketable points of background. Generally KeyWords are such nouns as "writer," "Excel," "Spanish."	Don't assume your action verbs will place you among the candidates chosen for an interview.

(continued)

YES, DO THIS	NO, DON'T DO THIS
Do incorporate the resume-writing guidance given in other chapters of this book (with the exception of heavy reliance on action verbs). For example, focus your resume. If you use a job objective with a KeyWord profile, remember to make sure the profile supports your objective.	Don't throw out all you have learned about writing formatted paper resumes; the problem-solving concepts also apply to digital resumes.
Do handle with care shortfalls in education. Suppose a job calls for a bachelor's degree and you only have two years of college. Put an asterisk (one space away from the name of the college so the job computer doesn't misread it), then use a footnote to write your plans or reasoning: "Pursuing bachelor's degree. Expect to receive in 20##" or "Bachelor's degree equivalent by study and education."	Don't (in an educational shortfall) put down two dates (the date you started and the date you left college) beside the name of your college. Double dates flag your disqualification If you are a graduate, the graduation year is enough.
Do handle with care shortfalls in experience. Suppose the job ad calls for five years' experience in manufacturing technology, and you have only three but you have an engineering degree. Computers don't handle the counting of years of experience very well. If you've had two jobs in manufacturing technology but one lasted two years and the other three years, the computer won't add it up. So just say it: "Have five years' experience equivalent: three years' direct experience plus two years' college training in subject." In this technique use "years' experience in" (apostrophe replaces the preposition "of") or "years of experience." The five years' experience requirement may be somewhat arbitrary. What employers want are skills; if you can come close to the requirement and you've got the skills, you've got an excellent chance of being chosen.	Don't write more years than a job ad asks for. If the job requires five years and you write you've got eight years, some software programs will whiz right by your resume. So write "more than five years' experience." By mimicking the job's requirements, older applicants also get a fair chance to be seen. Maybe you've got 30 years' experience; still write "more than five years' experience." Some programs search for double dates, such as 2000–2005; in this five-year example, if you have one job with five years' experience, the computer will pick it up. Computers look for experience in both ways: years' experience and double dates.

YES, DO THIS	NO, DON'T DO THIS
Do keep your resume updated with new KeyWorded skills and achievements; computers automatically date and call up the last resume received with your name and telephone number.	Don't send multiple resumes with differing objectives to the same database using the same name and telephone number; you'll look unfocused.
Do call to follow up and be assured your resume was received, is in the database, and has been routed to the appropriate line managers. If you can determine which line managers received your resume, try calling them before or after the start of the normal business day.	Don't end your follow-up with a call to a specified number for an employer's automated applicant tracking system. An impersonal inquiry to an automated response system android won't do much to make you stand out in the candidate pool.
Do use industry jargon and familiar, standard words that computers are likely to search for. Say "candidate sourcing," not "candidate locating," for example. Some OCR software can come up with synonyms but other software can't. If you use initials (MIT) in a KeyWord preface, spell it out later in the text (Massachusetts Institute of Technology).	Don't use unfamiliar words that computers may not be programmed to search for. Industry jargon is an exception to this caution — employers almost always use jargon in searching for the best candidates.

Finding Out Who's Scanning

Nowadays, you can safely assume that any mid- to large-size company is scanning resumes. So are most third-party recruiters, and so are some government agencies. Even companies with fewer than 500 employees are outsourcing their resume databases to service bureaus, especially high tech companies and those with high turnover.

If you're not sure your resume will be scanned, you can telephone the human resource department or company receptionist and ask "Do you scan your resumes into a computer database?"

Some employers ask that you fax your resume, which should be scannable. If you do so, you'll get better quality of reproduction by faxing from your computer, rather than from a fax.

The following pages provide a tongue-in-cheek look at good and bad examples of scannable resumes.

Bad Scannable Resume

WALDO DOOFUS

4400 MacBeth Circle
Central City, CA 94322

Messages: (414)332-2999
Home: (414)332-8765

EXECUTIVE MANAGEMENT ... BUSINESS DEVELOPMENT
MBA

Double column, lines, and underscores are risky for computer's eyes.

Even if made scanner readable, where did all this experience occur? What years?

PROFESSIONAL EXPERTISE

Product Marketing

Sales Management

Business Development

Customer Service

Operations Management

Manufacturing Processes

Material Flow

Inventory Management

Accounting & Finance

Financial Justification

Risk Management

Human Resources

Public Relations

Skills will be extracted, but what do they mean?

Total lack of dates plus huge list of functional talents ages candidate.

EDUCATION:

M.B.A. Degree,
University of La Morris
La Morris, CA

B.S., Accounting/
Business, Catfish &
Crystal College,
Portland, OR

PROFILE

A professional manager with many years of successful business experience gained in private industry, non-profit and government sectors. Accustomed to profit and loss responsibilities. Effective leader with imagination and vision. Marketer of industrial equipment in multi-level channels. Former President/CEO and Regional Sales Manager.

FUNCTIONAL SUMMARY OF EXPERIENCE

General Administration

Thoroughly experienced in managing the efforts of others. Direct leadership involvement in accounting, banking, credit, insurance and risk management. Experience with hiring, training, redirection and safety programs. Examples of general administration accomplishments:

- As President/CEO of a start-up material handling equipment company, exercised full profit and loss responsibility for all operations.
- Planned and implemented company strategy, including selection of product lines, fabrication to accommodate special applications, outsourcing manufacture of component parts.

Marketing & Sales Management

Diversified experience marketing industrial equipment products through established and new independent distributors.
Experienced in all types of product marketing, including cooperative advertising programs, selecting and training new distributors, encouraging and replacing established distributors, interacting with customers; assisting in the bidding process; preparing sales reports and forecasts. Examples of marketing accomplishments:

- As Regional Sales Manager with a major industrial hardware manufacturer, managed annual sales of $1.5 million in five western states while faced with shrinking product offering, many production problems, sales office reallocations and major personnel changes.
- Developed and implemented marketing strategies to maintain profitability as many competitors were failing.

Bad Scannable Resume

Technically scannable, but lack of KeyWords dooms chances of notice

Esmeralda Fitch
2323 Sapphire Drive,
St. Paul, MN 89077
987-555-9876

No proof of brags.

PROFESSIONAL OBJECTIVE

Hot air

To obtain a career-oriented position with a goal toward acquiring any additional skills and information available to enhance my abilities and perspective in order to more effectively perform.

TECHNICAL SKILLS

Mac? IBM?

Computer literate. Familiar with numerous commercial software packages (too many to list) for use in word processing and graphics.

PERSONAL INTERACTION SKILLS

Like what? Excel? Word?

Self-motivated, professional and personable, good communication skills, coordinate schedules, meet deadlines, dependable, organized adaptable, maintain excellent relationship with staff and public.

EDUCATION

Grad? Where?
Grad? Where?

Santa Manta Journey College
Glendale Business School
La Belle School of Charm and Fashion Modeling
West Bend High School   *Where?*

Serious about white collar work? Where?

EMPLOYMENT HISTORY

What job titles?

Dr. Judy Armstrong	Ft. Wayne, Ind.
Representum & Howe, Attorneys	Lexington, KY
Dr. William Payne, Verdugo Hospital	Glendale, CA
Dr. Dianne Goodglove, UCLA	Los Angeles, CA
Findum & Getumm Bail Bonds	Resume Speed, MO

PERSONAL

Creative, dependable, visual, organized, outgoing, self-confident, adaptable, energetic, hardworking and resourceful.   *So what?*

PERSONAL REFERENCES UPON REQUEST ◄─── *Unnecessary; waste of space*

Good Scannable Resume

Mark Rawl Michovich

683713 Marilea Circle
Murrieta, CA 92562
(123) 456-7890
e-mail: mmichovich@jjnet.com

Note linear treatment with ample KeyWords.

OBJECTIVE

Microcomputer network administration/analysis/training

PROFILE

10 years' A+ Certified Computer Service Technician/ Includes laser printer maintenance and repair, network administration, PC hardware and software configuration

Professional societies are KeyWords that employers often search for.

- Software: MS DOS, All Windows inc. Windows 98, HTML
- "Excellence in Customer Service" award
- Member and past officer, S. Cal Computer Tech's Association
- Systems integration, analysis and trouble shooting experience
- PC, Macintosh, and multi-user system experience

EXPERIENCE

What would have to change to make this a resume to send via e-mail? Answer: Turn solid bullets into asterisks, make type all one size, and substitute uppercase for boldface.

Electrismart Inc.   Moreno Valley, CA   1997 to Present
Consultant/Webmaster

Consultant for local Internet Service Provider (ISP).

- Assist with e-mail setup and configuration.
- Provide instruction for use with Macintosh and IBM/Compatible computers.
- Help new clients with web page design.

FreshImports Inc.   Norco, CA   1993-1996
Marketing and Sales Representative

- Marketing and product management of electronic microcomputer components for electronic manufacturing company.

Candidate lacks bachelor's degree, often a requirement. Observe how education is handled for computer scans.

- Managed all help-desk technical support, troubleshooting (hardware/software), integration and interface to PC compatibles (desktop and notebook), Macintosh and server environments.
- Created support manuals and user guides for proprietary and distributed products. "Improved overall customer service and technical support by 65%" (Employer's quote).

EDUCATION B.S.B.A * - California Baptist College, Pasadena, CA
  * Pursuing, expect to complete in 2003.

Good Scannable Resume

NOT a First Rate resume, but easy-to-read layout scans well. Simplicity is seductive.

Michael Foley
761 West Noah Avenue
New York, NY 10013
(212) 345-6789 (Home)
(212) 546-0987 (Messages)

KeyWord paragraph works well for any job, including this service occupation.

OBJECTIVE

Retail position for experienced shoe salesman

SKILLS SUMMARY

Retail sales, customer relations, merchandising, inventory, control, supervisory, Excel, Microsoft Word Office '97, UPC scanner, Markdown, Floor planning, IBM PC

EXPERIENCE

1/00 to Present
Bunion Bait Women's Shoes - Buffalo, NY
Assistant Manager
Supervised retail store operations which generated over $220,000 in annual sales revenue. Supervised a staff of 2 sales associates. Responsible for day-to-day operations including bank deposits, returns, merchandising, store presentation, hiring, and scheduling. Interpreted and implemented corporate policies and procedures, and ensured employee conformance to established practices. Ensured proper training of staff, and prepared related reports and audit data.

3/91 to 9/99
Paymore Shoes - Erie, PA
Senior Sales Associate
Supervised junior sales associates, merchandise replenishment, employee scheduling, and customer relations. Used Microsoft Excel and Word to generate reports that my boss required. Customer relations skills were tested on a daily basis, especially on half-price sales promotions. Ensured that customers received the best possible service, considering the circumstances.

1/87 to 3/91
Size Twelve and Up Women's Shoes - York, PA
Sales Associate

Chapter 13

Readying Your Resume
to Live Online

● ●

In This Chapter

▶ Converting your resume to plain text (ASCII)

▶ Filling out e-forms

▶ Using resume builders

▶ Understanding Web (HTML) resumes

▶ Coming up with KeyWords

● ●

*W*hen you send your resume by e-mail, usually it will be handled in one of two ways:

✔ Sent directly into an electronic resume management system without being read, where it is stored until a search retrieves it from the database.

✔ Immediately read by a recruiter or hiring manager.

Before you can zap your resume online through cyberspace, you need to create a Net-friendly version. This means that you convert your resume to plain text, also called ASCII text (see Chapter 11).

Fast Key to ASCII: The Plain Text Option

ASCII is pronounced "askee." It is an acronym that stands for *American Standard Code for Information Interchange* and is used to describe files that are stored in plain text.

ASCII is no beauty queen, but it's the file format virtually every computer understands. Almost everyone uses the old one-size-fits-all file to avoid communications snafus between several popular word-processing applications floating around cyberspace (such as WordPerfect, Microsoft Word, and WriteNow) that operate on various computer platforms (PCs or Macintosh computers, for example).

ASC (II) and it shall be received

To create a plain text resume, start with your formatted, printed resume. After you open your existing resume, make a copy of the computer file, name it *resume.txt* (or *RezTex*), and tell the computer to save it as a *text only* document.

Alternatively, just type your electronic version from scratch in your favorite word-processing program, saving it as a *text only* document and naming it *resume.txt*. Chapter 21 shows examples of plain text resumes.

Here are some extra tips for creating your digital resume:

✔ In Microsoft Word, select the Save As option from the File menu, and then select MS-DOS Text with Line Breaks. (If you're told to use hard returns rather than lines to end paragraphs, save as text only, without the line breaks.)

✔ In WordPerfect for Windows, select the Save As option from the File menu, and then select ASCII (DOS) Text.

✔ In WordPerfect for DOS, press F7 to Save As, and then select ASCII Text (Standard).

Now use a text editor to edit the *resume.txt* file to get it as close in appearance to your printed, formatted resume as possible. Examples of text editors are *Notepad for Windows* and *Simpletext for Macintosh*. Follow these tips.

No plain, no gain: Ten big don'ts

Because your resume now has ASCII for brains, it won't recognize the formatting commands that your word-processing program uses. So be on guard against these common errors found in plain text resumes:

Typeface/fonts

Don't expect a particular typeface or size in your ASCII resume. The typeface and fonts will appear in the typeface and size that are the defaults of the RezReader's computer. This means that boldface, italics, and various sizes will not appear in the online plain text version.

Word wrap

Don't use the word wrap feature when writing your resume because it will look as weird as a serial letter "E" running vertically down a page. Goofy word wrapping is one of the cardinal sins of online resumes. Set your margins at 0 and 65, or set the right margin at 6.5 inches. Then end each line after 65 characters with hard carriage returns (just press the Enter key) to insert line breaks.

Proportional typefaces

Don't use proportional typefaces that have different widths for different characters (such as Times Roman). Instead use a fixed-width typeface (such as Courier). Then you will know you have a true 65-character line. For example, if you compose and send your resume in Courier 12 and it is received in the Arial typeface, it should still work well with most e-mail programs, surviving transport with a close resemblance to the original line length.

Special characters

Don't use any characters that are not on your keyboard, such as "smart quotes" (those tasteful, curly quotation marks, not the straight, wooden, inch-mark variety) or mathematical symbols. They don't convert correctly, and your resume will need fumigating to rid itself of squiggles and capital U's.

You know you're off in the wrong direction in creating material that you will send in ASCII if you have to change the preferences setting in your word processor or otherwise go to a lot of trouble to get a certain character to print. Remember that you can use dashes and asterisks (they're on the keyboard) but not bullets (they're *not* on the keyboard).

And although you can't use bullets, bold, or underlined text in a plain text document, you can use plus signs (+) at the beginning of lines to draw attention to part of your document. You can also use a series of dashes to separate sections and use capital letters to substitute for the missing boldface. When you don't know what else to use to sharpen your ASCII effort, there's the Old Reliable — white space.

Tabs

Don't use tabs because they get wiped out in the conversion to ASCII. Use your spacebar instead.

Alignment

Don't expect your resume to be full-justified. Your ASCII resume will be automatically left-justified. If you need to indent a line or center a heading, use the spacebar.

Attachments

Paste your resume with a cover note (see *Cover Letters for Dummies, Second Edition*) into the body of your e-mail. You can, if you wish, also attach a nicely formatted resume. But don't just send the attachment without including your ASCII resume in the unified e-mail unless an employer specifically asks for your resume to be sent as an attachment. Employers generally don't want the bother of opening an attachment, nor do they want to risk a computer virus by opening attachments from strangers.

If you do receive an atypical request for a picture-perfect resume as an attachment, the easiest thing to do is put it in Microsoft Word and attach it to your e-mail.

Page numbers

Don't use page numbers. You can't be certain where the page breaks will fall, and your name and page number could end up halfway south on a page.

Spell check

Don't forget to spell check before you save your resume as an ASCII file. (Yes, that's like a warning to look both ways before crossing a street, but you'd be amazed how many typos litter otherwise strong online resumes.)

The subject line of your online resume

Don't forget the subject line when whisking your resume on electronic wings.

- ✔ When responding to an advertised job, use the job title or, if one is listed, the reference number.

- ✔ When stashing your unsolicited resume in a database, write a short "sales" headline. Example: *Bilingual teacher, soc studies/6 yrs' exp.* Or *Programmer, experienced, top skills: COBOL, C++.* Never just say *Bilingual teacher* or *Programmer.* Sell yourself! Keep rewriting until you have crammed as many sales points as possible into your "marquee."

Should you show a "cc" for "copy sent" on your resume? If you are e-mailing a hiring manager, copy the employment manager; that saves the hiring manager from having to forward your resume to human resources and is more likely to result in your landing in the company's resume database to be considered for any number of jobs. If you are sending your resume directly to a company's recruiter and not sending a copy to anyone, leave the space blank.

Making a final check

After you finish your plain text resume, review it in a text editor or send it to yourself. Make sure that all left margins are lined up. You can see the likely finished product in a text editor, also called a response form; it red-flags any non-ASCII characters that you mistakenly used, such as bullets (for which you then substitute asterisks or hyphens).

After you think your resume is ready to roll, write a short cover note (using the same guidelines as for your resume). Leading off with the cover note, cut and paste the text of both your note and resume into the body of an e-mail message. Send the message to yourself and to a friend, and then compare responses. This last check should reveal flaws in your technique; mend before you send.

E-Forms: Fill in the Blankety-Blanks

The e-form is just a shorter version of the plain text resume. It is usually found on company Web sites. The site encourages you to apply by setting your plain text into designated fields of the forms they post.

The e-form is almost like an application form, except that it lacks the legal document status an application form acquires when you sign it, certifying that all facts are true.

Follow the on-screen instructions given by each employer to cut and paste the requested information into the site's template. You are just filling in the blanks with your contact information supplemented by data lifted from your plain text resume. Remember that spell check isn't available in e-forms, which is why it's best to cut and paste parts of your resume into the e-form body, instead of typing them in manually. At least you know that all the words are likely to be spelled correctly.

When you're finished, send your e-form. That's all there is to it. No big deal.

Figure 13-1 shows an example of an e-form template.

Figure 13-2 shows how an e-form might look for the plain text of Della Hutching's resume shown back in Chapter 11.

If you do not receive an automatic acknowledgment that your resume was received, follow up with e-mail or call within a week to see that your e-form resume is where it's supposed to be and not lost in cyberspace. (For scripting on your follow-up, see Chapter 14.)

The biggest problem with e-forms is that, although they work well for job seekers in hot-shot occupations that all employers want to hire more of (talented information technology professionals, for example), they don't work so well for job seekers who need to document motivation, good attitude, and other personal characteristics and achievements that computers don't search for. When you rely on an e-form to get an employer's attention, you're playing 100 percent on the employer's turf.

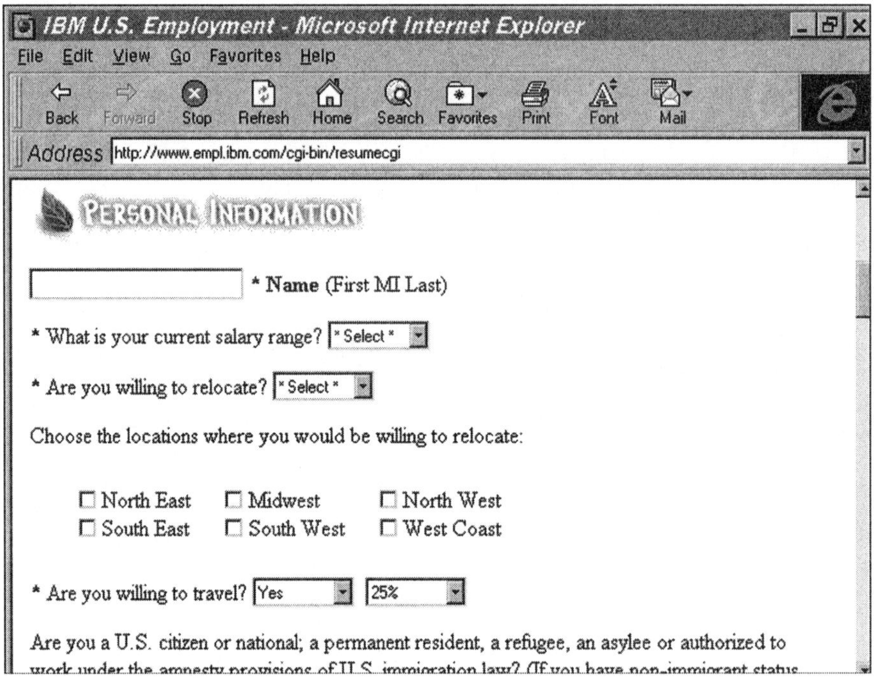

Figure 13-1:
With an e-form, you just fill in the blanks.

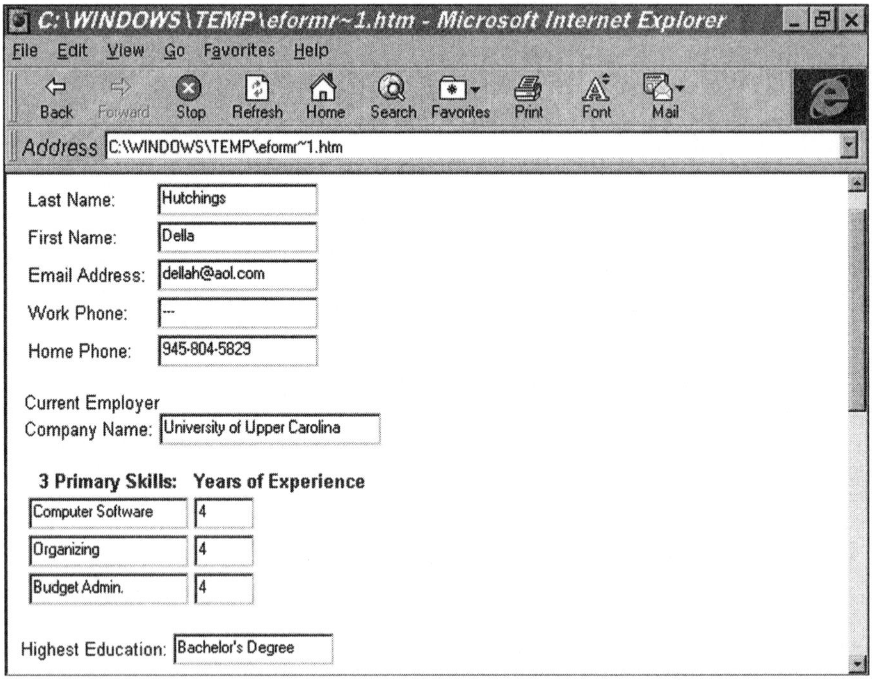

Figure 13-2:
An e-form for Della Hutchings based on her plain text resume.

Web Resumes: Sales Tools and Vanity Sites

The third type of digital resume is the Web resume, also called an HTML (HyperText Markup Language). HTML is a popular electronic file format, identified by its .htm or .html file extension. (Remember that ASCII files are identified by the .txt file extension.)

A Web resume can be a multimedia version with sound, film, and graphics, plus text (or any combination). A Web resume is posted on your own Web site. Chapter 11 has an example of a Web resume.

One caveat: Some Web resume guides suggest that you plaster a picture of yourself on your Web resume. Unless you're a model or performer, that's a big mistake. Employers don't want to set themselves up for charges of discrimination. Moreover, you may resemble an old enemy that the employer has consciously forgotten but subconsciously wants no part of. Ditch the photo of yourself!

The Web resume can be a colorful sales tool for those who are in creative jobs or who need to display their technical expertise. Who might that be? Graphics designers, artists, actors, singers, animators, photographers, architects, interior designers, models, and computer specialists are examples.

But for people in occupations where the visual presentation isn't central to their marketability, Web resumes may be seen as merely vanity sites, and recruiters say that they're too busy to drop by for a visit unless they're already interested in the applicant and need to get further information.

I, too, see the chief value of Web resumes as a follow-up after a successful contact. You can even use your Web resume as an excuse to initiate further contact. Calling is always best, but you can e-mail this basic message: "I'm really perfect for this job. If I've left any questions unanswered, please give me a call, or look at my Web resume at www.myWebaddress."

You can, of course, make note of your Web resume address on your formatted paper or plain text digital resume, but holding it back for a follow-up may be just the opening you need to jar action on hiring you.

Use plenty of KeyWords

As I discuss in Chapter 12, KeyWords permit your resume to be *searched* to *retrieve* you. The KeyWord concept is critical to online resumes, so I elaborate in this chapter.

KeyWords are chiefly nouns and short phrases (more rarely adjectives and action verbs) that identify your experience and education in terms of these categories:

- ✔ Skills
- ✔ Technical and professional areas of expertise
- ✔ Achievements
- ✔ Professional licenses, certifications
- ✔ Other distinguishing features of your work history
- ✔ Prestigious schools or former employers

Employers identify KeyWords, often including industry jargon, that they think represent essential qualifications necessary for high performance in a given position. They specify those KeyWords when they search a resume database.

If your resume has the sought-after KeyWords, the employer zooms you into focus; if not, you're overlooked for that particular job. (The good news is that after you're in a resume database, you'll be considered for other jobs too.)

Obviously, KeyWords are arbitrary and specific to the employer and to each search-and-retrieve action that the employer wants done. The following lists provide a few examples of KeyWords for selected career fields and industries.

Administration

operations manager

bachelor's degree

production schedule

project planning

data analysis

office manager

Banking

credit guidelines

loan management

construction loans

Uniform Commercial Code Filing

FIFO

branch manager

Childhood Development

master's degree

associate degree

preschool

evaluation training programs

educational administration

child development center

Information Technology

client-server architecture

Lotus network administrator

Java

UCSD supercomputer center

MIT computer lab

SQL server

Office

administrative assistant

Windows 98

Excel

records management

appointment scheduler

project planning

Human Resources

5 years' benefits experience

BSBA

recruiting

succession planning

ADA

sourcing

Choose your KeyWords with care. In the words of a Texas employer in an e-mail to me:

> *I am a lot more likely to call someone in for an interview when the resume says the applicant 'Wrote end-user manuals for a PC-based general accounting system developed in Visual Basic' than an applicant whose resume says 'Wrote end-user manuals.'*

The same Texas employer adds:

> *It annoys me no end when someone lists a tool on the resume and then can't talk intelligently about features of the tool or what they like about it in comparison to other tools — they don't really know the tool; they just used it once a long time ago and there's a difference.*

KeyWord: The plain text resume of choice

A KeyWord resume (see Chapters 4 and 12), adds a summary or profile of KeyWords anywhere on any type of format.

For pure text and e-form resumes, you should lead off with a KeyWord summary because that's what RezReaders see first when your resume hits the screen. RezReaders use the summary to decide "Shall I read on — or shall I move on?"

Keep in mind these KeyWord resume tip-top tips:

- ✔ Use as many valid KeyWords as possible in your resume, but if you place a KeyWord summary at the top of your online resume, 20 or 30 KeyWords are enough in one dose.

- ✔ Computers read KeyWords in any part of your resume so if you use a summary, avoid redundancy.

    If you use UCSD in your summary or opening profile, spell it out later — University of California at San Diego. If you mention that you have "four years of experience with three PC-based software programs," name the programs elsewhere: Excel, RoboHELP, QuickBooks.

A Game Plan for Digital Resumes

If all the data in Part IV is beginning to sound like digi-babble, here's a quick-and-slick way to forge ahead.

- ✔ Write a core resume the old-fangled way: formatted to flatter your background and styled in an eye-appealing manner with boldface, indentation, underlining, italics, and any graphic features that look good. Use all the action verbs you want. Hold on to this good-looking, *formatted* resume and take copies with you to job interviews. Advantage: SUPER PRESENTABLE.

- ✔ Working from the formatted resume you prepared in the previous bullet point, strip away the graphic baggage of underlines, italics, designs, and so forth. Advantage: SCANNABLE.

- ✔ Tank up your *scannable* resume with KeyWords even if you have to delete some action verbs. Advantage: SEARCHABLE.

- ✔ Working from your scannable resume, convert your resume to plain text (ASCII). Advantage: SENDABLE.

- ✔ Add a KeyWord Summary at the top of your *plain text resume* if it doesn't already have one. Advantage: SALEABLE.

- ✔ Working from your plain text resume, copy and paste requested data into employers' *e-forms* posted on their Web sites. Advantage: SPELLCHECKABLE.

Save all versions of your resume on your hard drive and a diskette, ready to print, revise, update, or e-mail in an instant.

One more tip: Suppose one day you hear about a job that you'd convert to alienism for, but you need to move fast and you're not sure which type of resume the employer wants. **Easy answer:** Right now, before that day comes, create an e-mailable, plain text resume that is scannable and also looks good printed on paper.

Chapter 14

Getting Your E-Resume to the Right Places

*W*here should I send my digital resume so that it does me some good? That's a question I hear a lot.

This chapter has much of the answer to that quandary. It shows you the big picture of Web sites where you can put your resume on display and hope that the right employers will notice it, or look for job listings (ads) that seem to call out for your resume. The other part of the answer is search-site strategy, which I discuss in Chapter 15.

Check Out These DotCom Resources

The following overview of DotCom (digital) resources illustrate what's available to you. *Except where noted, all resources in this sampling are free to the job seeker.*

Big national sites

The full-service sites boast databases of tens of thousands of job openings and active resumes. Generally, they offer all the specialty functions noted — executive employment, niches, information technology, and so on — plus newsletters, polls, and other attractions.

CareerPath, for example, with its job ads from 90 newspapers, allows you to search by city. JobOptions works with Business Women's Network. Monster.com maintains a talent auction division.

When you're looking for something special, you may find it at a specialty site or at a big national employment site.

America's Job Bank	www.ajb.dni.us
Monster.com	monster.com
Headhunter.net	headhunter.net
JobOptions	www.joboptions.com
HotJobs	hotjobs.com
NationJob Network	nationjob.com
CareerBuilder	careerbuilder.com
Career Mosaic	careermosaic.com
CareerPath	careerpath.com
Careers.wsj.com	careers.wsj.com
BrassRing.com	brassring.com
FlipDog.com	flipdog.com

Publication sites

Only a few years ago, Net naysayers were dismissive in their estimate of one's ability to use online resources to find a job locally. To a man, they thought the Net was best used for relocation. One of the most intriguing developments on the Net is the emergence of local sites with job offerings. Newspapers are a prime example — most have online editions that help you target a job in the city where you want to live, including your own backyard. The following sites can connect you.

AJR News Link (most newspapers)	ajr.newslink.org
Newspaperlinks.com (most newspapers)	newspaperlinks.com

NewsCentral (most newspapers)	`all-links.com/newscentral`
American City Business Journals	`amcity.com`
Inc.	`inc.com`
U.S. News	`www.usnews.com`
Business Week	`businessweek.com`

Search engines

What once were sites designed to help you find what you needed online —
search engines — are now virtual mega-malls. Jobs and careers are nearly
universal offerings.

Google	`google.com`
Yahoo! Classifieds	`yahoo.com`
Alta Vista	`av.com`
Lycos	`lycos.com`
Infoseek	`infoseek.com`
Excite	`excite.com`

One-stop sites

If you believe that the only one who got anything done by Friday was
Robinson Crusoe, you haven't looked for job listings on sites that aggregate
them. These resources gather under one cyber-roof the job openings listed
on 30 or more job boards.

Upseek.com	`upseek.com`
infoGIST (free trial, then pay)	`www.infogist.com`
RecruitUSA	`recruitusa.com`
WantedJobs 2K	`wj2k.com`

Executive sites

When you're looking for high-end positions, consider specialty ventures that often charge a couple hundred dollars for a six-months' subscription. But not all the management-only job sites charge to view their wares.

SixFigure Jobs	6figurejobs.com
NetShare (subscription fee)	www.netshare.com
Exec-U-Net (subscription fee)	execunet.com
Search Base (subscription fee)	www.searchbase.com
Search Bulletin (subscription fee)	searchbulletin.com

Niche sites

One of the best types of places to search and list your self-marketing materials are the specialty sites for career fields. Many are maintained by nonprofit professional associations. Others are commercial.

Society of Human Resource Management	shrm.org
Medzilla (biotech, pharmaceutical, medical)	medzilla.com
StarChefs (foodservice)	starchefs.com
Chronicle of Higher Education	chronicle.com
Public Relations Society of America	prsa.org
Project Management Institute	pmi.org
Assn. of Internet Professionals	association.org
Law Jobs	www.lawjobs.com
Advertising Age	adage.com
Financial Job Network (global)	fjn.com
Gamasutra (computer animation, video games)	gamasutra.com
MBA Central	careercentral.com/mba

Keep your resume distribution process from getting out of control

Be certain to maintain good records of where you send your digital resumes and e-forms — and when you send them. Not only do you want to follow up on specific job leads, but if making deposits in resume banks, you should know that many of them drop your documents out of sight if you don't update within six months.

Guides to Professional Organizations

Similar to the niche category above, you can use associations to network and research as well as find job listings. (One technique: Find an Internet-published professional article you admire, contact the author, and ask who you should be calling for job openings in the author's field; this approach requires schmoozing talent and probably works best for new graduates.) These sites point you to people and organizations in your target field.

American Society of Association Executives	www.asaenet.org
Associations on the Net (Int. Public Library)	www.ipl.org/ref/AON
Yahoo Business&Econ/Organizations/Professional	yahoo.com

Information technology employment sites

Virtually all advertising media are courting high-demand, high-tech employees. So look for something extra, such as discussion groups where you, if a techster, can meet and greet your own kind who may help you solve technical problems — or tip you to your next good job.

Brainbuzz.com	brainbuzz.com
DICE High Tech Jobs Online	dice.com
Techies.com	techies.com
ComputerJobStore	computerjobstore.com

New college graduate sites

Web sites for employers with fresh mortar boards on their minds are a growth industry — they're everywhere.

JobDirect	jobdirect.com
JobTrak	jobtrak.com
College Central Network	www.collegecentral.com
College Grad Job Hunter	collegegrad.com
Best Jobs USA	bestjobsusa.com
Internships.com	www.internships.com

Diversity sites

If you're in the diversity category, you may get some special insights and advisories by taking your resumes to visit classy specialty sites.

Black Collegian Online	black-collegian.com
LatPro	latpro.com
Asia-Net	asia-net.com
Gay work	gaywork.com

Government sites

All levels of government have jobs to fill. Here are places to source those jobs.

FedWorld Information Network	fedworld.gov
State & Local Government	piperinfo.com/state/states.html
About.com (search on government jobs)	about.com

Company Web sites

In the old days, before 1997 or so, if you wanted to apply at a specific company, you made direct application in some way or tried to find a friend of a friend to get you in the door. In the Internet age, you still do all the same things only the companies give you a lot more help by making it very easy to find out what they're up to and if they have advertised openings. Just crank up their Web page and get enlightened.

Company WebPages (4,000 companies)	`www.interbiznet.com/hunt /companies`
JobOptions (6,000 companies)	`www.joboptions.com`
Fortune (Fortune 500 companies)	`fortune.com`
WetFeet.com (industries; companies)	`wetfeet.com`
CorpTech (high-tech companies)	`corptech.com`
Meta List High-Tech Companies	`job-hunt.org/companies.shmtl`
Google (insert company/click on "I feel lucky")	`google.com`

Auction and staffing sites

The Web has spawned a burst of ventures that border on being human auctions. The services enable you to offer your skills to the highest bidder. And sometimes you bid on projects employers offer.

Aquent	`www.aquent.com`
Contract Employment Weekly	`ceweekly.com`
NationJob's WorkExchange	`nationjob.com`
Interim	`interim.com`
Guru.com	`guru.com`
FreeAgent	`Freeagent.com`

Recruiters sites

Outside recruiters are responsible for spotting candidates for many of the very best jobs. Find them and their specialties online.

Recruiters Online Network	ipa.com
Recruiter's Network	recruitersnetwork.com
Net-Temps	net-temps.com
TheWorksUSA	theworksusa.com
Oya's Recruiter Directory	i-recruit.com/oya
Electronic Recruiting Exchange	erexchange.com
Riley Guide Directories of Recruiting Firms	www.rileyguide.com

International sites

The idea of working anywhere in the world is a temptation to individuals across the planet. The Net clears information hurdles that once kept all but the most adventurous at home.

Escape Artist	escapeartist.com
JobNet Australia	jobnet.com.au
NetJobs (Canada)	www.netjobs.com

U.S. regional sites

Would your resume like to take a trip to a specific region of America? These examples are merely the tip of the continent.

East Coast

Western New York Jobs (Buffalo, Rochester)	wnyjobs.com
Boston Job Bank	bostonjobs.com
PhillyWorks	phillyworks.com

Midwest

Missouri Works	`works.state.mo.us`
Connect Ohio	`www.connectohio.com/jobs`
Wisconsin JobNet Job Search	`www.dwd.state.wi.us/jobnet`

South and Southwest

Charlotte's Web JobPage (N.C.)	`www.charweb.org/job/jobpage.html`
Working in Tennessee	`www.state.tn.us/work.html`

West Coast

Bay Area Jobs	`bayareacareers.com`
Employment Wash. Seattle	`members.aol.com/gwattier/washjob.htm`
Hawaii Careers	`lava.net/~kbucar/html/hawaii_careers.htm`

Local employment sites

Okay, so there's no place like home. There are sites to search for your preferred and familiar turf.

City Search	`citysearch.com`
Yahoo! Metros (Search for jobs by city)	`local.yahoo.com`

Personal job agent sites

Would you like to be golfing or shopping while a job opening finds you? That's what personal job agent technology is all about. You fill out a profile of what you offer and what you want and when a position matching your requirements comes along, you're tipped off by e-mail. You decide if you want to follow-up.

CareerXroads 2000 coauthor Mark Mehler says their research team found 322 job sites offering personal job agents — more than twice as many as the number (144) in the 1999 edition.

FutureStep (Korn Ferry)	`futurestep.com`
Alumni Network (headhunters)	`alumni-network.com`
JobOptions Job Alert	`www.joboptions.com`

DotCom job riches: Finding the whole bounty

The sampling of where to send your resumes in this chapter is certainly not comprehensive. Some observers claim 100,000 sites dealing with jobs litter the Web. I never counted. But to compile your own list, here are books dedicated to job site discussions that I highly recommend.

✔ *CareerXRoads 2000: The Directory to Job, Resume and Career Management Sites on the Web* by recruiting industry leaders Gerry Crispin and Mark Mehler (MMC Group; `careerxroads.com`) is simply the best Net directory published. Five hundred sites are fully reviewed and cross referenced with hundreds of additional sites indexed for jobs and resumes. San Francisco State University human resources professor John Sullivan and other experts provide introductory editorial content. If you sign up online, the authors will send you free quarterly bulletins.

✔ *Job Searching Online For Dummies, 2nd Edition* by Pam Dixon (IDG Books Worldwide, Inc.; `dummies.com`). This wonderful 2000 update includes a 400-site directory of job-search Web sites, and Dixon tells you what she thinks about each. Dixon keeps the directory fresh on her personal Web site (`pamdixon.com`). But this book is far more than a directory: Known for

her exhaustive, precise research, the author, who has top-flight technological skills, has plenty to say about the best techniques to use in Internet job search, which is now "all grown up."

✔ *The Guide to Internet Job Searching 2000-01 Edition* by Margaret Riley Dikel and Frances Roehm (NTC/Contemporary Publishing Co.; `ntc-cb.com`). A former college librarian, Dikel is a pioneer Internet search consultant respected the Web over. Roehm is a public librarian who has a pulse on what readers want to know about job searching online. Together they produce a very easy to read and easy to understand guide to the Net, a guide heavy with listings of digital resources. Dikel periodically updates the resources in her famous free Riley guide (rileyguide.com).

✔ *WEDDLE's Guide to Employment Web-Sites, The Job Seeker's Edition,* an annual by Peter D. Weddle, provides in-depth profiles of hundreds of leading job and resume banks and career portals. Weddle, an early leader in electronic job search, publishes a multitude of useful products for online job hunting, all of which are described in the company catalog (`weddles.com`).

Finding Out about Companies

The following resources are useful both for compiling job sourcing lists and for mining details useful in writing your resumes.

Companies Online	`www.companiesonline.com`
PR Newswire	`prnewswire.com`
Hoover's Online	`hoovers.com`

Thomas Register Online	`thomasregister.com`
About.com (search on employer research)	`www.about.com`
Corporate Window	`corporatewindow.com`
Business Wire	`businesswire.com`
Superpages	`superpages.com`
FreeEDGAR (Securities Exchange Commission)	`www.freeedgar.com`

Employee Message Boards — New!

Would you still send a cover letter and resume duo to a company whose employees think it's the bottom of the food chain? Now, Web-working the trenches of corporate America is opening an unprecedented era in opportunities for preemployment research.

Employee message boards are becoming common, but, like talk radio, they tend to attract more complaints than compliments. So use common sense in deciding if you're reading the real skinny on advancement opportunities, coworkers, pay raises, and the names of scrappy managers to avoid. Small companies have yet to grow their own "fine whines," so stay on the prowl for personal one-on-one networking to find a friend of a friend who is an ex- or current employee who's willing to spill the company beans.

Vault.com (hundreds of various companies)	`vault.com`
Yahoo!/Business-Finance/Co.'s/Intraco.Groups	`clubs.yahoo.com`
Industry Insite (online networking)	`industryinsite.com`

A tutorial and tips for researching companies

Hundreds of Web sites are flush with helpful information about where your resume could help you find a job. But making sense of all of them is a reach. Debbie Flanagan, a human resource professional in Ft. Lauderdale, Florida, gets five gold stars for her terrific free tutorial, *Researching Companies Online*.

Find it at: `home.sprintmail.com/~debflanagan/index.html`. This resource is well worth the mile-long address.

Salary Surveys

Don't put your salary history or requirements on your resume, but if want to begin checking out the market for someone with your skills and experience, here are two helpful sites:

JobStar.com   `jobstar.com`

About.com   `jobsearch.about.com/library/blsalary.htm`

Why not post to newsgroups?

Newsgroups are noticeably missing from this compendium of places to post your resume. I agree that people have found good jobs by posting on newsgroups. Rebecca Smith of ere-sumes (`eresumes.com`) tells the tale of John, who went to a newsgroup, downloaded about 1,000 job postings, and extracted 600 e-mail addresses, to which he posted his plain text resume and cover letter. After a couple of days, John began receiving nibbles from recruiters (and angry recipients who said they didn't appreciate his littering their e-mail boxes). Bottom line: The job hunter had a new job within the week at more than twice his old salary.

Although good things come from this strategy sometimes, the problem is that, after you post your resume, you lose control of it as it is posted again and again on other newsgroups and spidered off to appear on commercial resume banks. If your name and contact information as a job hunter appear around the world, your value as a candidate is diminished. Your exposure is too much of a good thing. Think about putting up billboards all over town saying that you want a job.

And if you are an employed, passive job seeker, after you lose control of your resume, you may find yourself explaining to your boss why your resume is everywhere.

If you're an unemployed new grad and want the word out, newsgroups can be a good option. But using a voicemail screen and a post office box, as well as a separate e-mail address, are wise ideas. You don't want loonies or identity bandits on your trail. (See Chapter 15.)

If, despite this less than enthusiastic mention of newsgroups, you still want to pop in to them, here are several front doors to try:

Vault.com (hundreds of various companies)   `vault.com`

Yahoo!/Business-Finance/Co.'s/Intraco.Groups   `clubs.yahoo.com`

Industry Insite (online networking)   `www.industryinsite.com`

Before You Begin Posting Right and Left

You're almost ready to let 'er rip, but you still need to think about the finer points of parading your digital resume: What sites should you never post to? How will you protect your confidentiality? How can you enjoy a rock-around-the-clock, no-trouble job search while you're playing golf?

See Chapter 15 for answers to these questions and more.

Chapter 15

Playing It Smart: Cybersavvy Strategies

*T*o make the most of an Internet gold rush and a corporate resume scanning frenzy, take time to learn the new rules of digital self-marketing. I've already mentioned a few of the new rules, but a little repetition doesn't hurt in today's world of scan-through reading.

'Round-the-Clock, Work-Free Cybersearch

About one third of working Americans change jobs each year, voluntarily or involuntarily. Because of less job security, increased ambition, and new technologies, many people are locked into a perpetual job search.

Tomorrow's job hunters may never know how we in earlier generations have sweated bullets to grind out resumes — typing, copying, and mailing out baskets of our precious self-marketing materials. Even today, you must put forth effort to post your resume to the resume- and job-marts that operate on the Net's cyberscape. But that's changing.

Job seekers can now post resumes and then sit back and wait for employers to find them — including companies they never would have found on their own initiative.

That's interesting but what's really electrifying is the rise of the passive job seeker. The passive job seeker is employed and not actively on the market, but is always interested in exploring the "right offer."

Are you a passive job seeker? Then meet your new best friend: the smart software casually called a "personal agent" that gets in touch with you by e-mail whenever a job opening is posted to a site where you have indicated your preferences.

Hundreds of Net career sites now sport a "personal agent," which is known by various names: Job Alert, Job Search Agent, and P.J. Scout to name a few. Industry watercooler talk says some personal agents work much better than other personal agents but a rating system hasn't been devised. Informally, the personal agents at JobOptions.com and NationJob.com consistently get good marks for their technology's functionality.

The nitty-gritty of a personal agent is simple. You fill out a profile template on a Web career site specifying your desired occupation, industry, locale, and salary range. You supply your e-mail address and go on with your life. Whenever a fresh job listing comes to the career site that's a pretty good match for your profile, the site's personal agent tips you off with a circumspect e-mail message. The employer is identified in the message. This means you know exactly to whom you are authorizing the career site to release your resume.

If you're mobile and have high-demand skills, personal agents are the best thing since headhunters to come along in career management strategies.

Confidentially Yours: Choose Databases Wisely

In Chapter 14, I warn against splattering your resume all over the Net by posting to newsgroups, from which your resume may be widely copied.

In addition to losing control of your resume, its wide availability can cause squabbles among contingency recruiters over who should be paid for finding you. An employer caught in the conflict of receiving a resume from multiple sources, including internal resume databases, will often pass over a potential employee rather than become involved in deciding which source, if any, should be paid.

The same caveat about not being too well promoted applies to a certain type of resume bank.

Measured by issues of security and candidate control, we have three main types of resume services:

- **Open resume banks:** Anyone can look at your resume.

- **Password-controlled resume banks:** Employers must have a password to read resumes.

- **Private resume banks:** Not only does a private service require that employers and other viewers register and be assigned a password, but the job seeker decides, on a job-listing-by-job-listing basis, whether or not to release his or her resume. This is a *candidate-controlled* (not system-controlled) resume database. In a candidate-controlled resume database, you are asked for permission to release your resume each and every time it goes out. When you say "Okay, release my resume," it goes only to one employer at a time.

Here are my recommendations for each type of resume service:

- **Employed: Private is #1.** If you are employed and don't want anyone to know that you're a passive job seeker, post your resume only in private resume services. Any other model is too risky.

- **Employed: Password-protected is #2.** If you are employed and it's not critical whether anyone finds out that you're in the job market, put your resume in the password-controlled resume services.

- **Unemployed: Use all types.** If you are jobless and want to spread your word as widely as possible, file your resume in the open, password-protected, and private resume services.

But in the open services, remember to use cloaking devices (voicemail, postal box, and a different e-mail address) for security reasons.

A few services charge to post your resume; only you can decide if the cost is worth it to you when so many sites put your name in cyberlights for free.

Target your resume posting. Choose your start-up group of resume databases based on your target industry and occupation, your experience level, and the degree of confidentiality that you require.

Helpful Tips for Digital Resumes

Read this list of hints that can help you improve your management of digital resumes:

- ✔ **Get a free e-mail address:** You can get a free e-mail address from *Hotmail* (hotmail.com) or *Yahoo!Mail* (yahoomail.com) if you have a Net connection. You don't need a Net connection, only a modem, to get a free e-mail address from *Juno* (juno.com).

- ✔ You don't even need to own a computer to do these e-mail addresses. You can access them from computers at libraries, friends' homes, airports, schools, cybercafes — anywhere.

- ✔ Be sure to check each and every one of your e-mailboxes daily.

- ✔ **College students:** Get another e-mail address: Most college students get a free e-mail address on campus that ends with the extension .edu — a dead giveaway for student status. Many employers, who really want from one to three years' experience, won't consider resumes with .edu in the e-mail address. Get another address for job hunting to at least make the first cut.

- ✔ **Consider using split personalities:** Suppose you want to present yourself as a candidate in two occupations or career fields in the same database. You're looking for a job as a *convention planner* or a *market representative,* say. Or as a *controller* or *internal auditor.* Most databases are programmed to replace resume number one with resume number two, assuming resume number two is an update. If you wish to be considered for two types of jobs, consideration may come automatically as a job computer searches the resume database for KeyWords.

  But if you want to double up to be sure, use your full name on resume number one. On resume number two, cut back your first and middle names to initials and change telephone numbers and e-mail addresses.

- ✔ **Post where you can edit:** Your digital resume is a living document. Be sure that you can make changes, adding new achievements, tweaking text, and noting new job titles.

- ✔ **Use mix-and-match text blocks:** Working from your master resume suggested in Chapter 11, write a variety of paragraphs and store them on your computer. When you must quickly put together a resume targeted to a specific job, you'll have a running start.

- ✔ **Practice online testing:** Some employers, weary of having their databases crammed with candidates who don't meet their skill standards, are requiring that technical jobs seekers take a mini-technical (screening) test before their resumes are allowed inside (see Chapter 16).

✔ **Double-check your Web page:** Before making your Web resume URL (address) public by putting it on other types of resumes, review your site for links that you may have forgotten you added in a more carefree period. Stories of links to employment-killing naked lady pictures and bawdy jokes continue to circulate. And don't provide links to your school class or professional society; employers may slip out and find better candidates than you. Finally, if confidentiality is important, don't forget to password-protect your Web page. When employers call, give them the password. If you don't know how to password-protect, ask your Web host or Internet service provider for instructions.

✔ **Remember that resume banks must obey civil rights laws:** Don't reveal any potentially discriminatory information by e-mail to a representative of a resume bank or job service that you would not reveal on a telephone call or during an in-person job interview. Assume the information will be passed on to employers.

✔ **Self-send first:** Before unleashing your resume on employers and resume banks, send it to yourself and a friend to compare and correct.

✔ **Bookmark favorite job sites and search tools:** If you choose not to position your resume in any resume service but to answer ads instead, bookmark some sites (see Chapter 14) and on a regular basis, make a focused search by job title, industry, or geographic location. You could, for example, ask a site to show a list of all open jobs for emergency medical technicians in Illinois, for example. Then blast your resume to the ones that seem desirable.

✔ **Use meta career sites to save time.** Wanted Jobs 2K (`wj2k.com`) is an example of a service that pulls together content from many career resources and puts them in one place.

The Net Is Transforming Job Searching

What's ahead for the vast virtual job market? Here's my crystal ball: The online employment industry is concentrating. The trend is toward several dominant mega sites — *really big ones* — each with millions of resumes and job listings in their databanks, and each qualifying as a one-stop virtual job center. Boutique sites maintained by professional associations and other affinity groups will continue to operate, but the gigantic players dominate.

Chapter 16

Here Now: Cyber-Resume Alternatives

- -

In This Chapter

▶ New steps in recruitment

▶ Outlook for Web resumes

▶ E-screening and assessment

▶ Inventing tomorrow's "resumes"

- -

*O*nline job hunting is changing for everyone, but boldly so for information technology (IT) professionals — and the resume is feeling the heat. Many recruiters who use career Web sites say *profiles* — not resumes — is where online recruiting is headed. (Profiles are e-forms, also known as response forms; see Chapter 13.)

Other resume-alternative designs for the digital revolution include taking job seekers straight from job ad response to assessment of qualifications, all online.

Most recruitment management changes are designed to place recruiters (not job seekers) firmly in command. But to aid job seekers and level the playing field, some recruitment insiders are suggesting innovative power-sharing ideas for tomorrow's resumes.

This chapter takes you on a quick tour of the What's New Department in using a resume — or something like it — to advance your future.

High Tech Trumps High Touch

Everywhere you look on Web career sites that encourage resume responses to job ads or promote resume banks, you'll find a profile form to be filled out. You may have the option to paste in your own resume, but most people fill out the forms, at least those they feel are important. You can spend anywhere from minutes to hours fleshing out an online profile.

At some point in the recruitment process, recruiters may want an honest-to-gosh resume. But recruiters (of all stripes — third-party, in-house, contingency, and retainer) are cheerleaders for profiles, rather than resumes. Employers want more detail about a job seeker's specific skills and competencies and to get that data in a form that matches closely their requirements, and profiles deliver that information.

Overworked recruiters want to be able to jump quickly to the applicant's most recent position, then jump over to the skills and educational information. The more variance there is from a standard resume, the more difficult it is to compare apples to apples.

In the field of IT, profiles work very well for the group most wanted — IT professionals with between one and four years of experience, enough to have the latest skills but not so much that their salaries are high. And companies are looking for IT professionals who have narrowly defined skills, such as Visual Basic, Java, or ColdFusion — or whatever is the skill set of the day.

On the other hand, profiles are bad medicine for very good people who have broader but less easily described skill sets, or managers who have the valued ability to create and to build relationships, or abundantly talented individuals who may not have a perfect lockstep upward track record. I'll illustrate with one example.

Profiles limit putting best foot forward

Heath Rocera (not his real name, but this is a real case) is a master of several construction trades. The gifted man had done it all — he'd run big jobs, for himself and for others, for which he was the general contractor. When the construction business was slack, Rocera, to support a family, had done the hands-on work for a list of satisfied clients stretching across several states.

Rocera's favorite gig was the eight highly-paid years he'd worked as the independent project chief for a government contractor. His other construction work had been sandwiched around the government contractor — what Rocera called "his lead client." At age 45, Rocera's aching back told him it was time to find another way to earn a living.

After deciding on a project management career, the expert general contractor spent a year studying for and passing an exam for certification as a Project Management Professional. The question facing him: How can I show I've really got 20 years of project management experience without yo-yoing back and forth between self-employment, working on a project's payroll, and back to self-employment?

Rocera solved his problem with a resume that spotlights his project management background — an impressive eight-year government project for contracts exceeding millions of dollars. That's what the RezReader sees first: Rocera's main claim to project management experience, not a hodge-podge of various construction jobs. Following the contact information, objective, and a KeyWord summary, here are excerpts illustrating the critical construction of Rocera's resume:

Experience: Licensed General Contractor/Consultant   1980 to Present

    Projects for Lead Client

ABC ENGINEERING COMPANY   1990 to 1998
Atlanta, Georgia
Construction Project Manager

[Projects and their results are described here.]

Related Experience

[Projects and their results for the years before and after the government contract are described here.]

Yes, the resume worked for Rocera and he had his choice of good offers.

But the question in my mind is: *Can Rocera's qualifications be adequately communicated in a rigidly constructed profile form?*

On the upside of the rush to profiles, the new steps in recruitment include dramatic strides to link mid-level management talent to the right job.

Profiles accomplish matchmaking online

An automated variation of executive recruiting has made its appearance. Futurestep (`futurestep.com`) was the first of its breed to operate an online recruiting and career management service. It is the Internet recruiting division of the king-sized search firm Korn/Ferry International, which has partnered with the *Wall Street Journal* and is aligned with America Online. The service requires job seekers to fill out profiles online to participate in its database.

Its profile forms go on and on. The time investment is the chief criticism I hear from job seekers, although you may not care if you spend hours to get through the forms, considering that your career is at stake.

The forms ask for your salary, career, and lifestyle histories and preferences. The career assessment component of the process is comprehensive, probing, and designed to overlook nothing significant.

Futurestep recruiters search the database in the same way their counterparts at Korn/Ferry do. What's the difference? Job seekers fill out their own profiles, instead of recruiters doing it for them. The service claims that it can reduce to 30 days the typical 90-days-plus timeframe for executive searches.

What's the difference between Futurestep's process and the personal agent (job alert) services described in Chapter 14? Futurestep recruiters interview candidates before shipping them on to corporate clients. Personal agents respond directly to you by e-mail when a job opening appears to match your profile.

Heidrick and Struggles also operates an Internet-based service for job seekers interested in high-level jobs in the information technology field: Leaders Online (`www.leadersonline.com`). Other executive search firms are reported to be considering similar services.

Will the Web Resume Get Its Groove Back?

A glamorous alternative to the one-dimensional resume is the Web resume, also called the HTML resume. Once the hot news buzz of everyone who could handle the technology, the HTML resume with its links and graphics is on the skids if busy recruiters have their way.

Recruiters are less than lukewarm about resumes created with the Internet programming language HTML (and the newer XML) because they take too much time to read. Moreover, recruiters resent having to follow links to find information they say should have been in the original package.

But isn't a Web resume with its bells and whistles a wonderful way to show employers that you handle a mean information technology skill? Apparently not. Recruiters now say job seekers don't get brownie points by showing their prowess with HTML because it's not a high-demand IT skill. And most searchable databases are text-only, which means the HTML resume must be converted to text before it can be stored — one more step for recruiters.

The final HTML negative for recruiters is that they often send clients batches of resumes and not all of their clients have HTML-enabled e-mail, which means the resumes may arrive looking no better than clothing turned inside out with the HTML tags showing.

Despite panning by recruiters whose eyes roll like slot machines trying to get everything read, some good can come of a Web resume:

- 🗸 When you need to show your work, such as engineering, architecture, art, or modeling

- 🗸 When you've already been in contact with an employer or recruiter and there's enough interest to want to know more about you

- 🗸 When you're working the talent auctions (see "Bidding Sparse in Talent Auctions" in this chapter) and potential employers want to know more before calling you

Are you a graphic arts publishing professional? Adobe Job Connection (www.adobe.com) hosts a free online portfolio service you can use to showcase your work worldwide. Access is free to employers and recruiters seeking graphic arts talent to fill Web, print, and video jobs.

Bidding Sparse in Talent Auctions

The first thing I noticed about Internet talent auction sites that display the qualifications of independent professionals offering themselves for hire — usually for short-term projects — is that few bids are posted.

Online talent auctions which seem to be everywhere are yet another resume alternative of sorts. The auctions work two ways — individuals advertise their skills and invite employers to bid; employers advertise projects and invite individuals to bid. As a rule the talent auctions are free to job seekers but employers pay to participate.

Make the rounds of the Net's career sites and search engines and you find a recruitment market that's created lots of talk but little significant momentum to date. (See Chapter 14.) "It may just be a question of time [before auctions catch on]," says John Sumser, publisher of *Electronic Recruiting News.*

Unleashing E-Screening

Have you heard the Paris taxicab story about Sir Arthur Conan Doyle, creator of the fictional detective Sherlock Holmes? Climbing into a cab without saying a word, the driver turned and asked, "Where to, Mr. Doyle?"

Doyle was taken aback and asked the driver if he'd ever seen him before. The driver said "no" and went to explain that the morning newspaper had carried a story about Doyle being on vacation in Marseilles. Lots of people from Marseilles use this taxi stand and your skin color tells me you've been on vacation.

The driver continued, remarking that an ink-spot on Doyle's right index finger suggested writing and that his clothing was English.

"Adding together that information, I deduced that you are Sir Arthur Conan Doyle," the driver said.

"Fantastic!" the writer exclaimed, "You're a real-life Sherlock Holmes!"

The driver smiled. "There is one other thing," he said. "Your name tag is on the top of your bag."

Employers today may not only want your name on your bag of talents — but insist on knowing what's in the bag before they allow you inside the resume database door.

A new industry is dawning that automates and individually customizes pre-screening and assessment tools. These are tools that you must deal with online before your resume is accepted into an employer's database — or tools (customized forms with questions you answer) that serve in lieu of your resume.

In essence, you are required to pass a kind of pop quiz based on skills for the job itself and sometimes a psychological assessment as well, to prove your bona fides. If you fail, you're deemed to be a "nonqualified" applicant and politely escorted out the Web door.

This genre is still taking shape but here are four examples: Brainbench (brainbench.com), Development Dimensions International (www.ddiworld.com), InterviewNow.com (interviewnow.com), and Recruitsoft (recruitsoft.com). Some of the sites offer sample tests so you can familiarize yourself with what you may encounter applying for a job where they don't want to guess who you are.

Time-Release E-Portfolios

Both Foster City, California, career consultant Clara Horvath and *CareerXroads, The Directory to Job, Resume and Career Management Sites on the Web* coauthor Gerry Crispin believe there must be a better way, a fairer way, to communicate your value to employers.

"Wouldn't it be nice if you could keep a master portfolio on yourself and give selective access to it for people you want to connect with?" Horvath asks. "These profiles would contain much more than your work history. How about a profile of examples of your best work? Maybe you'd want to include psychological profiles and a record of your continuous learning activities. . . ." She emphasizes that such a portfolio would require reliable Internet security.

Employers should reciprocate, Horvath explains. The company you're applying to would have parallel information "about company culture, personality and style; reward systems; salary structures; performance management systems; hiring and firing histories; educational benefits delivered; and a myriad of other relevant factors that are frequently very difficult to research outside the hiring fence."

Crispin describes much the same thing in his book, calling the concept an "e-portfolio." In Crispin's version, a third-party serves as a kind of escrow service, holding the information and releasing it a portion at a time between job applicant and employer. The exchange of information would be accomplished on the Web site of a professional association, trade organization, college alumni organization, or nonprofit certification organization.

Like a time-release capsule, information is exchanged in three phases:

- ✔ **Phase 1**: The employer sends an order to the company recruiting center for candidates to fit a specific job, citing "must have skills and competencies." The recruiter prepares a job order and matches it against anonymous candidates registered with the escrow Web site, sending it along to appropriate candidates with a request that the escrow site release additional information. Interested candidates, remaining anonymous, respond with questions.

- ✔ **Phase 2:** The company recruiter responds to a customized set of questions posed by candidates, such as the status of a specific benefit, a supervisor's style, a telecommuting policy, or the average tenure in a department.

- ✔ **Phase 3:** Each candidate receives a report with details about the company and job in a form easily compared to his or her "ideal" company profile. Now the candidates who wish to continue to be considered for the job authorize the release of a combination of name, and a combination of certifications, experiences and results (authenticated by the Web site escrow host), as well as a personality assessment held on file from an independent assessment center. The recruiter agrees that only the recruiter and hiring manager will see this comprehensive e-mail package and that it will be destroyed within 30 days. If all looks promising, the ideal next step is a single in-person job interview.

Brave New Worlds of Information Exchange

From paper and e-mail resumes, to profile databases and e-portfolios, the self-marketing of our talents to employers will be different tomorrow. But who knows exactly how?

Part V

Answers to Specific Resume Stumpers

The 5th Wave   By Rich Tennant

"I can tell a lot from your resume. You're well educated, detail oriented, and own a really tiny printer."

In this part . . .

Age and experience — the wrong kind — can turn your resume into a candidate for the dead letter file. Responsibly upgrade any factor that RezReaders may perceive as negative. Lying is foolish, but positioning the issue in the best possible light can warm interview chairs.

Chapter 17

Spin Control against Deadly Perceptions

- -

In This Chapter

▶ Squashing the overqualified objection

▶ Battling ageism

▶ Stretching too little experience

▶ Coping with new-graduate challenges

▶ Standing tall as a reentering woman

- -

Spin control means that when you can't change the facts of your experience or age, you change their presentation.

Sorry, we found someone more qualified (read younger)

Sorry, you're overqualified

Sorry, you have too little experience

Sorry, you have no experience

Sorry, you have no recent experience

All of these common rejection statements call for spin control, or putting the best face on a perception.

You can't strip away 20 years. Nor can you wipe away a substantial background that causes you to be ignored because you're "overqualified."

You can't beef up experience you don't have. Nor can you, as a new graduate, magically add work experience to your resume if you "forgot" to hold a student job or to do the college internship or co-op job that your parents and counselors nagged you to death about.

Or perhaps you don't want to lose your place in the corporate line because, as a mom, you chose to stay home with the kids and infuse them with family values.

Spin control to the rescue!

This chapter spotlights major resume components that need spin control to ward off an early burial for your resume. These components are the quintessential and potentially disabling perceptions that stem from your age, old or young; the abundance of your experience; and the experience that seemingly isn't there when you start out or return to the job market.

If you're tempted to skip over this chapter, which deals with reshaping perceptions, you have my permission — if you're no older than 35 and have five years' experience that precisely matches the requirements for a job that you want. Otherwise, sit down, read up, and fight on!

Too Much Experience

Leading off the lineup of resume stumpers is a focus on the shady side of the four-letter word that's ten letters long: *Experience.*

The E-word's assignment to pejorative status is justified. Not only is inappropriate experience — too much or too little — often the real reason you're turned down, but it's also too frequently a cover story for villainous rejections really based on any factor from bias to bad breath.

Too many qualifications or ageism?

A reader of my newspaper column, "Careers," who is rounding the 50s curve, writes that his qualifications for a training position are superior but too ample. He explains:

Preoccupation with age seems to be the pattern. I'm rarely called for an interview; when I call after sending a resume in response to an ad or a networking contact, I'm told I'm too experienced for the position — "You seem to be overqualified." How can I keep my resume from looking like lavender and old lace?

Ageism often is the subtext in the *overqualified* objection. Deal with it by limiting your work history to the most recent positions you've held that target the job opening. To avoid seeming too old or too highly paid, limit your related experience to about 15 years for a managerial job and to about 10 years for a technical job. Concerns about how you moved up so fast will arise if you only go back 10 years for a managerial job, but 10 years is believable for a technical job.

What about all your other experience? Leave it in your memory bank. Or if you believe that the older work history adds to your value as a candidate, you can describe it under a heading of **Other Experience** and briefly present it without dates. Figure 17-1 shows an example of a resume that shows recent experience only.

The recent-experience-only spin doesn't work every time, but give it a try — it shows that you're not stuck in a time warp, and it's a better tactic than advertising your age as one that qualifies for carbon dating.

If the employer is notorious for hiring only young draft horses, rethink your direction. Try to submit your resume to employers who can take advantage of your expertise, such as a new or expanding company operating in unfamiliar territory. Fortunately, a new tool has come along in the past several years admirably suited to this purpose: FirstRate job hunters now turn to the Internet's discussion groups to check out job leads, to name names of saint and sinner companies, and to ask about company cultures and antidiscriminatory practices.

Based on your occupation, you can choose among the many thousands of discussion groups available through mailing lists (such as listservs) and Usenet newsgroups. You may, for example, want to connect with other architects, financial planners, or technical writers. To find them, use Deja News (www.dejanews.com), the classic search engine for finding newsgroups. Another good resource is called Liszt Select (www.liszt.com), which is a directory of 90,000+ mailing lists. Use the KeyWords of your target employment field and you'll find all the discussion groups you can use.

Additionally, America Online offers a wide variety of forums and chat rooms that you can use to find out how others handled the perception problem you're facing. AOL is widely advertised, or for subscription information you can call (800) 827-6364.

If this method is not crystal clear, read *Job Searching Online For Dummies, Second Edition,* by Pam Dixon published by IDG Books Worldwide, Inc.

What if the overqualified objection is just that and not a veil for age discrimination? The employer legitimately may be concerned that when something better comes along, you'll set a sprint record for shortest time on the job. Set your sights higher.

If you really prefer to take life easier or to have more time to yourself, you can be forthcoming with that fact in your resume's objective. Writing this kind of statement is tricky. You risk coming across as worn-out goods, ready to kick back and listen to babbling brooks while you collect a paycheck. When you explain your desire to back off an overly stressful work load, balance your words with a counterstatement reflecting your energy and commitment, as in this example:

Energetic and work-focused, but no longer enjoy frenzied managerial responsibility; seek a challenging nonmanagerial position.

Recent experience only

Work Experience.

FEIN AND SONS – Operates continuously in Long Beach.**Sole Proprietor, Broker.**
Real estate brokerage, development, asset management, and consulting. In-house brokerage
company, specializing in eight- and nine-figure acquisitions, shopping centers, and
commercial space, obtaining entitlements and economic analysis. Personal volume: over
$100 million.

SONNHAARD INC. – Solana Beach. 1995 – 20XX.**Marketing Manager.**
Real estate development corporation. Primary project: Le Chateau Village, a French-theme
100-lot residential development in Del Mar. Sourced architect, designers, and contractors.
Limited liability company built 60 upscale custom homes by architect Jacques Donnaeu of
Toulouse. Supervised 10 sales representatives. Sales gross exceeded $40 million, selling 58
homes ahead of project schedule by six months.

WEST COAST ASSOCIATION – Los Angeles. 1987 – 1995.**Executive Vice President.**
International trade association with 190 firms holding annual fairs, from 25 states and all of
Canada, including two theme amusement parks, 15 affiliated breed organizations and 300
service members who provide goods and services to members. Annual convention attended
by over 2,000 executives. Acted as legislative advocate for California district and county
fairs, nine of which have horse racing and pari-mutuel wagering. Increased membership by
200%, administering seven-figure budget, with staff of five professionals.

Other Experience.

• BBH & Co., d.b.a. ENVIRONMENT AFFILIATED,**Executive Vice President.**
Administered six-figure budget and supervised 27 managers. Directed recruitment and
marketing activities.

• CSU Long Beach, **Development Director.** Managed $40 million dollar project to expand
campus grounds 30%. Maintained lowest campus construction budget in state, including
contracting and materials.

• TRADE ALTERNATIVE, **Commercial Properties Manager.** Marketed, leased, and
acquired $900,000 in commercial property. Catered to such upscale clientele as high-end
law firms.

Figure 17-1: This resume focuses on recent experience to avoid the problem of "overexperience."

Too much experience in one job

A reader writes:

> *I've stayed in my current and only job too long. When my company cut thousands of workers, we received outplacement classes. I was told that job overstayers are perceived to lack ambition, are not interested in learning new things, and are narrowly focused. What can I do about this?*

Spin strategy A: Divide your job into modules

Show that you successfully moved up and up, meeting new challenges and accepting ever more responsibility. Divide your job into realistic segments, which you label as Level 1, Level 2, Level 3, and so on. Describe each level as a separate position, just as you would if the levels had been different positions within the same company or with different employers. If your job titles changed as you moved up, that makes your writing task a lot easier.

Spin strategy B: Deal honestly with job titles

If your job title never changed, should you just make up job titles? No. The only truthful way to inaugurate fictional job titles is to parenthetically introduce them as "equivalent to ..." Suppose that you are an accountant and have been in the same job for 25 years. Your segments might be titled like this:

- ✔ Level 3 (equivalent to supervising accountant)
- ✔ Level 2 (equivalent to senior accountant)
- ✔ Level 1 (equivalent to accountant)

To mitigate the lack of being knighted with increasingly senior job titles, fill your resume with references to your continuous salary increases and bonuses and the range of job skills you mastered.

Spin strategy C: Tackle deadly perceptions head-on

Diminish any perception you became fat and sassy while staying in the same job too long by specifically describing open-ended workdays: "Worked past 5 p.m. at least once a week throughout employment."

Derail the perception you don't want to learn new things by being specific in describing learning adventures: "Attended six semesters of word-processing technologies; currently enrolled in adult education program to master latest software."

Discount the perception you are narrowly focused by explaining that although your employment address didn't change, professionally speaking, you are widely traveled in outside seminars, professional associations, and reading.

Spin strategy D: When nothing works, try something new

When you have followed the experts' recommendations note for note but are still sitting out the dance, take a chance on something new. In a departure from the normal practice of omitting from your resumes reasons for leaving a job, consider indicating why you're making a change after all this time. Neutralize the issue burning in every employer's mind: "Why now? Why after all these years are you on the market? Excessed out? Burned out?" If the question isn't asked, that doesn't mean it isn't hanging out in the recruiter's mind. Even though you may be seen as a moss-backed antiquity, reveal yourself as interested in today's and tomorrow's developments by adding this kind of phrase in your objective:

> ✔ Focusing on companies and organizations with contemporary viewpoints

In an even more pioneering move to solve the same problem, create a whole new section at the tail of your resume, headed *Bright Future,* with a statement such as this:

BRIGHT FUTURE

Layoffs springing from a new management structure give me the welcomed opportunity to accept new challenges and freshen my worklife.

An employer's perception of highly experienced people may be that they are too rigid and hold expectations that the new environment will replicate the old — a perception that assassinates resumes.

Not too long ago, a number of a blue-chip corporation's $75,000-a-year executive secretaries who had been there forever were axed; they had a problem with a capital *P.* Potential employers feared that not only could they not match former salaries, but also that the secretaries were spoiled by expecting high employee benefits and generous corporate practices.

And in the technical field, many seasoned engineers and scientists are experiencing difficulty. Recently, several U.S. technical giants insisted to Congress that they can't find enough technical workers in the U.S. and asked that the cap on recruiting foreign workers be raised by 50 percent. After their request, I was blitzed with e-mail from over-40 U.S. scientists and engineers protesting what they call age discrimination and corporate welfare. The protesting e-mail writers said that what the companies really want is young, cheap labor.

As one Oklahoma City reader said: "I have a Ph.D. in physics and more than 20 years of computer programming experience, including Fortran, C/C++, ADA, HTML, and Java. At my own substantial expense, I'm currently completing a year's course work in Cobol, Visual Basic, Web-page administration, and advanced LAN theory."

The Oklahoma reader laments that he hasn't had a nibble on a job interview. Yes, he's tried the internship remedy. "I enrolled for an internship, but after I donated 40 hours to the company, building five computers for free for them, the company pulled out of the internship program, negating a verbal agreement to give me hands-on experience.

"Because I have a doctorate, almost routinely I'm asked, 'Why would you want to be a programmer?' The implication is that I'm overqualified. The reality is that ageism is alive and well, and employers are unwilling to pay for senior talent."

Another reader, 46 and a Texas resident, also has a doctorate in a technical field and traveled a similar rough road. The Texas reader, now employed at a company he admires, says the corporate request to bring in younger, cheaper help from abroad discriminates against older technical workers who are willing to upgrade their skills. Some of the older workers are themselves earlier immigrants, he notes.

In such cases, I advise seasoned technical personnel to consider contract work (see Chapter 14 for examples of names and Web addresses of contract firms), but pick and choose because many contract firms, says the Texas reader, treat their hires like "pieces of meat." For contract work, start your resume with a KeyWord profile and include as many skills as you legitimately can.

In addition to following the resume tips for seasoned aces offered in this chapter, get other ideas of how technical personnel can surmount "overqualified" objections and age discrimination by cruising the Web site "Science, Math, and Engineering Links" (www.phds.org).

Also, you can tap into the nation's largest database of information describing age discrimination against technical personnel and some ideas on how to fight it by subscribing to the University of California at Davis computer science professor Norman Matloff's e-mailing list. For a free subscription, e-mail Dr. Matloff and ask to be put on his eye-opening list. His e-mail address is matloff@cs.ucdavis.edu.

If you're over 35 and sense that ageism or perceptions of rigidity are doing you in, defend yourself. Make your FirstRate resume crackle with vitality, new words, and examples of your flexibility and motivation to learn. Create an image of your life as one of windows sliding open, not of doors creaking closed.

Too Little Experience

RezReaders root for conciseness because they want to cut to the chase. But new graduates often have the opposite problem — they need to beef up their entries — as this reader suggests:

> *My experience section looks emaciated. How can I feed it a little?*

Writing your first resume is as much fun as cleaning out the garage. Assuming you're not a lazy person, one reason you don't get it done on time is fear — your value as a human being is reflected on a page, and that's scary. Either your life is too big to consolidate on paper or your life is nothing to brag about. Furthermore, you fear you can't write very well. Other than that, you've never done it before.

Deal with all these footdragging excuses by faithfully following the worksheet cues in Chapter 8. If you're not sure how your finished product should look, cast your eyes on Figure 17-2, which shows a hybrid formatted resume written by a new graduate who maximized a lean employment history.

New graduate with some experience

The word is trickling down that internships and student jobs are increasingly the ticket to the jobmarket, as this question shows:

> *My school's career center is holding resume workshops for graduating seniors. I can't go because I'm doing as I was told — getting work experience. Do employers really believe that a student job produces valuable real-life experience?*

Absolutely yes. A FirstRate resume shows every shred of work experience, paid and unpaid, through internships, student jobs, co-op education, and extracurricular activities.

Stretching your experience is the spin, although you won't get away with claiming that you spent your summers as vice president of Microsoft.

Separate your jobs into fragments and explain them. For example, don't say that your job title was "office help" or "office clerk" and stop there. Divide the job into such functions as telephone reception, telephone sales, contract negotiations, purchasing, inventory, staff training, computer application training, public speaking, and written communications. Describe each one in terms of your accomplishments and their outcomes (see Chapter 5). Your inventory of worksheets like those you create in Chapter 5 is invaluable to pump up your experience without fibbing about it.

New Graduate – Some Experience

MARTINA RABINOVICH
#543-B College Drive, Boston, Massachusetts 45678, (910) 111-2131

OBJECTIVE
Position with environmentally and socially conscious public relations firm. Proven skills in public relations, research, and organization; demonstrated leadership qualities throughout university activities and professional experience. Computer skills.

HIGHLIGHTS OF PUBLIC RELATIONS EXPERIENCE

- **House of Representatives Intern,** Renee H. Glamer's District Office, Elvin, MA.
  Summers 20XX – 20XX
  Assisted Representative Glamer to resolve consituents' issues. Communicated with legislative committees, researched legislation through the House computer system, and attended town meetings. Accumulated invaluable public relations skills using interpersonal abilities effectively in high-pressure, deadline-oriented situations. Major project: Veteran's Festival, 50th Anniversary.

- **Student Body Vice-President,** Boston University, Boston MA. 20XX – 20XX
  Chaired Council Operations Committee. Conducted all student body elections, using strong leadership and public speaking skills to accrue 1,600 votes.

- **Medford Municipal Pool Lifeguard,** Medford, MA. Summers 20XX – 20XX
  Began as snack bar employee, earned certificate, promoted to lifeguard, and then to head lifeguard with managerial responsibilities. Supervised 11 employees.

- **OTHER PUBLIC RELATIONS ACTIVITIES:**
  Student advisor, tour guide, campus delegate, student ambassador for alumni, peer tutor for critical thinking.

RESEARCH EXPERIENCE

- **Republican Party Pollster,** Medford District, Medford, MA. May – Nov., 20XX, 20XX
  Distributed more than 50,000 sample ballots. Tabulated results, using math skills. Developed effective organizational skills, communicating with the general public and responding to their interests diplomatically.

- **Medford County Historical Society Intern,** Medford County Historical Society, Medford, MA. Fall 20XX
  Using practiced research skills, researched and designed an exhibit focusing on elections of Progressive party candidates. Exhibit is on display at Medford County Museum, visited by more than 200 individuals a day.

ORGANIZATIONAL SKILLS

- **Alpha Kappa Omega Sorority Leader,** Boston University, Boston, MA. 20XX – 20XX
  Chaired Assualt-Risk Management meetings, 20XX – 20XX. Organized events to minimize individual and group risks of physical assault on campus. Assistant Bursar, 20XX – 20XX. Used strong prioritizing and math skills to assist Treasurer in distribution of funds.

Figure 17-2: Sample resume of a new graduate.

Figures 17-3A and 17-3B show examples of before-and-after resumes that illustrate the spin on a moderate amount of work experience. A student wrote both versions and went on to be hired at a virtual (online) magazine in New York as an assistant art director.

Virtually no paid or unpaid experience

Need a job, get experience! Need experience, get a job! This predicament has frustrated new graduates since the polar ice caps retreated. Some graduates get the message almost too late. Frequently, a marginal new graduate not only drags along a low GPA (grade point average), say a 2.5, but has invested four or five years of nonschool time developing skills as a television watcher, shopper, or socializer. The new graduate not only had no career-related internship or job but also didn't bother to get a job on restaurant row to fund such frivolities as kegs before finals and skiing afterward. There were no co-op assignments, no volunteer stints — zippo! This reader writes with a challenging query:

> *I'm just a college brat — I have no experience, plus I didn't exactly distinguish myself with grades. How do I write a resume from air?*

Having nothing but education to work with makes for a difficult resume scenario. Only dedicated job research and continual customizing of each resume has a chance of producing a FirstRate product. Perhaps you've overlooked something; even child-sitting or pet-sitting offers experience in accepting responsibility and demonstrates reliability.

If an exhaustive search of your hobbies, campus activities, or community service turns up nothing worth putting on your resume, your education must carry the entire weight of candidacy for employment. Milk it dry, as the example in Figure 17-4 suggests.

Starting over with a master's degree

An advanced degree represents another kind of "too little experience" when you use it as a door-opener to a new career instead of continuing in your current field.

After career mishaps, many people see a master's degree as a born-again employment credential for a well-planned career change. And new beginnings often are the happy outcome. By contrast, if their goals were murky as baccalaureate graduates and are still murky as master's degree graduates, disappointed but better-educated people fail to get what they want. The resume takes the brunt of the blame, as this question from a reader of my column suggests:

> *I am seeking a job with a new master's degree — obtained at age 47 — and experiencing a lot of difficulty. I have mailed out at least 500 resumes and received only one response — from a telephone company suggesting that I install telephone equipment. What is wrong with my resume?*

NEW GRADUATE – BEFORE

Dominic Preisendorfer

123 45th Way
Washington, OR 67891
(011) 121-3141

Muhlenberg College
Box 321
Allentown, PA 18104
(141) 312-1110

Education:
-Upper Washington High School: Graduated w/scholars diploma. Vice President of class.

-Muhlenberg College, Allentown, PA
  anticipate BA in Spring 20XX.
  visual arts major with a concentration in graphic design involved w/campus arts festival.

Internships:
-Drury Design: Fall 20XX semester. Making mechanicals, layouts on computer, jersey design, research.

-Washington Magazine (art dept.): Summer 20XX. Assisted with layouts in the "well" of the front of the book.

-Net Line Design: Spring 20XX semester. Helped in business side of office with filing, billing, typing. Prepared comps for presentation.

Work Experience:

-R.R. Manning: Fall 20XX-current. Stock, sales, display, delivery

-Freelance: Summer 1999

Computer Skills:
  Macintosh programs: Macwrite, Quark, PhotoShop, Aldus Freehand, Pagemaker, Illustration IBM programs

Figure 17-3A: Even a thin-looking resume can be fleshed out.

NEW GRADUATE -- AFTER

Dominic Preisendorfer

123 45th Way
Washington, OR 67891
(011) 121-3141

Muhlenberg College
Box 321
Allentown, PA 18104
(141) 312-1110

EDUCATION

Muhlenberg College, Allentown, Pennsylvania
BA, Art, June 20XX. Chair, Campus Arts Festival

INTERNSHIPS

Drury Design, Green Mills, Oregon
Fall 20XX
- Contributed to all aspects of a cutting-edge, multifaceted design firm.
- Researched trends as part of "Genie for the New Century" campaign. Drew sketches for new Genie: resulted as subject of article in New Yorker magazine.
- Developed mechanicals for *U.S. Museum of Film Profiles* magazine.
- Transformed BMX Bicycle Company's logo to evoke 21st Century image for racing jersey.
- Assisted with layout for the first Dark Horse style guide to be used by comics firms for licensing.

Washington Magazine, Washington, Oregon
Summer 20XX
- Assisted in day-to-day operations of the art department and in each aspect of production schedule.
- Helped evaluate and provide solutions for layouts in well of book.
- Contributed to redesign of book front. Recommended changes in typefaces, colors, and sizes.

Net Line Design, Allentown, Pennsylvania
Spring 20XX
- Provided extensive clerical support for office, including billing, data entry, filing.
- Prepared samples for presentation.

WORK EXPERIENCE

Freelance, Cafe Paradise, Green Mills, Oregon
Summer 1997
- Graphic Design: Designed logo, letterhead, business cards, and brochure.
- Advertising: Developed, implemented ad campaign including media purchasing.
- Interior Design: Worked with architect to design funky, eclectic bar, interior environment.

R.R. Manning, Washington, Oregon
Sales, Fall 1999-Present. High-end country furnishing and accessories store.
- Create windows and furniture displays, developing visual marketing skills and strategies.
- Servicing clients based on customer satisfaction and responses to marketing strategies.
- Train and supervise new hires in stocking and inventory.

COMPUTER SKILLS

- Macintosh Programs: Macwrite, QuarkXPress, Photoshop, Aldus Freehand, Pagemaker, Type Styler, Super Paint, and Illustrator.
- PC Programs: Microsoft Publisher and Works for Windows 2000.

Figure 17-3B: A new graduate adds a different spin.

New Graduate – Little Experience

Deanna R. McNealy
(111) 213-1415

1234 University Drive,#56B
Irvine, California 78910

Seek entry-level retail sales position. Offer more than three years' intensive study of public communication. Completed Bachelor's degree, developing strong research, language, interpersonal, computer, and disciplinary skills. Proven interactive skills with groups and individuals. Energetic, adaptive, fast learner.

BACKGROUND & EDUCATION

- **Bachelor of Arts, University of California at Irvine (UCI), May, 20##, Literature & Social Studies**

Self-Directed Studies   20## - Present
Focusing on mainstream culture and trends, study merchandising and population demographicsof individuals between the ages of 18 and 49. Browse media and advertising extensively, developing an in-depth understanding of material consumption in U.S. culture.

University Studies
8/1 – 12/29, 20##   Literary Philosophy, Graduate, UCI, Irvine, California
Accumulated skills in prioritizing, self-management and discipline, accomplishing over 90 pages ofcommentary on the subject of philosophical thought.

1/23 – 5/25, 20##   Social Text and Context, UCI, Irvine, California
Developed in-depth understanding of public consensus and modern value systems.Concentration: the relationship between ideals and historical and economic patterns.

1/23 – 5/25, 20##   Critical Thinking, UCI, Irvine, California
60 hours of self-directed research and lecture attendance, studying essential elements of critical thought. Developed skills in argumentative dialogue, logic, analysis, and approaching perception from an educated and diverse persepctive. Focus: anatomy of critcal thought.

1/23 - 5/25, 20##   Public Communication, UCI, Irvine, California
Intensive study of the psychological and social techniques of speech and communication. Developed comprehensive understanding of debate, physical language, formal and informal delivery, subliminal communication, and advertising. Focus: written and visual advertisingtechniques.

Other Experience 20## - Present, UCI, Irvine, California
15th and 16th Century Rhetoric, French Poetry, Literature in Music, Women, Words & Wisdom, FilmTheory, Shakespeare, British Fiction, U.S. Fiction, World Literature.

SKILLS
Computer: All word processing applications on Macintosh and PC, Internet savvy.
Interpersonal: Experienced in working with groups and individuals using teamwork and collaboration, setting goals, delegating and communicating effectively.

Figure 17-4: The resume of a graduate with little experience.

The resume isn't the real problem here. If the reader, a man, sent the same resume to 500 potential employers, he's clearly not focused on what he's best fit to do — one size does not fit all. This individual should learn a great deal more about job hunting and then write a career plan to be reviewed monthly. *Job Hunting For Dummies, Second Edition,* by Max Messmer from IDG Books Worldwide, Inc., is a good place to start.

Returning to the resume treatment, if your master's degree is intended to facilitate a career change, see the career-transition resume discussion in Chapter 19. If your master's degree upgrades your credentials in the same field in which you now work, begin your resume by reporting your work experience; follow up with the education section, leading off with the newly minted master's degree. Make use of a resume-ending section titled *Other Information* to say that you view learning as a life-skill, as evidenced by the master's degree.

When the Ph.D. is a liability

You slaved and skimped in school to earn a doctorate. Now that you're seeking to use that knowledge and credential, your head is being thrust into a brick wall. This dilemma calls for all the critical thinking faculties you developed in your educational pursuits, as this plaintive appeal reveals:

> *But ... I went through six years of learning at tough schools, and now that I'm $80,000 in debt for my Ph.D., nobody wants to hire me. Isn't my education supposed to ensure my employment?*

Unfortunately, that's not how it works. A doctorate traditionally has been reserved for research or teaching, but even those job prospects aren't living up to expectations. Doctorate-holding job hunters return day after day with reports of rejection because they are said to be "overqualified." Here are two viewpoints on this issue:

- From a career adviser to Ph.D.s: "Although the jobmarket for Ph.D.s is tight, disastrously so in some fields, unemployment rates are very low, and those earning doctorates almost always end up in professional positions that use their intelligence, if not their training. It may take a few years to find their niches."

- From an outplacement consultant: "Ph.D.s are hard to place. Companies assume they will not be contented in a job that doesn't make use of their education. If they are older, it is twice as hard. Many companies have given up their R&D (research and development) labs.

- "Universities look for someone who can bring in grant money. I ask Ph.D.s to make two resumes — one with the degree and one without. The one without at least gets them interviews."

View number two gets my vote because not everyone has several years to launch a career. Although it's disheartening, I suggest that, unless you are certain a Ph.D. is required for the position(s), you omit the Piled High and Deep degree from your resume.

As I discuss in Chapter 5, you are not writing an autobiography but rather a selected view of your strengths as they apply to the job market.

Too Long Gone: For Women Only

The reentering woman still has it tough. Usually, it's Mom who puts her career on hold to meet family responsibilities. When she tries to reenter the job market, by choice or economic necessity, she feels as though she's been living on another planet, as this letter shows:

> *Employers don't want to hire women if they've been mothers and out of the market for more than a year or two. Hey, ya know, for the last 10 years, I've worked my tail off! Don't they understand that? Doesn't intelligence, willingness to work hard, creativity, attention to detail, drive, efficiency, grace under pressure, initiative, leadership, persistence, resourcefulness, responsibility, teamwork, and a sense of humor mean anything these days?*

Every characteristic that this reader mentions is still a hot ticket in the job market, but the burden is on her to interpret these virtues as marketable skills.

- ✔ Grace under pressure, for example, translates to *crisis manager,* a valuable person when the electricity fails in a computer-driven office.

- ✔ Resourcefulness translates to *office manager,* who is able to ward off crank calls from credit collection agencies.

- ✔ A sense of humor translates to *data communications manager,* who joshes a sleepy technical whiz into reporting for work at two in the morning for emergency repair of a busted satellite hovering over Europe.

Here's what the returning woman must do to develop a FirstRate resume that connects what she can do with what an employer wants done.

Look back in discovery

Review your worksheets to spot transferable skills that you gained in volunteer, civic, hobby, and domestic work. Scout for adult and continuing education, both on campus and in nontraditional settings.

Reexamine the informative television programs you've watched, the news magazines you've monitored. Go to the library and read business magazines and trade journals to make a lexicon of up-to-date words, such as *Please compare my skills* (not *I'm sure you will agree*).

Avoid tired words like *go-getter* and *upwardly mobile.* Yesteryear's buzzwords, such as *management by objective* and *girl Friday* won't do a thing to perk up your image.

Incorporate professional terms

The use of professional words can help de-emphasize informal training or work experience. But you must be careful when doing this to show good judgment about the work world.

Professionalizing your domestic experience is a tightrope walk: Ignoring it leaves you looking like a missing person, yet you can't be pretentious or naive. Don't say *housewife;* say *family caretaker* or *domestic specialist.* Refer to *home management* to minimize gaps in time spent as a homemaker. ***Important:*** Fill the home management period with transferable skills relevant to the targeted position.

Delve into what you did during your home management period. You did not hold a paid job, but you did do important unpaid work. Dissect your achievements to find your deeds — they can be impressive. Examples range from time management (developing the ability to do more with less time) to budgeting experience (developing a sophisticated understanding of priority allocation of financial resources). Other examples include using the telephone in drumming up support for a favorite charity (developing confidence and a businesslike telephone technique) and leadership positions in the PTA (developing a sense of authority and the ability to guide others).

Despite almost three decades of media attention to skills developed by homemakers, employers continue to be dismissive of parenting and other abilities acquired inside the home. Many employers believe identifying yourself as a domestic specialist is no more workplace-useful than claiming to be a "seasoned husband" or "experienced friend."

Make your homemaker skills difficult to disrespect by showing their relevance to a given career field. Be careful to avoid sounding as though you attended a workshop where you memorized big words.

Whatever you do, you can't ignore the issue — like where have you been for the past few years? When you lack skills developed outside the home in community work, you have to do the best you can to pull out home-based skills.

INSIDER HINT

Selected home-based skills

Don't overlook these skills you may have acquired inside the home. I've included a few examples of occupations in which they can be used. This illustration assumes you lack formal credentials for professional-level work. If you do have the credentials, upgrade the examples to the appropriate job level.

✔ Juggling schedules: Paraprofessional assistant to business executives, physicians. Small service business operator, dispatching staff of technicians.

✔ Peer counseling: Human resources department employee benefits assistant. Substance abuse program manager.

✔ Arranging social events: Party shop manager. Nonprofit organization fund-raiser. Art gallery employee.

✔ Conflict resolution: Administrative assistant. Customer service representative. School secretary.

✔ Problem-solving: Any job.

✔ Decorating: Interior decorator. Interior fabric shop salesperson.

✔ Nursing: Medical or dental office assistant.

✔ Solid purchasing judgment: Purchasing agent. Merchandiser.

✔ Planning trips, relocations: Travel agent. Corporate employee relocation coordinator.

✔ Communicating: Any job.

✔ Shaping budgets: Office manager. Department head. Accounting clerk.

✔ Maximizing interior spaces: Commercial-office real estate agent. Business furniture store operator.

Use years or use dates — not both

Some advisers suggest that in referring to your home management years, you use years, not dates, which avoids the gap in paid work experience, like so:

• *Family Care 10 years*

Child care, home operations, budgeting and support for a family of four. Participation in parent/school relations, human services, and religious organization

• *Leadership Positions*

Vice President, Curriculum Committee, PTA; Chair, Fund-Raising, American Humane Society; Subcommittee Chair, Budget Committee, First Baptist Church

This *years-only approach* is unlikely to make a favorable impression on a person who hires often. Employment professionals prefer concrete facts and dates. But the years-only resume can work at small businesses where the hiring manager also wears several other hats and doesn't pay much attention to hiring guidelines.

Don't make the mistake of using both forms on the same resume, assigning dates to your paid jobs but only years to your homemaker work.

Showcase your best work: An example

Figure 17-5 shows a resume sample of interest to reentering women.

Know the score

Gender bias lives, and, of course, you should omit all information that the employer is not entitled to, including your age, marital status, physical condition, number and ages of children, and husband's name. Even though the law is on your side, in today's interview-rationed job market, your resume must qualify you more than the next guy. If you've been out of the job market for some years, you have to work harder and smarter to show you're a hot hire. Seek out seminars and services offered to reentering women to help in your quest.

Spin Control Is in the Details

A white ruffled blouse stained only slightly with one dab of spaghetti sauce is 99 percent clean. But every person who sees me wear it remembers the red spot, not the rest of the blouse. You can have a 99 percent FirstRate resume, but any one of the deadly perceptions identified in this chapter can ice it without your knowing why. Practice spin control — present possible negative perceptions in a flattering light.

REENTRY

JOY R. NGUYEN

12 Watt Road, Palmira, Florida 34567   (321) 654-9876

SUMMARY OF EXPERIENCE

More than five years' experience in event-planning, fundraising, administration and publicity. More than nine years' experience in administration for retail and manufacturing firms. B.A. in Business. Florida Teaching Certificate.

NONPROFIT/VOLUNTEER SERVICE

1997-Present Palmira Optimists' Association, Palmira, Florida
                       Membership Committee Chair
Planning, organizing programs, exhibits and events to recruit association members. Coordinated annual new member events.

1989-1999   Okeefenokee County Y.M.C.A., Okeefenokee, Florida
                       Member, Board of Directors and Executive Committee
Spearheaded first Y.M.C.A. organization in county. Designed programs, procedures, and policies, monitoring trustees in the construction of $3 million facility. Led $2.5 million fundraising campaign.

- **Fundraising Chair,** 1992-1998 Raised funds for entire construction project, establishing hundreds of donors and supervising project. Sourced contractors and directed fundraising activities, using strong interpersonal and networking skills.

HOME MANAGEMENT EXPERIENCE

- **Scheduling:** Assisted business executive and two children in the scheduling of travel and 160,000 miles of transportation. Arranged ticketing, negotiated finances of $12,000 in travel expenses.
- **Conflict Resolution:** Arbitrated personal, business issues. Effective interpersonal skills.
- **Relocation:** Launched inter state relocation of entire family, coordinating moving services, trucks, and packing schedules.
- **Budget & Purchasing:** Managed family finances, including budgeting, medical, dental, insurance packages, two home purchases, three auto purchases, expenses, and taxes. Developed finance and math skills.

ADDITIONAL PROFESSIONAL EXPERIENCE

1989-1991   Sunrise Books, Cabana, Florida
                       Assistant Manager, Sales Representative
Managed daily operations of coffee house and bookstore, directing staff of 35. Supervised entire floor of merchandise and stock. Purchased all sideline goods.

- Spearheaded store's first sales campaign, resulting in tripled sales.
- Designed system for inventory analysis, streamlining purchasing, and display control.
- Redirected staff duties for more effective work hours.
- Promoted from sales to supervisor in 38 days; three months later to asst. mgr.

EDUCATION

- **Bachelor of Science in Business,** 1989, University of Miami, Miami, G.P.A.: 3.75
- **Florida Teaching Certificate,** Business and English, 1996, Florida State, Palmira

Figure 17-5: Sample resume of a domestic specialist reentering the work world.

Chapter 18

Spin Control against Special Issues

• •

In This Chapter

▶ Guarding against negative information

▶ Dealing with disability issues

▶ Patching over employment gaps

▶ Spin-controlling a demotion

▶ Adding focus to the busy resume

▶ Constructing resume-accessory references

• •

Chapter 17 focuses on FirstRate spin-control techniques that apply to various aspects of experience, a traditional issue that affects most people during their lifetime. In this chapter, I examine selected special issues that concern fewer people but can be most difficult to handle.

Some issues, such as disability or criminal justice problems, may never relate to you. Other issues, such as job tenure, have gained new urgency in an era when more and more companies buy your brains and skills for a period of time and then cut you loose.

I know a few people with a "perfect" job history — but only a few. Most job seekers are burdened with special issues that won't survive a standard-issue resume. Here are spin-control techniques for various resume predicaments and concerns.

Omit Inappropriate Data

The best way to handle some land mines on your resume is to ignore them.

As explained in Chapter 7, generally it's a mistake to reveal negative information on a resume. Save troublemaking information for the all-important job interview, where you have a fighting chance to explain your side of things.

Generally speaking, stay away from these topics when constructing a resume:

- ✔ Firings, demotions, forced resignations, and early termination of contracts
- ✔ Personal differences with coworkers or supervisors
- ✔ Bankruptcy, tax evasion, or credit problems
- ✔ Criminal convictions or lawsuits
- ✔ Homelessness
- ✔ Illnesses from which you have now recovered
- ✔ Disabilities that do not prevent you from performing the essential functions of the job, with or without some form of accommodation

Should you ever give reasons for leaving a job?

In most instances, resume silence in the face of interview-killing facts is still the strategy of choice. But the time has come to rethink at least one special issue: losing a job.

Now that jobs are shed like so many autumn leaves, losing a job is no longer viewed as a case of personal failure. It may be to your advantage to state on your resume why you left your last position, assuming that it was not due to poor work performance on your part. If you were downsized out, the RezReader may appreciate your straightforward statement "Job eliminated in downsizing."

But remember, if you elect to say why you lost one job, for consistency you have to say why you left all your jobs — such as for greater opportunity, advancement, and the like.

Job Seekers with Disabilities

More than 40 million Americans are protected by the ADA (Americans with Disabilities Act), which covers a wide spectrum of disabilities. These disabilities include acquired immunodeficiency syndrome (AIDS) and human immunodeficiency virus (HIV), alcoholism, cancer, cerebral palsy, diabetes, emotional illness, epilepsy, hearing and speech disorders, heart disorders, learning disabilities such as dyslexia, mental retardation, muscular dystrophy, and visual impairments. The act does not cover conditions that impose short-term limitations, such as pregnancy or broken bones.

The ADA makes it illegal for an employer to refuse to hire (or discriminate against) a person simply because that person has one or more disabilities. Generally, the ADA forbids employers who have more than 15 employees and who are hiring from doing the following:

- ✔ Discriminating on the basis of any physical or mental disability
- ✔ Asking job applicants questions about their past or current medical conditions
- ✔ Requiring applicants to take preemployment medical exams

The ADA requires that an employer make reasonable accommodations for qualified individuals who have disabilities, unless doing so would cause the employer "undue hardship." The undue hardship provision is still open to interpretation by the courts.

If you have a disability that you believe is covered by the ADA, familiarize yourself with the law's specifics. Call your member of Congress, visit your library, or obtain free comprehensive ADA guides and supporting materials from the splendid Internet World Wide Web site maintained by the Job Accommodation Network (http://janweb.icdi.wvu.edu/).

The ADA watches your back to prevent discrimination based on your disability, but RezReaders may still weasel around the law to avoid what they perceive as a liability. Use street savvy: When you can't win and you can't break even, change the game.

In your game, spin control begins with not disclosing your disability on your resume.

When should you disclose your disability?

- ✔ If your disability is visible, the best time to disclose it is after the interview has been set and you telephone to confirm the arrangements. Pass the message in an offhanded manner: "Because I use a wheelchair for mobility, I was wondering if you can suggest which entrance to your building would be the most convenient?"
- ✔ Alternatively, you may want to reserve disclosure for the interview.
- ✔ If your disability is not visible, such as mental illness or epilepsy, you need not disclose it unless you'll need special accommodations. Even then, you can hold the disclosure until the negotiating stage once you've received a potential job offer.

Either way, be confident, unapologetic, unimpaired, and attitude-positive. Disclosure in the job-search process is a complex quandary.

What can you do about gaps in your work history caused by disability?

In years past, you might have been able to obscure the issue. No longer. New computer databases make it easy for suspicious employers to research your medical history. And with health insurance costs so high, they may do exactly that. If your illness-related job history has so many gaps that it looks like a hockey player's teeth, I've never heard a better suggestion than writing the no-pretense "Illness and Recovery" next to the date. It's honest, and the "recovery" part says, "I'm back and ready to work!"

If you have too many episodes of "missing teeth," your work history will look less shaky in a functional format, discussed in Chapter 4. Online resume discussion groups, which you can find through the Job Accommodation Network, are further sources of guidance on this difficult issue.

Finally, should you mention on your resume a need for adaptive equipment, such as a special kind of telephone?

I wouldn't mention the need for adaptive equipment — even if the equipment is inexpensive or you're willing to buy it yourself. Instead, stick with the time-release capsule method of sharing information: Dribble out those revelations that may stifle interest in hiring you only when necessary. Never lose sight of your objective: to get an interview.

When Demotion Strikes

Kevin Allen (real person, phony name) was the district manager of five stores in a chain when he was demoted to manager of a single store. The chain was sending him a message — the chain's top managers hoped he'd quit so they could avoid awarding a severance package of benefits. Kevin ignored the message, retained a lawyer, kept his job, and started a job hunt after hours.

He finessed his resume by listing all the positions he had held in the chain, leaving out dates of when each started and stopped. Achievements were combined.

> Demoting Store Chain, Big City
>
> District Manager, 5 stores
>
> Store Manager, Windy City
>
> Store Assistant Manager, Sunny City
>
> Store Clerk, Sunny City

Throwing all of Kevin's titles into one big pot seemed a clever idea, but it didn't work for him. After a year of searching, Kevin got interviews, yes; but at every single face-to-face meeting, he was nailed with the same question: "Why were you demoted?" The interviewers' attitudes seemed accusatory, as if they'd been misled. Kevin failed to answer the question satisfactorily — he did not receive a single offer during a year's search. How did all the potential employers find out the truth?

Among obvious explanations: (A) Kevin worked in a "village" industry where people know each other and gossip. (B) Employers ordered credit checks on him; credit checks show employment details. (C) Employers authorized private investigations, an uncommon but not unheard-of practice in private business.

No one knows what really happened, but in hindsight, Kevin might have done better had he accepted the message that the chain wanted him out, negotiated a favorable severance package that included good references, and quit immediately while his true title was that of district manager.

After two humiliating years of demotion status, Kevin took action by "crossing the River Jordan," a Biblical phrase that universities have adapted. It refers to those who seek a new beginning by returning to college for a law or business degree. Kevin enrolled in law school.

In cases like Kevin's, a strategy that may work better is forthright but doesn't flash your demotion in neon lights. Combine only two titles together, followed quickly by your accomplishments and strengths:

1994 - 1997 Demoting Company Name

Assistant Manager, Manager

As assistant manager, support the manager and carefully monitor detailed transactions with vendors, insuring maintenance of products and inventory; use skills in invoicing, billing, ordering, and purchasing. As manager, supervise all aspects of purchasing, display, and merchandise sales. Trained team of more than 30 employees in two-week period. Trained three assistant managers in essential functions of customers, employees, and finance. Increased sales revenues 25 percent in first six months.

No matter how well you handle your resume entry, the reference of the demoting employer may ultimately end your chances of landing a new job that you want. In trying to mend fences, you may appeal to the demoting employer's fairness or go for guilt. Point out how hard you worked and how loyal you've been. Find reasons why your performance record was flawed. Ask for the commitment of a favorable reference and a downplaying of the demotion. If fairness or guilt appeals are denied, see an employment lawyer about sending the demoting employer, on law-firm letterhead, a warning against libel or slander.

The basic way to handle demotions throughout the job-hunting process is akin to how you handle being fired: by accentuating the positive contributions and results for which you are responsible. *But being demoted is trickier to handle than being fired.* It's a weirdish fact, but being fired no longer suggests personal failure; being demoted does.

Sealing Gaps in Your Record

Periods of unemployment leave black holes in your work history. Should you (A) fill them with positive expressions such as *family obligations,* (B) fill them with less positive but true words such as *unemployed,* or (C) show the gap without comment?

Choosing B, *unemployed,* is dreary. Forget that! Choosing C, *leave-it-blank-and-say-nothing,* often works — just hope it won't be noticed. My choice is A: Tell the truth about what you were doing but spin control it in a dignified, positive way. A few examples: *independent study. . . foreign travel. . . career renewal through study and assessment.*

An infoblizzard of tips has been published on how to repair resume holes. Unless you were building bombs in a terrorist training camp, the principles are simple:

- ✔ Present the time gap as a positive event.

- ✔ Detail why it made you a better worker — not a better *person,* but a better worker with more favorable characteristics, polished skills, and mature understanding, all of which you're dying to contribute to your new employer.

How can these principles be applied? Take the case of a student who dropped out of college to play in a band and do odd jobs for four years before coming back to finish his biology degree and look for a job. The student knows that employers may perceive him as not committed to a career. In the resume, he should treat the band years like any other job: Describe the skills that were polished as a band leader. Identify instances of problem solving, teamwork, leadership, and budgeting.

The real problem solver has to come in the cover letter that accompanies this resume, as Abilene Christian University Director of Career Services Jack Stewart outlines:

After completing two years of undergraduate study, it was necessary for me to work to continue my education. Using my talents as a musician, I organized a band and after four years was able to continue my education. I matured and learned much about the real world and confirmed that an education is extremely important in fulfilling my career goals.

The chief mistake people make is assuming that a positive explanation won't sell and fudging dates from legitimate jobs to cover the black holes. You may get away with it in the beginning. But ultimately, you will be asked to sign a formal application, a legal document. When a company wishes to chop staff without paying severance benefits, the first thing that happens is an intense investigation of the company's database of application forms. People who lied on their applications can be sent out into the mean streets with nothing but their current paychecks on their backs.

Lying isn't worth the risk — it's a mistake.

Another method of papering-over glaring gaps is to include all your work under "Work History" and cite unpaid and volunteer work as well as paid jobs.

Suppose you've been unemployed for the past year. That's a new black hole. Some advisers suggest the old dodge of allowing the RezReader to misperceive the open-ended date of employment for your last job: "2000 – " as though you meant "2000 – Present." The open-ender solution often works — until you run into a RezReader who thinks it's way too calculating.

The consultant/entrepreneur gap

Professional and managerial job seekers are routinely advised to explain black holes by saying that they were consultants or that they owned small businesses. Not everyone can be a consultant, and there's substantial risk in the small-business explanation.

If it should happen to be true that you were a consultant, name your clients and give a glimmer of the contributions you made to each. If you really had a small business, remember: Employers worry that you'll be too independent to do things their way, or that you'll stay just long enough to learn their business and go into competition against them. Strategic antidotes: Search for a business owner who is within eyeshot of retirement and wouldn't mind your continuing the business and paying a monthly pension. Resume antidotes: Describe yourself as "manager," not "CEO" or "president," and if you have time, rename your business something other than your own name: "River's End Associates, Inc.," not "Theresa K. Bronz, Inc."

Application forms: Take them seriously

Although many job hunters tend to blow off formal application forms, these tiresome profiles are legal documents. Lies can come back to bite you. Stick to the facts as you follow these rules and push some paper:

✔ If allowed, take the application home; photocopy it in case you spill coffee on your first effort.

✔ Verify all dates of employment and salaries to the letter.

✔ Enter the full name and last known address of former employers. If former employers are no longer available, don't substitute coworkers.

✔ If asked for salary history, give your base salary (or add commission and bonuses), omitting benefits.

✔ Give a complete employment history in months and years, including trivial three-week jobs that you wisely left off the resume. If you stint on telling the whole story, you leave a loophole of withholding information that later can be used against you if the employer decides you're excess.

✔ Unless you have a condition directly affecting your ability to do the job for which you are applying, you need not elaborate on it.

✔ Divulge any criminal record unless your records are sealed; consult a lawyer before job hunting.

✔ Be honest about having collected unemployment benefits (but remember that purposeful repeaters are frowned on); if you're caught lying about it later, practice your farewell speech.

✔ Autograph the application; you have been honest — why worry?

Black holes are less obvious in a functional format, as discussed in Chapter 4. *If you can't find a positive explanation for a black hole, say nothing.*

If you possess a not-so-pristine past, stick with small employers who probably won't dig into the minutiae.

Here a Job, There a Job, Everywhere a Job, Job

I once interviewed a man who had held 185 jobs over the course of his 20-year career, ranging from dishwasher to circus clown, and from truck driver to nursing aide.

He wrote to me, not requesting resume advice, but to complain that a potential employer had the nerve to call him a *job hopper!*

Talk about an antiquated term — in the late 20th century, the notion of job hopping is as far out of a reality circle as the concepts of job security, company loyalty, and a guaranteed company pension. The Great American Dumping Machine will continue to sack people who then may have to take virtually any job they can to survive.

The risk of having too many jobs in your background is one of focus. *Unfocused* is an ugly word in job-search circles. Being judged as "unfocused" is saying that you lack commitment, that you are perpetually at a fork in the road. It's a reason not to hire you.

The jobs-impacted resume problem is exploding, affecting large numbers of people. The harsh realities of business are forcing people to detour from a single career pathway to the acquisition of new skills and experiences, even if they are not skills and experiences of choice. Serious creative writing will be needed to keep a resume focus on the work history that is relevant for the next job sought.

Many superbly talented and hard-working job hunters today have too many jobs in their history by circumstance, not by choice. If you're in this cohort:

✔ Start by referring to your *diversified* or *skills-building* background.

✔ Use a functional or hybrid resume format, presenting *only your experience relevant to the job you seek.*

✔ Express your work history in years, not months and years.

When your resume looks as though it will collapse under the weight of a mishmash of jobs unconnected to your present target, eliminate your previous trivial pursuits. Group the consequential jobs under a heading that says, *Relevant Work Experience Summary.*

What if this approach solves one problem — the busy resume — but creates another, such as a huge, gaping black hole where you removed inconsequential jobs? Create a second work history section that covers those holes, labeling it "Other Experience." Figure 18-1 shows an example.

Dealing with an unfocused career pattern on paper is easier when it's done under the banner of a temporary service company. The spin in this case lists the temporary services company as the employer. You choose one job title that covers most of your assignments. Under that umbrella title, identify specific assignments. Give the dates in years next to the temporary services firm, skipping dates for each assignment. Figure 18-2 shows an example.

IMPACTED RESUME WITH FOCUS

Professional Experience

UNITECH, Hamburg, Germany
Computer Laboratory Assistant, 1997-Present
> Manage and troubleshoot hardware and software systems. Recover data, create programming architecture, and install parts and software. Assist a team of 18 engineers.

TECHNIK TECH, Hamburg, Germany
Assistant to System Analysts, 1993 - 1996
> Participated in construction, repair, and installation of systems at local businesses. Diagnosed faulty systems and reported to senior analysts, decreasing their workload by 25%.

TRADE NET, Berlin, Germany
Applications and Network Specialist, 1991-1993
> Set up and monitored a Windows-based BBS, including installation, structure, security, and graphics. Authored installation scripts for Trade Net, licensing U.S. software use in Europe.

Other Experience

AMERICAN TOY STORE, Berlin, Germany, Sales Representative, 1996-1997
Arranged and inventoried merchandise, directed sales and customer relations. Developed strong interpersonal skills and gained knowledge of retail industry.

CAMP INTERNATIONAL, Oslo, Germany, Activities Director, 1991-1993
Organized daily activities for more than 300 children from English-speaking countries, including sports, recreation, and day classes. Supervised 10 counselors and kitchen staff of five, developing responsible and effective management skills.

Figure 18-1: Solving the black-hole problem in a jobs-impacted resume by creating a focus plus a second work history section.

What if you work for several temporary services at the same time? The simple answer is that you use the same technique of dating your work history for the temporary service firms, not for the individual assignments. This dating technique is a statement of fact; you legally are an employee of the temporary services firm, not of the company that pays for your temporary services.

When Substance Abuse Is the Problem

Substance abuse is a disability under the Americans with Disabilities Act. If you are recovered from the addiction, you are entitled to all of the Act's protections. If you are still abusing a substance, such as alcohol or illegal narcotics, you are not covered by the Act. Do not disclose previous substance abuse on your resume.

FOCUSING WITH TEMP JOBS

Professional Experience

Relia-Temps   1997-present

Executive Secretary

- North Western Banking Group
Perform all clerical and administrative responsibilities for 10-partner investment and loan firm, assisting each partner in drafting contracts, reviewing proposals, and desiging various financial programs. Supervise 7 staff members. Introduced 50% more efficient filing system, reducing client reviews from 4 to 3 hours.

Administrative Assistant

- Mosaic Advertising
Supervised 3 receptionists and 4 clerical specialists, reporting directly to president. Administered daily operations of all accounting and communication transactions. Using extensive computer savvy, upgraded company computer networks withWindows 98.

- Blakeslee Environmental, Inc.
Assisted 8 attorneys at interstate environmental protection agency, scheduling meetings and conferences, maintaining files, and updating database records. Redesigned office procedures and methods of communication, superior organizational skills.

Figure 18-2: Listing your temporary job assignments without looking unfocused.

Cover gaps in your work history with the "Illness and Recovery" statement (see the "Job Seekers with Disabilities" section of this chapter) or simply do not address the issue at all. Be careful what information you put on a job application — remember that it is a legal form and that lies can come back to haunt you (see the "Sealing Gaps in Your Record" section of this chapter).

If you were ever arrested for smoking pot or being intoxicated — even once in your life — the fact may surface to damage your employment chances. Asking about arrest records is illegal, but a few private companies don't let that stop them — they compile electronic databases of such arrest information and sell them to employers.

The upshot: Avoid a resume mention of booze or drugs, be careful about application forms, and be honest at interviews — *if* you have recovered or *if* the experience was a brief fling or two. If you are still held prisoner by a chronic, destructive, or debilitating overuse of a chemical substance that interferes with your life or employment, no resume tweaks will benefit you. Get help for your addiction.

Suggestions for Inmates and Ex-Inmates

The best resume advice for prison inmates is to get additional education, not only for education's sake but because you can explain gaps with it. You could, for example, write "2000–2006 Bachelor's in Education, Regents College, New York." (Regents is a highly regarded distance learning university.)

If you're an ex-inmate and you missed out on educational opportunities, write what you did during your incarceration — cook, carpenter, clerk, and so forth. Listing "1996–2006 Masonry Foreman" beats "1996–2006 Alcatraz Penitentiary."

The strategy to use on your resume is to show that you made constructive use of your time during your lockup.

Ask your prison administrator or parole officer to refer you to nonprofit organizations that provide employment assistance to former offenders. A comprehensive work on the subject is the second edition of *The Ex-Inmate's Complete Guide to Successful Employment* by Errol Craig Sull, available by mail from The Correctional Education Company, 433 Franklin St., Patio Suite, Buffalo, NY 14202; telephone 716-882-3456; e-mail: correctionaled@juno.com.

References Gain New Importance

Do not include your references on your resume. Do create a second document filled with the names, correct telephone numbers, and addresses of references. Supply this sheet only when requested by an interested potential employer — don't burn out your references by allowing too many casual callers access to their names and contact information.

In an earlier time, when supply and demand were roughly in balance, employers didn't always bother to check references. Small employers still may not, but midsized and large companies, afraid of making a hiring mistake, are taking aim on your past. Reference-auditing companies that specialize in uncovering reasons not to hire candidates contract with employers.

Rules vary slightly in different states, but employers can legally investigate not only references but an applicant's credit history, record of criminal convictions (not arrests), moving violations and accidents, performance at previous jobs, and workers' compensation claims.

Because so much information is available about you — probably more than you or I like to think about — make a project of handling your references. Key suggestions include the following:

- ✔ **Choose your references carefully.** List references who have direct knowledge of your job performance. If necessary, go beyond your immediate supervisor and include past or present coworkers, subordinates, customers, suppliers, members of trade associations, or anyone else who can praise your work. With the exception of your immediate boss, never — *never* — list a reference until you have gained that person's permission to do so. Make a dry run: Have a brave buddy call your references to make certain that no sly naysayers are hiding behind friendly faces.

- ✔ **Coach your references.** Providing your resume is standard operating procedure. Go further: Write a short script of likely questions with a summary of persuasion points under each question. In addition to general good words about your industriousness, creativity, and leadership, focus on the industry. If you're applying at a financial institution, suggest that your references dwell on trustworthiness, conservatism, and good judgment. If you're applying at a high-tech company that has proprietary software and inventions, ask your references to stress your ethics and loyalty.

- ✔ **Write your own reference letters.** A letter of reference is not particularly effective, but it is better than nothing in cases where a company tanks out, your boss dies, or the reference is difficult to reach. When you want a reference letter, go after it FirstRate style: Offer to draft or even to prepare for signature a letter of praise on your reference's letterhead. Routinely arrange for a reference letter when you leave a job.

✔ **Stamp out bad references.** If you were axed or pressed to resign, or you told your boss what you thought and quit, move immediately from spin control to damage control. Even if you were cool enough to obtain a letter of reference before you left, you absolutely must gulp down the bile and try to neutralize the reference.

As mentioned earlier in this chapter, appeal to a sense of fair play or guilt. Sometimes just saying you are sorry and you hope the employer won't keep you from earning a living will be enough. Sometimes it won't.

When you have done all you can to overcome a bad reference, you have three options:

✔ Drown the poor reference in large numbers of favorable references.

✔ Find a lawyer who, for $100 or so, will write a letter threatening legal action for libel or slander. This approach is surprisingly effective.

✔ Continue your job hunt, concentrating on small firms that may not check references or who may be more inclined to take a chance on someone.

No matter how super-powerful you've made your resume, weak or poor references can wipe out your job chances. That's why you write the sample question-and-answer scripts and the reference letters, and that's why you take the first step to patch things up with former adversaries. Your employment is a much higher priority by far to you than it is to reference-givers.

Corking the Bad Credit Rap

Credit histories — called *consumer reports* — hold much more than payment history. A consumer report on you contains data from names of previous employers and residential stability to divorces and estimated prior earnings.

Employers are wary of hiring people awash in debt because they fear stress impacts on job performance, or they fear that you have inadequate management skills or even that you may have sticky fingers with the company's funds.

Consumer reports have serious implications for students who graduate with sky-high education loans and credit card balances. They or their families may have missed payments to keep up college study. Divorced individuals often need spin control to address credit problems.

An amendment to the Fair Credit Reporting Act took effect in 1997; among new consumer protections against unfair credit treatment is the requirement that employers must get your permission in a stand-alone document to check your credit — no blending the request into fine print in the employment application.

And after an employer receives the report on you — but before any adverse action is taken, such as rejecting your application for a job — the employer must give you a free copy of the report with related legal documents. This gives you a chance to correct mistakes and spin control your issues.

For details of your rights, get a free copy of the Federal Trade Commission's publication, *Fair Credit Reporting,* by writing to the Public Reference Branch, FTC, Washington, DC 20580. Or you can get the publication online at www.ftc.gov/bcp/conline/pubs/credit/fcra.htm.

Credit checking isn't a resume concern as such, but after you understand how a negative consumer report — true or erroneous — can torpedo your employment chances, you'll work all the harder on getting great references.

Positive Statements Draw Interest

A positive explanation goes a long way in overcoming a resume land mine. It won't work all the time, but it will work some of the time, and all you need — for now — is one good offer to hit the job jackpot.

Chapter 19

Core Concepts for Career Changers Today

In This Chapter

▶ Motivations for career change

▶ Skills to take with you

▶ Tips on transition resumes

*A*re you interested in changing careers?

Technically speaking, a *job* is a position of employment within an organization; you can have lots of jobs in the same occupation. An *occupation* is your vocation, business, profession, or trade. A *career* is your entire work history. Changing careers really means changing occupations, not changing jobs.

Some people pursue different paths because their careers have left them; others wake up nights wondering "Is this all there is?" Still others retire only to discover that their blood doesn't flow to their brains as well when they put their feet up.

Among other reasons people seek career transitions:

✔ In their late 20s and early 30s, some dissatisfied workers take a candid look at their lives and declare "Oops, that's not me, try again."

✔ In their late 30s and early 40s, some men and women who have climbed the pinnacle of success feel that their lives lack meaning: What will it matter 500 years from today whether they lived or died?

✔ At any age, some mothers of older or grown children seek salvation from terminal homemaking and housecleaning.

✔ In their 20s to 40s, some military personnel find themselves passing through the separation-from-service gate, exchanging their uniforms for civvies.

For resume purposes, it doesn't matter why you're looking elsewhere when you're thinking about changing careers. Your challenge is the same:

You must learn to leverage your skills in a new direction. At every turn in your decision-making process, ask yourself: How can I bridge the future with the past?

Regardless of your age, if you cannot find a way to use what you already know in a new place, understand that you'll be a beginner competing with younger and cheaper graduates, so you need to find an edge.

What else can you do to ease your change of direction?

✔ Compensate for your lack of experience in a new career field by showing specific crossover skills and how you would use those skills to solve problems or deliver benefits in the job you want. (Most people handle this strategy in cover letters or proposals, but problem solving or benefit delivery can lead off a targeted resume.)

✔ Be cautious about asserting what you can do for a specific employer. A number of candidates take this good idea, fail to do righteous research, and come away looking foolish. Not only do they try to fix what ain't broken, they have misguided suggestions that don't really improve what's working. Try to avoid setting yourself up for failure when you use crossover skills to solve problems or deliver benefits.

✔ Use your resume to start communicating your adaptability, drive, intelligence, and highest accomplishments that can bring rewards to a new employer.

✔ Bury experience that is irrelevant to your new target in a brief *Other Experience* section at the tail end of your resume.

Portable Skills Can Turn Your Life Around

Skills, not preferences, entitle you to be employed. (Tough, but the money doesn't always follow when you do what you love.)

The molecules of self-discovery are elusive. Self-discovery in a group setting is more fun than sitting alone scratching your head. Enroll in a career workshop and get help. The group dynamics are similar to those that motivate members in a weight-control organization: "How many pounds did you lose?" equates to "How many skills did you come up with?"

Start trolling for portable skills as you review abbreviated lists of KeyWords and GoodWords in Chapters 6 and 13, respectively. And see my book, *Cover Letters For Dummies,* Second Edition. Plan to spend as many as 20 hours over the next few weeks in putting a name to each of your marketable skills.

For help beyond the scope of these pages, see a terrific and inexpensive book very useful to career changers, *Five Steps to Career Success: The Essential Guide for Students, Job Seekers and Lifelong Learners* by Urban Whitaker. The guide contains a substantial discussion of skills and includes discovery activities. The author, Dr. Whitaker, is a leader in adult career change circles. Order the book for $14.50 (includes postage) by mail from the West Coast Print Center, 747 Rosemount Road, Oakland, CA 94610; phone (510) 663-7061; www.westcoastprintercenter.com.

Still other resources found at libraries include software programs that relate skills to occupations, such as *Choices, Systems 2000, Discover, SIGI Plus* and *SkillsUP.* The latter, *SkillsUP,* is my favorite software program. The first part of the program shows you how skills are used in each of 250 occupations; the second part steps you through a personal skills improvement plan. Once you've rounded up your core skills, you can use the SkillsUP software to tell you which occupations use your skills.

Acquire more skills

Figure on two indispensable skills for most career changers:

- ✔ Computer literacy, with the ability to use word processing and spreadsheet programs at minimum
- ✔ Internet literacy, with the ability to use e-mail and search engines at minimum

If you didn't grow up digital, take seminars and find a tutor (a neighborhood teenager will be perfect), or enroll in community college courses or adult education classes at a high school. Possessing computer and Internet skills make you seem not old and rigid, but young and flexible, which encourages employers to look at you and see reduced training costs along with a new source of technological support.

What if you don't have the transferable skills you need to ply a new trade? Maybe you can use volunteerism as a stepping stone to a new career. Volunteer for a brief period of time through a volunteer referral service to make sure that you're legally working without pay.

Volunteering allows you to test drive a new career choice and pick up substantial skills (and their all-important KeyWords) that you can ride to a new resume and talking points that you can use to hammer home your benefits in job interviews. You won't, of course, say on your resume that you were a volunteer, but instead note your skills acquired and achievements made.

You may decide that new education will put you on the right job map. Even if you don't take a full-blown certificate, diploma, or degree program, an evening course at a local college will give you related marketable points for your resume. (As a bonus, your classmates may be professionals who have jobs in your target area, allowing you to develop new contacts.)

Match your target job description

When you've firmly labeled your mobile marketable skills and found more than you expected (thank you, God), what's next? Here's a practical idea to begin your career shift:

Find or write job descriptions of your target occupations. If you like your current field and are leaving involuntarily because it's disappearing from under your feet, start with job descriptions in closely related jobs. Compare requirements of related jobs with your transferable skills profile. If you don't like your current field, forget I mentioned it.

To identify occupations closely related to your current field, check a library copy of the *Occupational Outlook Handbook* published by the U.S. Department of Labor. Or see it online at http://stats.bls.gov/ocohome.htm.

Knowing the name of what you have to offer gets you up off your knees, out of the past, and into the future. You no longer have to say, "This is what I have done; can you use me?"

Now you can write a resume that RezReaders will respect, by saying, "This is what I can do for you that will add to your productivity, efficiency, or effectiveness. Not to mention a little bump on the bottom line."

A career changer's resume lesson

The most dramatic example of a career change resume I've seen was created by resume expert and author Yana Parker. She took on the case of Marguerite Avery, a 68-year-old homemaker who was trying to join the workforce but missing success and wrote a resume that prompted several job leads. See the resume on Yana Parker's Web site (www.damngood.com/jobseekers/reentry.html).

Five FirstRate Tips for Transition Resumes

If you're a career changer in transition, these tips can help smooth the ride:

1. **Choose the functional format or its hybrid offspring (described in Chapter 4).**

   This class of formats emphasizes the transferable skills in your pocket. Your presentation must help the employer see what you can do, not merely what you have done. A lockstep reverse chronological format doesn't give you the flexibility to change your image.

2. **Place the skills relevant to your intended change up front in your resume.**

   (If you don't have any, start the analysis process again or get a night job to cover your bills while you gain relevant experience or education.) Relevant skills are what RezReaders must hit on immediately. Your big message must be the first message. Everything else is in a distant second place.

3. **Take care to use appropriate headings.**

   If you are using freelance, hobby, or volunteer experience, use the heading *Work Experience* and list it first, unless you have changed your focus through education. Then begin with the heading *Education*. To refine this heading, substitute target-job related education, such as *Accounting Education* or *Healthcare Education*. Your employment history follows.

   What do you do with all the experience that was great in your old job but means zero where you want to go? Lump it together at the end of your resume under *Other Experience* or *Earlier Experience*. Shrink it to positions, titles, employers, and/or degrees and educational institutions. If extraneous experience is older than five years, squash it entirely.

   In Chapter 17, I suggest that you omit jobs that go back further than 10 to 15 years as a tactic to combat ageism without changing careers; an even shorter five-year cutoff refocuses your career direction.

4. **Avoid jargon connected to your former occupation.**

   Jargon used in your old place makes you sound like an outsider in new career fields. Former members of the armed forces, in particular, must be careful to speak in English to avoid confusing RezReaders with military jargon. A little research in appropriate trade magazines reveals the buzzwords for your target occupation, making you sound like an insider. Whom would you hire, an outsider or an insider?

5. **To follow the FirstRate approach to career-transition resumes, target each position.**

   The help wanted section of your major metropolitan newspaper is a convenient road map of essential functions for various jobs. An Internet search engine can direct you to resumes that others have posted in career fields of interest; compare their content with your efforts and spice up your resume as needed. Check out Chapter 1 for more on ways to research your new occupation.

Hitting Pay Dirt on Career Changing

When your job disappears or you'd like to disappear from your job, first look in the *horizontal job market* — related jobs in the same career field or related career fields. These are the areas where your transferable skills are most likely to fit and count as experience. When you cannot or will not incorporate your transferable skills into a new career field, you'll be paid as a beginner.

That's why you're wise to understand the skills-transferring process. Experiment with ways to interpret your multi-industry skills on paper — from the very first moment a RezReader sets eyes on your resume, the answers to these questions must be apparent:

Why are you qualified for the position in my company?

Why doesn't your last position relate to this one?

Answer these, and you're on your way to the career change you seek.

Part VI

Samples of FirstRate Resumes

The 5th Wave   By Rich Tennant

"The magazine didn't hire me, but they are paying me $50 to print my resume on their joke page."

In this part . . .

Some things you've got to see to believe. And these resume samples have been carefully crafted so you can see different ways to handle your own FirstRate effort. Your resume is really your marketing piece — make it a strong sell. You have lots of options. Be creative.

Chapter 20

A Sampling of FirstRate Resumes

In This Chapter

▶ Model resumes in 15 career fields

*P*repare to meet the graduates of FirstRate boot camp, from entry- to management-level job seekers. Real people wrote the originals of these resumes, but I tore them up and rewrote them to meet FirstRate standards. All names and contact information are fictional, but the raw selling power behind every one is real.

Although FirstRate formats (illustrated by the templates in Chapter 4) are loaded with sell-power, they are by no means rigid — not every section heading works for every resume. Choose your section headings to flaunt your strengths.

In the interest of not chopping trees, I chopped material — that is, some resumes to follow would have been two pages had I not eliminated text. Occasionally, as another conservation measure, I used ampersands (&) to replace the word "and." Should you use ampersands on your own resume? Yes, but very gingerly. Ampersands are okay for

- ✔ Company names
- ✔ Copyrights
- ✔ Logos
- ✔ Familiar phrases — "P & L Statements"

Otherwise, spell out the word "and."

Here is a selection of FirstRate model resumes.

Assistant Retail Manager
ACCOMPLISHMENT/COMPUTER UNFRIENDLY

> Contact data too close together to scan.

Jack Straw

2424 Heavensent Lane, Wichita, Kansas 67056 (316) 446-5513   E-mail: jstraw@aol.com

OBJECTIVE
Position as **assistant retail manager** using my eight years of experience in retail, technical sales, and software experience.

SUMMARY
- Hard-won and successful experience in many aspects of retailing: sales, marketing, operations, training, and service.

- Can open and manage retail software and other technical products. Qualified as assistant manager of retail store; qualified as department manager of superstore. Managed new retail location ranking in top ten of 64 stores within first year.

- Internet/World Wide Web merchandising start-up study.

> Web merchandising is buzzword; "start-up study" means Straw studied topic, is ready to implement new selling technology for new employer.

HIGHLIGHTS OF SKILLS

- Opening, operating **new locations**
- **Growing sales:** make **customer first**
- **Budgeting, extending credit**
- **Recruiting** and interviewing
- **Training** and retraining staff
- **Telemarketing**
- Product display
- Promotion, advertising strategies
- **Software licensing, electronics, purchasing**

- All major **point-of-sale equipment**
- **Computer skills:** PCs and Macs; General Store, Excel, Lotus 1-2-3, QuickBooks, Aldus PageMaker, CAD, CorelDraw, Desktop Publisher, Superpaint, Windows Office including Word.
- **Internet skills:** World Wide Web, e-mail, FTP

> Can be made computer friendly by eliminating vertical design lines.

PROFESSIONAL EXPERIENCE

Video Tape Tub, La Costa, KS -- Customer Representative   1998-Present
Customer service, product display, inventory maintenance, video rentals and returns. "Best help I've had in five years" (Owner Cal Showers).

Custom Names, Delmar, KS -- Consumer Service Representative   1997
Extensive retail sales and technical support for software, computer equipment, satellite TV, electronics and home theater equipment. Maintained average monthly sales of $30,000, ranking fourth in sales. Heavy telemarketing component.

(1 of 2)

Jack Straw

The Cutting Edge, Rancho, KS -- Assistant Manager   1995-1997
Serviced upscale clientele in high-end software, electronics and video game retail store. Handled sales, purchasing, staff training, work schedules, product inventory and display, technical support for electronics and software, bank deposits and staff management.

Software Bug, Carlsbad, KS -- Night Manager   1992-1995
Evening management of software retail store. Innovative sales strategies brought store from 47th in sales ranking to 8th in a 64-store chain. Other work: employee recruiting and dismissal, training, retraining, scheduling, staff management, technical support. Awarded Employee of Month four separate months.

Temp-a-Medic, La Jolla, CA -- Healthcare Staffer   1991-1992
Matched healthcare temps with hospitals in Los Angeles and San Diego. Developed organizational skills, calm resilience when chaos threatened and acceptance of high-pressure, detail-reliant environment. Sold new accounts at seven hospitals.

EDUCATION

62 academic hours toward bachelor's degree; have kept nose to grindstone taking 3-6 hours per semester for past five years. Anticipate testing out of 18 hours; expect degree June, 2003.

VOLUNTEER AND PERSONAL EXPERIENCE

-- Coach, Roller Hockey Little League of North County. Coached winning North (San Diego) County team of more than 30 youths, ages 7-12. Grateful for opportunity to develop strong interpersonal, cross-generational, cross-cultural and community networks. Proven talent with teamwork, organization, people of various economic classes.

-- Interests include computers, electronics, ice hockey, computer drafting and freehand illustration.

> Straw's goal is completion of college degree. To indicate intent to enroll for more than 3 to 6 hours per semester while working in retailing, noted for long hours, would be risky.

(2 of 2)

Chemist
PROFESSIONAL/COMPUTER FRIENDLY

DIXON MARBEND
123 Moon Road, Flanders, New Jersey, 07836 (201) 584-0150

Chemist ←——— *Objective repalced with job title, summary follows – personalizes the format.*

Six years' research experience with increasing responsibility and successful record of instrumentation and scientific achievement. Specialty: Silicon. Designed computer systems (mainframe to micro) for laboratory instrument automation, including patented design. Published presenter.

EDUCATION

- Ph.D., Chemical Design & Engineering, University of Rochester, Rochester, New York.
  Dissertation: Manipulation of Luminescent Porous Silicon Structures
- Master of Science, Chemistry, University of Rochester, Rochester, New York
- Bachelor of Science, Physics, Honors, University of New Jersey-Elizabeth, Elizabeth, New Jersey

EXPERIENCE AND ACCOMPLISHMENTS

Quantifies achievements and responsibilities.

1995-20XX   **Research Assistant, University of Rochester, Rochester, N.Y.**
- Patented procedure for "Engineering of Luminescent Images on Silicon" and coauthored seven publications (see addendum).
- Conducted research investigations of luminescent silicon, and spearheaded procedure for abricating structures with photoelectricity; managed staff of 5 assistants.
- Delivered 14 presentations of results and research in progress to professors in department.
- Tutored 37 undergraduates in research and chemistry theory, increasing teaching skills.
- Purchased $79,000 in chemicals and equipment for starting research lab .

1994-1995   **Research Assistant, University of New York, New York City**
- Built non-vibrating 1.5 ton aluminium platform for NMR management.
- Assisted professor with construction of super-conducting NMR spectrometer.
- Designed and manufactured integrated circuits in lab.

Shows results of achievements.

Minimizes less relevant jobs.

1994   **Research Assistant, University of New Jersey-Elizabeth, Elizabeth, N. J.**
- Investigated methods for feature distortion in scanning tunneling microscopy.

1993-1994   **Laboratory Assistant, University of New York, New York City**
- Prepared and maintained delicate equipment and chemicals for chemistry labs, ensuring maximum performance and efficiency.
- Worked with 57 teacher assistants and students, developing training skills.

Skills section added to format, enhancing abilities and using more KeyWords.

TECHNICAL SKILLS ←———

Steady state photoluminescence	Machining aluminum and Plexiglas
Raman, FTIR and UV-Vis spectroscopy	Macintosh: Word, KaleidaGraph,
Inert atmosphere (Schlenk and dry box)	Canvas, Aldus PageMaker, MacDraw,
Standard electrochemistry/photochemistry	Hypercard, Chem 3D, Excel, Internet
AFM, STM, and SEM	

(1 of 2)

Dixon Marbend (201) 584-0150

PUBLICATIONS

"Engineering of Luminescent Images on Silicon." Marbend, U.S. Patent No. 1,234,567; Jan 1, 2000

"Silicon Technology." Saynor and Marbend in 1999 *Martin-Marietta Yearbook of Science Technology*; Martin-Marietta: New York, N.Y. 1998, 123-4

"Optical Cavities in Silicon Film." Saynor, Curbin, and Marbend in *Electrochemic Journal*, 1998, 21

"Emission from Etched Silicon." Marbend and Piner in *Material Research Symposium*, 1998, 12, 3456-7

"Color Image Generation on Silicon." Marbend and Saynor in *Chemical Science*, 1997, 123, 4567-8

"Porous Silicon Micro-Dension." Marbend and Saynor in *Physics Applied*, 1997, 45, 678-9

"Stoichiometric Cadmium Electrodeposition." Krass and Marbend, *MaterialChem*, 1996, 1, 23

HONORS, MEMBERSHIPS & PRESENTATIONS

Chemical Symposium Research Fellow, Undergraduate Honors Fellows, Winter Research Fellow

Chemical Symposium, Chemical Alliance, Electrochemistry Association

Marbend, Saynor and Curbin. *Emission from Etched Silicon.* Presented at 123rd Chemical Symposium, Detroit, Michigan, January 2000

Marbend. *Porous Silicon Micro-Dension.* Presented at 234th Chemical Alliance, New York City, New York, January 1998

> New scanning software reads italics; old ones do not. Marbend telephones RezReader to determine scanning software. When old programs are used, Marbend substitutes a second version of his resume, replacing italics with quotes around same typeface used in rest of resume.

Health Club Manager
REVERSE CHRONOLOGICAL/COMPUTER FRIENDLY

Hilda Larson
347 Appleview Drive, Chicago, IL 60611
(312) 555-9876

Larson leads with graduate degree because health clubs are subject to legal liability for client injuries, aggravated by employees without formal credentials.

*** CONFIDENTIAL ***
Work (brief messages only) (312) 555-9876

Larson's boss doesn't know she's job-hunting; note "Confidential" and work telephone number with mention to keep calls to arrangement-making only.

Objective and Qualifications:

Health and Fitness Industry Management: Master's and undergraduate degree in Health and Fitness. Eight years' individual and group health education and exercise leadership. Extensive background in equestrian skills, dance, gymnastics, martial arts, swimming, and strength work. Use wellness and preventive-medicine techniques.

Professional Experience:

5/96-Present University of Chicago Center for Disease Research & Health, Chicago, IL
- **Health Promotion Specialist, Researcher, Exercise Physiologist**
Provide monthly nutrition testing and counseling to 120 individuals, 300 in group. Conduct health and fitness classes -- 350 per month. Organization and promotion skills recognized with selection for Health Promotion Coordinator to Chicago Executive Program.

10/94-5/96   Wheaton College Health and Fitness, Wheaton, IL
- **Instructor and Program Consultant**
Produced bimonthly newsletter, wellness counseling, and campus-wide publicity, leading to 25% membership increase in health and fitness club in 3 months.

11/94-5/96   Fitness Plus Enterprises, Inc., Winnetka, IL
- **Personal Fitness Trainer, Group Exercise Instructor**
Taught group exercise classes and designed personal fitness programs for 550 individual clients. Popular trainer among special groups (disabled and elderly).

5/94-7/94   Aerobics Activity Center, Winnetka, IL
- **Assistant to the Associate Director**
Designed activity program, teaching, lecturing, and performing market research.

9/93-5/94   University of Chicago, Chicago, IL
- **Graduate Teaching Fellow**
Designed and taught. Advised 24 independent study projects for undergraduate students. Wrote two proposals to Health/Fitness Department Chair, initiating development of new graduate instruction program; result $5,000 grant from school.

(1 of 2)

Hilda Larson
(312) 555-9876

Education:

Master of Health Science, Health Education Concentration, University of Chicago, 1995
Bachelor of Science, Honors, Kinesiology, Adult Fitness Concentration, University of Chicago, 1991
Guest Scholar, Physical Education Professional Division, University of Chicago, Winter and Spring 1994

> It's OK to list the education section on the 2nd page because Larson refers to it in the qualifications section.

Certifications:

1998   Exer-Safety Associates Step/Bench Certification
1996   American College of Sports Medicine Health and Fitness Instructor
1995   American Council on Exercise Certified Personal Trainer

Presentations:

- University of Chicago Executive Program, Summer 1998 and 1999
- Sport Cardiologists and Nutritionist National Conference, Spring 1995
- Buen Salud Annual Gathering, Mexico City, Mexico, Spring 1995
- University of Chicago Individual Fitness Design, Fall 1994

Conferences:

- World Fitness IDEA International Conference, Las Vegas, NV, 1999
- IDEA Personal Trainer's Conference, San Jose, CA, 1998
- Regional Northeast Wellness Conference, Boston, MA,1995

Awards and Honors:

- Academic Honors, University of Chicago, 1988 and 1989
- Harriet Wilson Award for Kindness and Receptivity to Others, 1986
- Cross Cultural Awareness Award for Achievement in Cross Cultural Skills, 1986
- Varsity Letters in Dance and Gymnastics, University of Chicago, 1986
- Honored as "Outstanding in public relations and efficiency," 1992
- National Amateur Champion at the National Horse Show, Madison Square Garden, 1986

> Despite national standing in equestrian skills, urban health clubs aren't known for horse stables, thus award is placed last. Yet such a prominent skill can't be omitted -- further, RezReader may be a rider and identify with Larson.

(2 of 2)

Public Relations Representative
REVERSE CHRONOLOGICAL/COMPUTER FRIENDLY

Lorna Quito
Roßmarket 12, 12345 Frankfurt/Main, 12-8907-87, Germany
Telephone 2323-90000
E-mail: lquito@gold.com.de

Objective

Communications or public relations position, using high-stakes
skills: writing, editing, placement, promotion, speaking, production,
and Web page design. Employ all media: newspaper, magazines,
radio, television, multimedia, online.

> Note: Larger
> type for
> summary hook.

Employment

1997-Present   **Publicist**, European Red Cross, European Region, Berlin, Germany

Coordinate communications for greater Germany area. Work with 16 service
groups to develop written standards for Red Cross Shelters. Media
spokesperson for local and major disasters. Currently writing and designing
Web page.

➤ Write newsletters, annual reports, press releases, articles, speeches, and
fact sheets distributed across Germany and outlying areas, with plans to
implement Internet distribution.

➤ Initiate and plan media relations, publicity events, annual meetings, and
projects (designers/printers) for Red Cross endeavors; working with team
of 11.

> Several
> mentions of
> electronic
> technology
> important
> because
> international
> communications
> demands
> Internet &
> online
> publishing
> competency.

1996-1997   **Public Relations Assistant**, International Publicité, Paris, France

Designed and produced copy for 12 brochures, 12 proposals, and 5
presentations in France. Developed Web page and company Internet-
published magazine. Led team of 17 developing PR proposals. Coordinated
mailings. Maintained employee morale during rumors of pending bankruptcy.
"Ms. Quito was indispensable. We would have lost half our employees if she
had not remained calm, continuing to produce for our clients," according to
Jacque DuPris, Senior Public Relations Manager.

> Includes praise
> from a
> supervisor.

1995-1996   **Manager**, Law School Records and Admit Specialists, Paris, France

Managed publication, sales, and distribution for $20 million nonprofit legal
education services organization. Promoted company's 16 publications

(1 of 2)

Lorna Quito

Sentence break on first page signals reader there is a second page.

through direct marketing, law school forums, and book publishers. Established positive relationship with press, radio, and television contacts. Led creative team of 14 members to develop effective publicity strategies.

1986-1994   Cooper-Cologne, U.S. Division, Los Angeles, CA

(1990-1994) **Senior Coordinator of Publicity Services** for $45 million management consulting company with offices in 18 countries. Managed 8 activities and 41 staff members involved in database development, list purchase, publication schedule, and in-house communications.

(1986-1990) **Special Projects Coordinator:** Planned logistics of monthly executive forums in selected U.S. cities. Directed key facets of annual 200-member business conferences for U.S. and Canadian markets.

Education

1983, Bachelor of Fine Arts, cum laude; The Mary and Joseph Institute, Maryland
1996-1998, Riddell University, Los Angeles; courses in journalism

Place highest education first, although noting more recent education. Modest GPA not mentioned.

When hand delivered, this creative person's resume lends itself to portfolio treatment (showing samples of your work). Because RezReaders say they want less, not more, paper, think about making two collections of portfolio content:

Collection 1: The "pony pack" contains just two or three outstanding examples of public relations coups, such as major feature stories featuring your client.

Collection 2: The "race horse pack" contains a more generous representation of your public relations success. During a job interview, begin with Collection 1, holding Collection 2 in reserve until you receive signals the timing is right to offer more.

Restaurant Manager
REVERSE CHRONOLOGICAL/COMPUTER FRIENDLY

Trisha S. Dunbar
123 Massachusetts Street, Salem, KS 66146   (913) 345-9876   E-mail: dunba@aol.com

> Note: The apostrophe after "years" replaces "of."

Objective

General Manager position in a fast-paced, family-oriented restaurant

Summary of Qualifications

- 14 years' experience in family-oriented restaurant management
- Implemented strategic marketing plan which increased patronage 43% at Maggie McGee's
- Designed award system for waitstaff, increasing sales 36% and decreasing employee turnover
- High energy and optimism motivate employees, thereby increasing guest satisfaction
- Graduated summa cum laude with Bachelor's in Business Management while working full-time

Professional Experience

1994-present **General Manager**   Maggie McGee's, Salem, Kansas
Direct operations of this family-oriented restaurant which serves over 600 meals daily.
Oversee activities of 6 assistant managers, supervising staff of 150.

> Notes specific customer base.

- Developed marketing plan, increasing business by 43%
- Implemented new computer system which decreased degree of error by 25%
- Redesigned kitchen for greater efficiency and ease of movement
- Programmed computer system for new restaurant in Missouri

1988-1994   **Assistant Manager**   Teller's Restaurant, Lawrence, Kansas
Assisted general manager with guest satisfaction, daily operations, staffing, inventory control,
training, and business and marketing plans. Supervised staff of 100, serving over 400 meals daily.

- Designed and implemented computer program to assist in staffing
- Implemented training program which restaurant chain adopted as company policy
- Assisted general manager in developing marketing plan, increasing business 18%
- Designed program for greater inventory control, decreasing loss 26%

> Gives documentable results.

1985-1988   **Bar Manager**   The Lion's Roar, Chico, California
Responsible for guest satisfaction, staffing, inventory control, policy implementation, budget
control, and marketing and promotional plans. Supervised staff of 25, serving 500 customers
daily.

- Developed promotional plans that increased student business by 55%
- Assisted restaurant managers in developing staff award system
- Developed "Home-We-Go," an alcohol awareness program offering rides to bar guests

1983-1985   **Head Cocktail Server**   The Lion's Roar, Chico, California
Responsible for guest satisfaction, responsible alcohol service, and daily scheduling.

- Improved scheduling system, increasing efficiency and eliminating confusion
- Promoted to Bar Manager

> Including this position and promotion indicates that Dunbar has substantial restaurant experience prior to her management experience.

Education

Bachelor of Arts in Business Management with minor in Computer Science
California State University at Chico, Chico, CA, 1985
Honors: Summa Cum Laude; GPA 3.95/4.0

Real Estate Agent
REVERSE CHRONOLOGICAL/COMPUTER UNFRIENDLY

○○○○○○○○○○○○○○○○○ **Tanner Childs** ○○○○○○○○○○○○○○○○○

4190 Parkside, New Rochelle, New York 10801 (212) 720-0504
E-mail: tchilds@cdl.com   Pager: (212) 485-7894

Note pager and e-mail -- current with technology.

○○○

Summary
More than 12 years' real estate and financial experience. Skilled in negotiating and administering subcontractor submittals, architectural draftings, cost containment and recoveries contracts, estimates, bid packages, project development, and field work.

Computer reads hollow bullets as letter "o," thus name becomes "ooTanner Childsoo" and bulleted items become "oProcurement," "oPrimary," and so on.

Experience
1995-Present   **Franklin Contractors Corporation, Financial Specialist**
New York City, NY
FCC is the Federal Deposit Insurance division for failed savings and loan liquidation.

Briefly describes prestigious employer.

1998-1999   **Contract Specialist -- New Rochelle, NY**
○ Procurement and administration of 93 financial service and consulting contracts valued at $100 million
○ Primary Contract Administrator for 12 firms, including Lloyd & Donner, Hilteron Consulting, and Carrington & Associates
○ Contract oversight on 32 payroll contracts with Hill Services, valued at more than $17 million
○ Advisor to U.S. Office of Inspector General and Office of Contractor Oversight and surveillance for contractor billing acquisitions of failed thrifts; conducted over 100 training seminars for agents

Names prestigious clients in field.

1995-1997   **Operations /Loan Portfolio Consultant -- New Rochelle, NY**
○ Advisor to acquiring bank executive management on operational mergers and acquisitions of failed thrifts, conducted training seminars for agents. Redding Banks, Green Banks, NY Financial.

Consulting background verified by naming clients.

1987-1995   **Wholesale Loans Inc., Vice President -- New Rochelle, NY**
○ Managed sales department -- $4 billion in loan volume
○ Originated wholesale of 37 mortgage loan packages

Education
Bachelor of Science, Business Economics, University of California, Santa Barbara, 1983

Professional Licenses and Designations
New York: General Contractor's License, Real Estate Brokers License, Notary Public
California Real Estate License
Residential Member, American Institute of Real Estate Appraisers
Warranted Contract Officer, Resolved Trust Corporation
Member, National Contracting Management Association

Sales Representative
REVERSE CHRONOLOGICAL/COMPUTER UNFRIENDLY

Richard Stanton

321 Ranch Lake Road, Houston, Texas 77081   (713)664-5678

> Stanton seeks to widen net for jobs, hence term "technical" frequently substituted for "auto."

Objective

Sales Representative position with technical and marketing focus. Over 15 years' sales, training, marketing, operations, and management experience in automotive industry.

Work History

President, Conversion Products, Inc., 1998-Present

◆ Relocated and streamlined manufacturing plant, recertified testing lab according to EPA
◆ Increased sales 28% in first quarter of 1998

President, Motoran Corporation, 1990-1998

◆ Increased sales 84% in eight years by revising product line, opening new distribution channels, and expanding markets
◆ Engineered new product development, supervising team of 45 sales representatives
◆ Provided technical service and support to resolve client dissatisfaction

Director, Auto-Serve Center, 1987-1990

> "Director" substituted for "Owner" of business to seem more agreeable to taking direction.

◆ Invigorated repair shop by strengthening teamwork, productivity, and cost control
◆ Initiated a 527% sales increase and achieved first-year profit goals in three months
◆ Led national sales in October 1997 out of 100 Auto-Serve Centers

Technical Service Manager, Good Tire Corporation, 1984-1987

◆ Managed product engineering, quality assurance, warranty administration, and technical marketing activities for replacement parts division
◆ Supervised 37 chief and staff engineer activities
◆ Integrated technical activities into domestic and international sales and distribution, including trade show participation and international travel

Service Training Manager, Truckline Inc., 1983-1985

◆ Led customer technical service and training; instructed 112 staff
◆ Involved in ad agency operations and coordination of 9 trade shows
◆ Established team of 90 national distributors in two years

Education

Master of Business Administration, University of Texas at Austin, Austin, TX, 1996
Bachelor of Science, Industrial Technology, Southern University, Dallas, TX, 1982

> Omitted lengthy list of automotive publications and professional affiliations to avoid typecasting.

> Computer will gag on graphics and decorative typeface at top.

Editor
TARGETED/COMPUTER FRIENDLY

> Resume could be made computer friendly by moving e-mail address to separate line below the telephone number. Computer will read numerical e-mail address as a street address.

Ron Bohart-Smithy

123 Albany Road, College Park, MD 20742
(301) 456-7891 E-mail: bohartsmithy@juno.com

Position as Sunbright Community Newspapers publisher and business manager, using more than 15 years' experience in print media publishing and management.

Summary of Qualifications

- Unassailable record of increasing sales and cost-containment management of newspapers, magazines, shoppers and journals. Experienced in supervising temp workforce.

- Launched shopper: current circulation 50,500, grew revenues in 18 months to $40,000 per issue.

- Dynamo in business area -- increased profits to highest point in four years for leading industry guide. Trimmed costs by 18%.

Summary of Skills

- PUBLISHING SKILLS: In-depth knowledge of weekly and free-circulation newspaper industry -- Awarded by National Newspaper Association for outstanding weekly.
- RAINMAKING SKILLS -- Boosted ad revenues for 100,000 weekly circulation by 300% in one year; enjoy civic activities with community leaders.
- MANAGEMENT SKILLS -- Produced largest issues in recent history for 85,000-circulation weekly.

Accomplishments and Experience

> Note larger font size used to hook reader, smaller size for job description fill-in.

- **Successfully started a new business newspaper**
Reader's Business Journal, Baltimore, MD   September 1997-February 20##

> As General Manager, launched gazelle business journal for Pale Moon Printing, opening its office and hiring, supervising and training all staff.
> - Publication currently maintains free-circulation exceeding 50,500. | Note high-impact presentation of achievements & experience.
> - Grew revenues from 0 to $40,000 per issue.

- **Increased profits to highest point in four years, established leading industry guide**
Georgetown Associates, Washington, DC   June 1996-May 1997

> As Publisher, directed newspapers, magazines and books for coin and paper money collectors at world's largest hobby publisher. Trained new editors newsstand techniques to increase sell-through.

Georgetown News, Minter's Economy Reporter, and Penny Prices.
- Total distribution exceeded 200,000. Sold a new $200,000 per year ad insert contract.

(1 of 2)

Editor
TARGETED/COMPUTER FRIENDLY

Ron Bohart-Smithy

> *Computer expects to find employer name before accomplishment, but for human eyes, this presentation is great.*

- **Won award for finest large weekly (managed three with 30 employees)**

PDR Publishing, Northampton, MA and Boston, MA   November 1993-May 1996

  As Group Manager and Publisher, superintended three weeklies with 85,000 circulation.
  - Direction of 30 full-time employees led to surpassing sales goals.
  - Won Boston Press "Sweepstakes" for finest large weekly, listed in 1995 "Who's Who."

- **Quadrupled advertising sales at the National Newspaper Association**

Publisher's Auxiliary, NNA, Boston, MA   December 1989-November 1993

  As General Manager, supervised trade publication, recognized as the leading "how to" guide in the field.
  - Personally cited as NNA's most valuable service in member survey.
  - Judged National Best Paper Contest.
  - Represented NNA at state press meetings, Amer-Eastern Shows and American Press, familiarizing and selling with newspaper executives and vendors.

- **Launched new, special sections in subsidiary of Worrell, managed employees**

Daily Voice, Worrell Newspapers, Albany, NY   October 1987-December 1989

  As Co-operative Advertising Manager, oversaw circulation of 31,000 daily, solicited manufacturers and distributors, launched successful new sections.

- **Produced largest issues in the recent history for an 85,000 free-circulation weekly**

"10-Storey" (news & Hebrew weekly), Albany, NY   April 1986-September 1987

  As Publisher, produced three weeklies and supervised 45 employees.

- **Promoted publication to nation's finest small weekly, 11 awards, record profits.**

New England Talk, Bangor, ME   February 1985-March 1986

  As Publisher, increased paid circulation to an all-time high of 14,083, increasing ad lineage; New England Talk showed record profits.
  - Awarded by National Newspaper Association as nation's finest small weekly.
  - 11 awards from the Maine Press Association.

Education
Bachelor of Arts, Marketing, University of Boston, MA
Dean's List in Major, awarded for outstanding performance.

> *Older newspaper guy adroit at presenting strengths -- publishing, revenue generation, management -- media owners seek. He limits number of years' experience. In private he jokes that he started working during the St. Louis World's Fair in 1904.*

Nonprofit Manager
REVERSE CHRONOLOGICAL/COMPUTER FRIENDLY

MARSHA ANN WHITELAND

231 Montrose Heights
Manchester, NH 03104

(603) 456-9876
E-Mail: mwhite@mci.mail.com

> *Nonprofits struggle for funds; a manager who is an attorney is a value-added candidate -- a resume opener.*

....

NONPROFIT MANAGER-ATTORNEY: Significant experience with urban issues and nonprofit organizations. Successful manager of complex multimillion-dollar programs requiring constant attention to bottom line. Skilled advocate effective in stressful environment requiring personal diplomacy mediation among conflicting groups.

....

PROFESSIONAL EXPERIENCE

STANFORD RESOLUTION, INC., Montpelier, Vermont

Senior Counsel, Professional Liability Section, June 1999 to present

> *Quantifies all achievements.*

> *Upward mobility shown by dividing jobs by heading.*

Manage professional liability (34 members including section chiefs, attorneys, paralegals, and clerical staff), and substantive legal work involving approximately 175 failed savings and loans. Close investigations, bring suit, and settle litigation. "With Marsha in charge, we are a legal powerhouse!" -- Jack Ricemaster, Co-Senior Counsel.

Counsel, Professional Liability Section, November 1993 to May 1999

> *Quantifies all achievements.*

Managed investigation and litigation of civil claims against 25+ failed savings and loans, as well as liaisoned with attorneys, accountants, brokers, appraisers, insurers, and fidelity bond companies; supervised investigators and counsel, assuring cost-effectiveness. Budgeted more than $15 million for S&L project. Coordinated with federal agencies: Department of Justice, Office of Thrift Supervision, and Federal Deposit Insurance Corporation.

OSWALD, LEICHT, AND SCHULTZ, Washington, D.C.
Associate, September 1991 to September 1993

Focused civil litigation on real estate issues, HUD regulations, and franchise laws.

> *Minimizes less pertinent jobs.*

LEAGUE OF FEMALE CITIZENS' FUND, Washington, D.C.
Project Director, October 1987 to September 1991

> *Includes apt volunteer services in work history.*

Directed 100+ volunteers in national Community Development Block Grant Monitoring Project; executed volunteer training program; organized national conference allowing volunteer participant conferences with officials of Department of Justice and Housing and Urban Development resulting in grant extensions.

> *Shows results with achievements.*

EDUCATION

STANFORD LAW SCHOOL, Juris Doctorate, Bar Admission, Washington, D.C.

NEW HAMPSHIRE UNIVERSITY, Bachelor of Arts, Urban Studies, Magna Cum Laude

Freelance Graphic Artist
HYBRID & TARGETED/COMPUTER UNFRIENDLY

> *Computer sees e-mail address too close to telephone number.*

MICHELLE M. SMARTS
123 National Ave., Apt. B, Wise, VA 24293

Graphic designer/5 yrs exp/Virginia
(703) 456-7891, E-mail: arts@iii.com

OBJECTIVE: Graphic designer for medical center.

HIGHLIGHTS OF EXPERIENCE:

> *Advanced degrees count in targeting academic setting of medical center.*

Education: Master of Arts, Graphic Design, 1998
Graduate Program, University of Virginia at Richmond,
Division of Biomedical Visualization

Graphic Designer and Artist Programmer
See Biomedical Visualization departmental WWW home page, University of Virginia, Richmond

> *Clean layout emphasizes design skills as well as mastery of computer skills.*

Broad-based experience in computer and hard copy image processing skills:

computer animation	3-D modeling	Web page graphics
graphic design	interactive multimedia	production graphics
HTML programming	Internet home page	book layout

> *Maximizes white space by using columns. Stand-alone words are OK in columns, but not in text. Vertical lines are not computer friendly.*

Software skills:

Macromedia Director	Adobe Illustrator	Imageworks XV	NetScape
Visual Basic	Freehand	PageMaker	Mosaic
HyperCard	Photoshop	QuarkXPress	StrataStudioPro
CorelDRAW!	Photostyler	PowerPoint	Infini-D
	Lumena	Persuasion	Crystal 3-D
		Alias	

> *Includes KeyWords in all skills listings.*

Freehand imaging skills:

high rendering	photography	pastel/pencil	oil painting
life drawing	airbrush	pen & ink	biological imaging
sculpting	charcoal	watercolor	

EMPLOYMENT:

> *Showcases most pertinent experience on first page.*

Freelance Illustrator, Lexington, Virginia   1998-Present

Illustration of medical poster, advertisement and manual images, computer graphics, logos, NetScape and Mosaic home page design. Captain and collaborate with a team of seven artists.

Graphic Design Intern, Presbyterian Hospital, Wise, Virginia   1997-Present

Illustration and graphic design for health and medical-related subjects. Primary focus on creative advertising of medical services and health care plans. Campaign resulted in $225K revenue increase.

(1 of 2)

MICHELLE M. SMARTS

Graduate Assistant, Computing Systems Aid, University of Virginia   1995-1996

Updating and troubleshooting existing computer systems, instructing 375 of students, alumni and faculty in use of all software on Macintosh and DOS/Windows systems.

Illustrator and Computer Consultant, Word Crafts, Butterfield, Virginia   1994-1995

Page layout and illustration for products and product labels, graphic design for advertisements and catalogues, new product design and development, updated production system and streamlined and computerized all corporation's file storage.

ASSOCIATIONS AND HONORS:

Association of Medical Illustrators, 1997-Present
International Interactive Communications, 1998-Present
Graduate Student Council, Communications Chair, 1997-1998
Distinguished Student, 1994-1996

> Maximizes 2nd page with humanizing testimonials.

COMPLIMENTARY QUOTES:

"It's important to be able to distinguish between a good designer and a great designer; Michelle distinguishes herself!"
-- Dr. Mary Landsforth, Director of Presbyterian Hospital Communications Department

"I thought *I* was the hot computer imaging genius, until Smarts came along and taught *me!*"
-- Kyle Day, Resident Programmer, Div. of Biomedical Visualization, University of Virginia

"When Michelle joined us, we all had to work a little harder -- her speed and originality made us look bad by comparison!"
-- Lizel Delosrios, Lexington computer graphics freelancer

> Newer scanner software can read italics; old ones can't. Smarts called her target medical center and determined they have newer software. When in doubt, don't use italics.

Brian N. Hawes
123 Northumbridge Avenue Nashville, Tennessee 37203
(615) 456-7891   E-mail bhaw@aol.com

> Replaces objective with job title.

→ **Speech-Language Pathologist**

EDUCATION

1991 to 1993, and 2000   **University of Tennessee, Chattanooga, TN**
Ph.D., 1993; dissertation pending.
Minor: Audio/Visual Media, G.P.A.: 4.00
Awarded assistantship for clinical research.

> Includes top achievements.

1989 to 1990   **Wolgrel University, Bartlett, TN**
Master of Science in Speech-Language Pathology, Minor: Psychology, G.P.A.: 4.00
Wrote and produced radio and television commercials and promotional videos.

1980 to 1984 and 1990   **Tuskeegee University, Tuskeegee, TN**
Bachelor of Arts in Language, Minor: History, G.P.A.: 3.86
Graduated summa cum laude, after three study-abroad terms, serving as multimedia laboratory
assistant, student government representative, and club president.

> Shows extra-curricular achievements.

> Skips summary-- saved for cover letter.

PROFESSIONAL EXPERIENCE AND ACCOMPLISHMENTS

1992 to Present   **Radius Vox Laboratories, Millington, TN**   **Director**

> Describes prestigious employer.

Firm delivers computer and video imaging and audio signal analysis (voice spectrography). Marketing
targets hundreds of physicians and healthcare providers treating laryngeal, craniofacial dental, and
neurologic disorders.

1991 to 1992   **University of Tennessee, Chattanooga, TN**   **Lecturer, Researcher**
Restructured research laboratory, adding new facilities for voice analysis, videoendoscopy, and
biofeedback. Employed sound spectrography, stroboscopy, photography, and electrophysiologic
measurement techniques. Lectured to 233 Linguists on articulation and voice disorders analysis.
Supervised Orofacial Clinic (staff of 37), developed familiarity with fiberoptic endoscopy,
videofluoroscopy, and nasometry.

> Quantifies achievements.

1990 to 1992   **The Sound & Sight Center, Bartlett, TN**   **Speech-Language Pathologist**
Provided assessment and therapy to over 3,000 patients (neurologic, orofacial, vocal and pediatric).
Designed medical forms and computer-based therapy, decreasing procedure time by 30%. Coordinated
patient referral plans with local medical centers.

> Shows industry knowledge.

OTHER SKILLS AND CERTIFICATIONS
Computer: Windows (latest version), numerous applications, Microsoft certified, AI (Prolog), SAS, and SPSS.
Specialized Certifications: American Speech Association, International Association of Forensic Phonetics,
Association of Phonetic Sciences, Zertifikat Deutsch, Goethe Institute Summer Abroad Fellowship, and Lake
Search and Rescue Team. Licensed Tennessee Speech-Language Pathologist, FCC Radiotelephone Operator's
Permit.

Financial Executive
LINEAR/COMPUTER FRIENDLY

Contact information placed on right so it can be read easily when RezReader thumbs through a stack of resumes.

Diana Carter
12 Wollenstromcraft Way
Princeton, NJ 07921
(908) 345-6789
dcart@aol.com

Objective: FINANCIAL MARKETS MANAGEMENT POSITION

Experience:

Great Eastern Bank, Princeton, NJ   July 1995-July 2000
Second Vice President -- Global Markets Project Manager
- Developed, outlined, and scheduled 98 conferences covering spectrum of financial risk management issues
- Launched 53-page quarterly newsletter on new products and fluctuations. Researched and edited copy from technical specialists and regulatory agencies
- Expanded circulation of client newsletter more than 500% in three years
- Managed $1.2 million budget and monitored department expenses
- Provided marketing support for Senior Vice President
- Traveled to Hong Kong, Singapore, and London delivering educational seminars on derivative products and uses
- Administered 17 bank personnel policies for seven staff members
- Directed office closure due to downsizing

Divides job by title, emphasizing upward mobility.

Reason for leaving OK here -- widespread banking mergers.

Assistant Treasurer -- Global Risk Managment Project Coordinator
- Assisted establishment of Risk Management Education & Marketing department
- Created presentation materials for over 30 conferences and education programs in 1996
- Promoted to Project Manager/Second Vice President

Trims down less relevant jobs to focus resume on target job.

PC Leaser Inc., Newark, NJ   November 1992-June 1995
Assistant Vice President
- Negotiated and prepared loan documentation for 23 financing lease transactions
- Scheduled and finalized fundings with 15 financial institutions

Computer Borrowers Corporation, New York City, NY   May 1991-November 1992
Lease Finance Administrator
- Managed company's secured credit lines, market activity, and interest rates
- Arranged financing for transactions up to $2 million and interim financing for all leases
- Served as financial liaison with 5 departments within the company

Education:

Graduate School of Management, University of New York, New York City
- Currently pursuing an MBA (part-time), credits earned: 38 of 60
Cambridge College, Cambridge, MA
- Bachelor of Arts in Sociology, May 1988

GPA not high, thus not mentioned.

Nuclear Engineer
Reverse CHRONOLOGICAL/COMPUTER FRIENDLY

Anthony T. Barbosa

Graceland Avenue
St. Louis, MO 677777
319.789.3393 Home
319.366.2525 Mobile
atbarbosa@earthlink.net

CONFIDENTIAL RESUME

Also a KeyWord resume; no KeyWord summary but KeyWords throughout — good technical jargon

EXPERIENCE

Text is well separated from horizontal lines; asterisks (rather than solid bullets) mean easy transfer to plain text.

2000-Present   Giant Power & Light Co.   St. Louis, MO
Reactor Operator Candidate, Hot License Class 97-01

* Chosen by management to attend Reactor Operator-Hot License class 97-01

* Passed the National BWR GFES Exam with a score of 93%

1996-2000   Giant Power & Light Co.   St. Louis, MO
Auxiliary Operator Nuclear - A

Entire resume stresses accomplishment, impressive striving to demonstrate skills.

* Member of operations unit which upgraded the San Bern Nuclear Plant from a forced shutdown condition on the NRC watch list to both NRC SALP-1 and INPO-1 ratings, company dual unit record breaking performance, and established world records for BWR single and dual unit continuous operations.

* Operated reactor, turbine, and auxiliary support systems to support the safe, reliable, economical, and environmentally sound production of power.

* Selected by operations management as one of three operators for extended assignments as Radwaste Control Operator, to pursue system, operational and programmatic upgrades. Received awards for results produced in this area.

Note how candidate divides tenure at a single employer into segments reflecting advancement.

* Developed several computer programs to assist the operations unit with managing operator exposure and error free performance.

1995-1997   Giant Power & Light Co.   St. Louis, MO
Radiological Engineer

* Developed a remote valve decontamination device that saved the utility in excess of $450,000 of critical path time during its first use.

* Performed a hydrogen water chemistry impact study to determine the impact of increased injection hydrogen rates on site exposure.

* Designed the containment and developed procedures used for the recovery of a damaged Americium-Beryllium neutron calibration source.

CONFIDENTIAL RESUME

Anthony T. Barbosa
Page 2

1993-1995	Nuclear Associates	Various sites

Health Physics Supervisor/Lead Technician

*   Clemente Nuclear Generating Station, Towanda, GA (BWR)

*   Paired with GE on full system decon (fuel installed) testing for EPRI

*   Heddon's Fort, Cincinnati, OH (PWR)

1992-1993	Careful Waste Management, Inc.	Tampa, FL

Field Chemist

*   Supervised packaging and shipping of hazardous materials

*   OSHA 40-HR Hazmat trained

*   On-call emergency supervisor/safety officer for field ops

1984-1992	U.S. Navy	Bangor, WA

Engineering Watch Supervisor/Lead Engineering Lab Tech

*   Managed 13-man engineering watch section in port/underway for Trident sub

*   Supervised chemistry and radiological control department

*   Article 108 rad con monitor

*   Navy prototype staff instructor

EDUCATION

New York Regents is a well-regarded distance education institution; candidate studied while aboard submarine.

2000	Virginia Polytechnic University	Blackburn, VA

Bachelor of Science in Nuclear Engineering

*   GPA 3.8/4.0

1994	New York Regents College	Albany, NY

Associate Degree in Liberal Arts

INTERESTS

*   Competitive offshore sailing, computers, bicycling, backpacking, Frisbee dog competition.

Personal interests convey image of competitiveness, technology priority, yet rounded out with healthful activities.

Information Technology
REVERSE CHRONOLOGICAL/PLAIN TEXT

> Plain text resume can go over the Net and slide right into a scannable database.

```
GEORGIA K. ESTRADA
107 Begonia Terrace
Lexington, MA 02165
Pager: (617)999-0808
Email: gkestrada@bu.edu
```

> Giving pager number is a good idea; adds immediacy to contact.

```
JOB OBJECTIVE
+++++++++++++++++++++++++++++++++++++++++++++++++++++++++++++++++++++
MICROSOFT WINDOWS OR NETWORK PROTOCOL DEVELOPMENT

SKILLS
+++++++++++++++++++++++++++++++++++++++++++++++++++++++++++++++++++++
C, C++, CGI, CScript, DOS, HTML, HTTP, Java, Javascript, MFC, SQL,
SSI+, TCP/IP, UNIX, Lotus, Visual Basic, Visual C++, WebDBC,
Windows NT/98

EMPLOYMENT
+++++++++++++++++++++++++++++++++++++++++++++++++++++++++++++++++++++
Clarion Systems, Inc.                                  2000-Present
PROGRAMMER
Develop, maintain, and monitor product-building tools and
processes using Visual C++ and MFC on Win NT 4.0. Began as intern;
promoted to regular status job.

Wonderwheels, Inc.                                  09/1999-01/2000
JUNIOR SOFTWARE ENGINEER
Internship: Team member responsible for design and development of
Windows 95 real-time, manufacturing application. Implement code
to improve application's performance. Enhance GUI features, assist
in test and troubleshoot application.

RHI Labs, Inc.                                      05/1999-08/1999
APPLICATION PROGRAMMER
Co-op job: Designed and developed two project tracking programs
using MS SQL, Javascript, and HTML. Member of team to maintain,
enhance, and create NTSQL server applications. Tested programs,
gathered user requirements, and created help documentation and
released applications.

Boston University Computer Sci. Dept.                    1997-1999
PROGRAMMING ASSISTANT/TEACHING ASSISTANT
Assisted undergraduate students in C & C++ programming. Provided
technical support and acted as lab assistant. Projects: Java
Poker Game, War Gamescore, Inventory Database Manager, Assembler
and Linker.

EDUCATION
+++++++++++++++++++++++++++++++++++++++++++++++++++++++++++++++++++++
Boston University
Boston, MA
BACHELOR OF ARTS COMPUTER SCIENCE - May 2000.
GPA: 3.75; Attended on 4-year partial scholarship; internships
```

Business Specialist
REVERSE CHRONOLOGICAL/PLAIN TEXT

This one-page resume is shown for technique; in real life, elaborate on skills, name software, explain skills claims. Back up your brags. Remember, digitals can be longer than paper resumes.

```
ALBERTO LAFUENTE
7806 Palm Drive
Plano, TX 70890
(832) 704-2694
e-mail: alf@newbiz.com
www.newbiz.com
```

Skills summary at top, skills summary at end: Resume is stuffed with skills, just what computers feed on.

```
NEW BUSINESS SPECIALIST
>>>>>>>>>>>>>>>>>>>>>>>>>>>>>>>>>>>>>>>>>>>>>>>>>>>>>>>>>>>>>>>

Client relationship management. Client planning. Product
Development. Marketing materials. Capitalization. Venture funding.
Start-up specialist.

EXPERIENCE

Sawyer Enterprises, Inc.  Kansas City, MO
Director of Marketing
2000-2002
Founding principal in this health-product corporation. Produced
300% revenue increase in second year of operation from six-figure
base. Travel up to 75%, including distributor contact and
training, site demos, trade shows.
* Sourced medical and technical services.
* Wrote company marketing plans.
* Served on executive team.
* Brought in company's largest contract, $875,000.
* Bid with procurement contracts from government; 45% success.

Contintentwide Bank            Kansas City, MO
New Business Account Executive
1998-2000
Responsible for soliciting large corporate accounts and loans;
enlarged base by $2.8 million. Hired and trained associates.

EDUCATION

The Ohio State University      Columbus, Ohio
Bachelor of Arts, History
1998
Continuing Education:
Marketing, Sales, Finance, Accounting
1999-Present

HARD SKILLS
PC programs: word processing, spreadsheets (accounting and
analysis). Heavy Internet research skills. Technology savvy.

SOFT SKILLS
Communications: technical information to technical and
nontechnical managers. Bilingual (English and Spanish).
```

No mention that company folded.

Chapter 21

A Sampling of Special Needs Resumes

• •

In This Chapter

▶ Model resumes for new graduates, reentry homemakers, career changers, people with gaps in their records, and other situations

• •

*H*aving to fight to advance your career isn't unusual — neither are the job-war wounds on your resume. Many who seek employment today have a few special issues that should be stamped "handle with care."

New graduates and reentry homemakers need jobs but lack extensive paid experience. Career changers, including ex-military personnel, face the challenge of transferring skills and learning entire new job languages. Seasoned aces may have "too much" experience, and must defend themselves against labels of "overqualification." People who have gaps in their records, who were demoted down the power chain, or who were exposed to too many temporary jobs must manage their resumes to sell skills rather than experience.

The model resume samples to follow generally match the templates in Chapter 4. In some instances, the sample section headings may not match the templates exactly. The templates contain the whole range of heading options so you can pick and choose the best way to market your unique needs and interests.

Gap in History
TARGETED/COMPUTER UNFRIENDLY

> Computer can't read graphic or shading; name will not retrieve. For human eyes only.

Paula G. Cramer
271 Redus Ave.
Mustang, OK 73064, (405) 123-4567

OBJECTIVE: KELLEY-KENNEDY PRINTING COMPANY PRODUCTION MANAGER
to use 12 plus years of print production management experience and graphic art knowledge

QUALIFICATIONS SUMMARY
- Handle all print project phases from design through prepress to final
- Budget management — competent, careful
- Education (college degree plus seminars) in management backs up experience-based skills

SKILLS SUMMARY

Desktop Publishing	Staff Management
Color Separation Technology	Vendor Contract Negotiations
WP 8, Word 97, Lotus 123, MS Excel, QuarkXPress,	Purchasing
PageMaker, Internet, All Word-Processing Software	Blueline Approvals

> Good treatment of two gaps — the first one was nearly three years, the other was six months. You have to read carefully to find the gaps because they are buried in the copy.

ACCOMPLISHMENTS AND EXPERIENCE

Lewisburg Marketing, Inc., Ada, OK
PRODUCTION MANAGER AND PRINT BUYER (Direct Mail):
Managed direct mail print production from design development through mail date for 40+ concurrent projects, meeting deadlines for 2.5 million per week, 12/96-3/00
- Directed prepress, design review, proofing, blueline approval, layout, print and finishing schedules. Insured compliance with U.S. Postal requirements.
- Purchased for all job components and effectively managed $13 million annual budget; price and contract copywriters, designers, and printer negotiations.

The Maupin Company, Edmond, OK
PRODUCTION COORDINATOR AND PLANNER
Planned and executed print production needs for clients, coordinated efforts of Account Executive, Designers, and Production Staff, 4/95-6/96
- Managed estimating, purchasing, job production layout, and projects submission to graphic design, camera and stripping, providing proofreading, scheduling, and blueline approvals, working closely with press room manager to meet delivery deadlines.

PRIOR EXPERIENCE

Investment Litho Company, Edmond, OK
GENERAL ASSISTANT
Worked part-time throughout college. Learned printing business from master printers, 6/88-6/92

EDUCATION Bucknell University, Ada, OK - B.S. in Business and Marketing, 1991
Massbank Management Institute, Edmond, OK - 12 seminars, management

College Intern

HYBRID/COMPUTER FRIENDLY

This resume puts all contact data on the same line although general scanning rules call for separate lines; newer systems will read one line, but put a minimum of six spaces between address, telephone, and e-mail.

Hard-sell language omits Chinese proficiency and is designed to counteract employer's potential assumption that Davidson (in USA on student visa) will return to Asian nation. Otherwise, bilingualism should appear in objective. Using professors' names and testimonials encourages further interest.

Alexander Davidson

36 W. Garnet #4   Pacific Beach, CA 92012   (619) 435-5555   E-mail: alexd@ddd.edu

Objective   **Internship or career-related summer position in Electrical Engineering;**
"Highly motivated — an all-American go-getter" (says professor Bob Smith) ...
"Fast-learning, earnest and hard-working graduate student" (professor Joan Roberts) ...
"Smart, friendly, outgoing — real stick-to-it-iveness" (professor Tim Horrell)...

Education   San Diego State University, San Diego, CA
Degree: Masters of Science in Engineering   Major: Electrical Engineering
GPA: 3.0/4.0   Graduation: December 2000

Degree: Bachelor of Science   Major: Electrical Engineering
GPA: 3.86/4.0   Minor: Mathematics
Honors: Magna Cum Laude   Graduation: May 1999

Honors   National Dean's List, Dean's List at San Diego State University, Member of College's National Engineering Honor Society, Member of Alpha Chi National Honor Society

Software Skills   MathCAD, MathLab, Pspice, Microcap, Fortran, Altera Logic Design System, programming M68HC11 microcontroller using Assembly language, C Language and other software utilities (word processing, spreadsheets)

Includes KeyWords in skills and courses sections.

Relevant Courses
- Systems, Signals and Noise
- Data Communications
- Fiber Optics Communication
- Digital Image Processing
- Random Signal Theory 1 and 2
- Transform Theory and Application
- Digital Spectral Analysis
- Communication Network Design

Work Experience   **Tutoring Lab Supervisor**
San Diego State University   Fall 1995-present
- Tutor students in Engineering, Mathematics, and Science courses

Assistant Engineer
Rilerad Projects Engineering, Hong Kong   Summers 1995-1999
- Collected data from engineers, produced progress reports
- Assisted bidding team, preparing documents and breakdown quotations

Administrator
National Service Hong Kong Armed Forces   March 1992-June 1995
- Scheduled military training and vocational upgrading courses
- Improved mobilization system to increase Reserve Corps processing rate during mobilization exercise

Activities   Vice President, Institute of Electrical and Electronic Engineers (IEEE), student chapter
Secretary of student chapter of National Society of Professional Engineers (NSPE)
Society of Physics Students
Intercultural Club
Intramural sports at San Diego State University
Fluent in Chinese

This is not a KickButt resume. What's wrong? Hint: Other than GPA, not high at master's level, where are measurements? Where are achievements? How could this resume be kicked up a couple of notches?

REANNA DUMON

123 Dane Street, Portland, OR 97504

(503) 456-7891

E-mail: rdumo@aol.com

Qualifications Highlights:

Seek physical therapist position using eight years' physical therapy and nursing experience in Canada, Switzerland, and the United States. Fluent in French, English, and Spanish. Trauma life-support, ECG, pediatrics, obstetrics, emergency and general nursing, internal medicine.

> Includes KeyWords in summary.

Education:

- Laval University, Quebec, Canada, Physical Therapy Certificate, 1998-2000
- Ste-Foy College, Ste-Foy, Quebec, Canada, D.E.C. in Technical Nursing (equivalent to RN diploma in U.S.), 1987-1990
- Garneau College, Ste-Foy, Quebec, Canada, D.E.C. in Physical Therapy, 1983-1985

Experience:

Ungava Hospital, Nunavik, Canada, 1995-20XX
- Designed 25-page physical therapy clinic manual distributed to injured patients regarding methods of therapy and preventative procedures to eliminate further injury.
- Nurse: Clinical work: physical therapy, pediatric, obstetrical, and long-term follow-ups, child vaccination, laboratory procedures, home visiting, physical exams, medical evacuations, mutidisciplinary case discussions.
        Community Health: school vaccination programs.
        Administration: patient transfers, medical visits, arranging meetings.

> Includes KeyWords in job descriptions.

Ungava Hospital, Nunavik, Canada, 1993-1995
- Coordinated physical therapy schedule and program for 16 patients.
- Pediatrics, obstetrics, general medicine nurse. Monitored staff of 30 pediatric nurses; managed 57 patients.
- Coordinated schedule for 37 nurses in general medicine unit, maximizing hospital efficiency in patient care and personal organizational skills.

Canntonnal Hospital of Fribourg, Fribourg, Switzerland, 1992-1993

> Gives results.

- Nurse, Department of Internal Medicine. Managed 26 patients, 8 with PT needs.
- Trained 11 interns on internal medicine procedures, enhancing leadership, management, and interpersonal skills to implement teamwork ideal of hospital.

Bassee-Nord Health Center, Quebec, Canada, 1990-1992
- Performed daily physical therapy sessions with 13 pediatric patients.
- Head Nurse – emergency care, general medicine and pediatrics nurse.
- Promoted to Head nurse in emergency-care unit within first eight months.
- Supervised 23 nursing interns and coordinated medicine schedules for 35 patients.

> Because physical therapy, not nursing, is goal, Dumon leads with physical therapy experience, although nursing experience is dominant. Dumon moves in and out of the two professions – PT and nursing.

Seasoned Ace
ACCOMPLISHMENT/COMPUTER UNFRIENDLY

Romero Cortez
42 Plains Road
Mystic, CT 06493
(203) 555-6932
E-mail: romeroc@drd.sfi.com

Senior Creative/Marketing Executive
Experienced in major account management, new product and strategic concept development, advertising and promotion; spearheaded revenue growth from $13 million to $180 million in 5 years.

Omits section headings for more direct impact.

- Increased one company's value from $50 million to sales price of $225 million
- Revitalized company by effecting $10 million sales increase

Effective leader skilled in building, training, and motivating highly profitable creative teams and directing major projects to completion on time with strong cost control. Track record of developing and maintaining corporate relationships.

Creative/Marketing Success Highlights

"Advertises" marketing achievements.

Marketing Theme	Client
Tannik's Capitalist Tool	Tannik's Magazine
Call them with clarity	RTO Telephones
Fly us	Abroad Airlines
Oil No More	Oil Gleaners Inc.
Let Our Machines Work, You Think	Mattison Products
Feel sensitive	Crimson Skin Products
Every Bit Crystal Quality	Crystal Diskettes
Moist and Flavorful Food	New-Taste Dog Food

Awards
Clio, American Institute of Graphic Arts, Rissoli Award, Best Read Ad-Rosser Reeves, Communications Arts Award, Outdoor Billboard Design Award, and Andy Award, International Film Festival Silver Medal, Connecticut Art Directors Club Gold Medal

(1 of 2)

Can change to computer friendly by switching "Creative Marketing Success Highlights" with "Professional Experience." That's the order in which computers expect to find data. But for human viewing, current presentation is different and effective.

Romero Cortez

Developed all RTO-TV Network advertising for 2 years. Directed turnaround of Morning brand cereal division. Other creative assignments in advertising, direct marketing and new product development launches for:

Generative Appliances	American Bottling Co.
International Athletics Association	New Foods
Sweet Candy Company	Crystal

Sells industry reputation before employment history.

Professional Experience

Vice President, Creative Director	Wilton Marketing & Communications, Wilton, CT 1991-Present
Vice President, Associate Creative Director	McConnell and McCarthy, Inc., Manhattan, NY 1988-1991
Vice President, Associate Creative Director	Mark Jenkins Company Advertising, Inc., Manhattan, NY 1981-1988

Romero Cortez shows he's a pro by using advertising skills on his resume — in this model, Cortez makes a virtue of open white space, citing only a few standout achievements.

Seasoned Ace

ACCOMPLISHMENT/COMPUTER FRIENDLY

Dana M. Brigham

123 Teal Way, Tujunga, California, 91042   (714) 222-4985
e-mail: dbrigham@infonet.com

Urban Planner: 15 years' experience in urban planning with substantial management experience in public and private sectors. Experienced in preparing and managing: general plan revisions; zoning code administration; redevelopment plans; environmental projects.

Different typeface than body text for more attention.

Qualifications and Accomplishments:

- Planner for city of Laguna Niguel, managing review of large-scale urban projects.

- Managed general plan preparation for Irvine, Palmdale, and San Jose including environmental analysis of plans' impacts, surviving court challenge.

Gives results.

- Supervised zoning section of Irvine Planning Department for over four years, developing commission agenda and preparing staff reports to commission and City Council.

- Supervised 37 planners in public sector for Irvine, Palmdale, and San Jose.

Brigham departs from template by combining qualifications and accomplishments.

- Assisted in establishing plan in Palmdale immediately following its incorporation.

- Directed task force in designing and implementing new hillside grading/development standards for Palmdale, developing builder sensitivity to community goals.

- Organized Hillside Development Panel for 1997 American Planning Association.

- Managed preparation of E. Santa Monica Boulevard Strategic Plan and East Irvine Specific Plan for Pasadena; coordinated with 56 planners, presented to large groups.

Employment:

CITY OF IRVINE, Irvine, California, 1998-Present
Special Projects Planner, Planning and Community Development Department.

LOCKEN AND CO., Santa Monica, California, 1995-1998
Director of Planning Department.

Maximizes white space.

CITY OF PALMDALE, Palmdale, California, 1991-1995
Senior Project Manager, Planning and Research Section.

KLO ASSOCIATES, Palmdale, California, 1989-1991
Senior Project Manager of preparing environmental impact reports.

WOLHBAHN & SONS, Santa Monica, California, 1987-1989
Senior Planning Consultant providing advisory services to local municipalities.

CITY OF SAN JOSE, San Jose, California, 1983-1987
Supervising Associate Planner, Zoning Division, Planning Department.

Education:

Bachelor of Arts, Political Science, University of Sacramento, Sacramento, California, 1982
Master of Science, Public Administration, California State University, Sacramento, California 1985

Professional Affiliations:

American Planning Association, American Institute of Certified Planners

Seasoned Ace
ACCOMPLISHMENT/COMPUTER FRIENDLY

Older human resource pro wishes to re-enter private sector after government stint; limits work history to 10 years.

ANDREW WALLACE
P.O. BOX 123, NEWPORT, LONG ISLAND, 11413
(212) 456-1997
awall@aol.com

Human Resource position using recruitment, appraisal and benefit skills, accumulated over 10 years

QUALIFICATIONS:

- ➤ Directed human resource systems for two mid-sized corporations
- ➤ Worked inside EEOC structure; bulletproof employee management
- ➤ Expert in recruiting, benefits, evaluations, training, and outplacement
- ➤ Use computer — or manual — applicant/employee tracking systems
- ➤ Can manage contingent workforce

ACCOMPLISHMENTS:

- ➤ Investigated and negotiated resolutions of 400 allegations of employment discrimination. Led investigation teams and instructed on negotiation procedures to maximize resolution success.

- ➤ Performed EEO consultation, trained more than 60 employer and university organizations in human resource skills to establish increasingly effective management-staff working relationship.

- ➤ Received 12 annual merit-based promotions; managed staff of 15 recruiters.

RECENT PROFESSIONAL EXPERIENCE:

- ➤ 11/96 to 12/99 — **Employment Equality Commission, New York, NY** — Federal Investigator
- ➤ 9/95 to 6/99 — **University Of New York City, Queens, NY** — Adjunct Faculty
- ➤ 11/95 to 11/96 — **Swanky Interiors, New York, NY** — Human Resources Director
- ➤ 6/89 to 9/95 — **Lucrative Corporation, Buffalo, NY** — Human Resources Manager

EDUCATION:

- ➤ **Central New York University** — Master of Sciences, Human Resource Administration
- ➤ **Mariner College** — Bachelor of Arts, Management of Human Resources
- ➤ **New York College of Law** — Continuing coursework toward Juris Doctor degree

PROFESSIONAL ASSOCIATIONS:

- ➤ Human Resource Association of New York
- ➤ Society for Human Resource Management
- ➤ American Society of Training & Development
- ➤ American Bar Association Student Division
- ➤ State Bar of New York Student Division
- ➤ Kiwanis International

New Graduate
REVERSE CHRONOLOGICAL & TARGETED/COMPUTER FRIENDLY

> *Lutwig's research on the target showed they wanted an energetic, young person with his degrees. Objective and education centered for formal look and to highlight degrees that employer favors.*

DALE K. LUTWIG

12 West 34th Street , Los Angeles, CA 91121
(213) 567-8910   E-mail: twig@nnn.gov

Objective : CONGRESSIONAL AIDE

JURIS DOCTOR INTERNATIONAL LEGAL STUDIES
Occidental University, College of Law 20XX

MASTER OF ARTS, POLITICAL SCIENCE
Adele School of Citizenship and Public Affairs, 20XX
Concentration in Government Planning & International Negotiation
Teaching Assistant in International Negotiation

BACHELOR OF ARTS, POLITICS AND SOCIOLOGY
University of California, Los Angeles, 20XX, Dean's List

Bar Admission: CA and NJ Passed entrance examinations. Admissions pending.

WORK EXPERIENCE

> *Summary omitted: saved for cover letter.*

1997-2000   **Office of the United States Trade Representative**
Assisted Deputy Assistant US Trade Representative in analyzing House and Senate bills. Reconstructed 25 legislative provisions which complicated international trade obligations. Corresponded with corporations, trade associations, congressional staff members and other Federal agencies. Developed working dexterity with international negotiations. Trade representative John Katan compliments my work: "Best intern we have."

> *Complimentary quotes accentuate skills and promise.*

1996   **Los Angeles Department of Consumer Affairs**
Assisted investigators in enforcing Attorney General's Guidelines for Fair Advertising. Accumulated strong background in advertising ethics proceedings.

1995   **Charles Swabb**
Assisted 19 account executives in management activities, including investor research, telemarketing, mass mailings, computerized clerical operations and communications. Tremendous experience with intercompany and public communications. Praised for follow- through and organization (office manager Tom Cannon).

1992-1995   **Reese, Riley & Thorne**
Assisted library staff, paralegals and attorneys with all library functions, including organization and research. Modernized 14 computers. Compiled legal information for 32 lawsuits from cases and articles, acquiring early experience with legal negotiations.

MISCELLANEOUS

> *Technical skills detailed to target employer's needs.*

• Proficient with all applications, including LEXIS/NEXIS/WESTLAW databases.
• Hobbies include sailboat racing and golf.

> *Personal interest included; Lutwig's research shows target company's RezReaders value interest in sports.*

New Graduate

LINEAR/COMPUTER FRIENDLY

> Grades speak for themselves. Testimonial backs up claim of favorable faculty comments.

Herman Ling

123 Northrop Avenue #4, Ft. Lauderdale, Florida 33308
(305) 566-6789   E-mail: hling@jkuafu.edu

Objective Marketing position in Agribusiness or Chemicals

Qualifications Focus: plant pathology. MBA/Master's in Plant Pathology/ agriculture undergraduate degree. Two years' international marketing experience. Bilingual — Chinese and English. Computer literate. Rated tops by grades and favorable faculty comments in graduate studies: ("Herman Ling is the most industrious student to come through here in several years" — U. of Colorado marketing professor Karl Weber.)

Communications Skills
- Computer: MS Word, Excel, Powerpoint, WordPerfect, Lotus 123, Freelance, Harvard Graphics, PSI-Plot, SAS JUMP, QBasic programming, and main frame
- Language: Chinese (Mandarin and several dialects)

> Gives details on bilingual and computer claims in summary.

Experience

8/96-7/99 **Graduate Research Assistant**
University of Colorado, Department of Plant Pathology, Boulder, CO
- Designed and implemented experiments in greenhouse, growth chamber, and field
- Developed weather-based advisory for improving control of plant disease with reduced fungicide

7/94-8/96 **Account Manager, Department of Marketing and Sales**
Detect Bio-Pharmacy Group, Beijing, PR China
- Developed channel strategies for entering Chinese marketplace
- Managed and developed sales accounts
- Developed promotion plan for marketing new medicine
- Participated in joint venture for manufacturing ingredients

> Prior experience in China. This experience is for U.S. job, thus quote from U.S. professor; for a job in China, would emphasize China connections.

9/91-6/94 **Social Coordinator, Department Student Association; Co-editor, Department Student Journal**
Beijing Agricultural University, Beijing, PR China

Education **Master of Business Administration,** 2001, GPA 4.0/4.0
University of Miami, Miami, FL

Master of Science, Plant Pathology, 1999, GPA 3.8/4.0
University of Colorado, Boulder, CO

Bachelor of Science, Plant Protection, 1994, GPA (comparable) 4.0/4.0
Beijing Agricultural University, Beijing, People's Republic of China

Publications **Ling, Herman,** Grant, P., and Milton, F. 2000 "Effects of precipitation and temperature on garden crop infection." *Plant Disease.*

Ling, Herman, and Kilkenny, E. 2000 "Comparison of weather-dependent crops based on soil concentration." *Plant Disease.*

Activities American Phytopathological Society

> Despite advanced degrees, placed experience first to show market orientation.

Re-Entry Homemaker
REVERSE CHRONOLOGICAL/COMPUTER FRIENDLY

Faith Marks

167 Vanderbilt Road
Harrisburg, PA 12101

(916) 779-1434
E-mail: fmarks@cts.com

Space between text and line.

Objective
Social Studies Teacher, grades 5-12
Teaching is my life. Comfortable with computers, daily communication and research via
e-mail and the Internet. Computer focus promises that children taught will not be left
behind in a competitive era.

Objective mixed with summary: concentration on e-mail & Internet shows stay-at-home is up-to-date.

Education
Bachelor of Science in Secondary Education
Pennsylvania State University, 1997

Pennsylvania Teaching Credential:
Economics, Geography, United States and
World History, Grades 5-12

Honors
• National Dean's List, 1996
• Alpha Lambda, 1994, Freshman Honor Society
• Phi ETA Sigma, 1994, Freshman Honor Society

Fast-learning, willingness to put self-interest aside for team good.

Teaching Experience

Substitute Teacher, Townville Elementary School   Fall 1997
• Became expert at instant lesson plan preparation. Never refuse last-minute assignments.
• Work with diverse student groups, expanding range of teaching capabilities. Not
  intimidated by challenge of middle-school behavioral problems.
• Use considerable experience with children, ages five - twelve. Create exciting and
  motivational lesson plans. Principal Morgan Rathbone says "Faith Marks gives
  110% to her substitute teaching assignments. Her students get energized by her
  classroom technique. I only wish we had a staff opening. I'd hire her in a second!"

Complimentary quote used to explain why she was not hired here if she's so great.

Student Teacher, Townville Middle School, 10 weeks   Spring 1997
                     Grant Middle School, 6 weeks
• Taught US History, Geography, and Government; developed multi-faceted
  daily lesson plans for each course.
• Perfected computer fluency. Strengthened supervisory roles, delegation ability,
  organizational skills and motivational techniques. Worked full-time while parenting.
• Instructed extracurricular activities, including softball and computer club.

Additional Experience
Advised graduate students, worked as student financial aid liaison. Analyzed student
financial information and matched to available funding.

Seasoned Ace
LINEAR/COMPUTER FRIENDLY

Alternative heading for Objective.

Lee Ralston

7702 Ridge Road   Tacoma, Washington 90543
(206) 555-9876   E-mail: lralst@aol.com

Ampersand OK — familiar phrase.

Profile: Property Management professional seeks to use high-quality history in supervisory position. More than 15 years' solid experience A to Z in property management.

Qualifications:
- Skilled in profit & loss, reductions, distribution, and financial administration
- Restructure marketing plans strategically, advancing returns in excess of 20%
- Record of enthusiastic achievement of corporate objectives
- LIHTC (tax credit), Bond, Section 8, HODAG, New Construction and Renovations
- Managed multi-family properties in Washington, California, Oregon, Arizona, Colorado, and Utah

Quantifies achievements.

KeyWords throughout.

Education and Training:
- **Bachelor of Arts in Education,** University of Puget Sound, Tacoma, Washington
- **College of Certified Property Managers,** Apartment Management, Real Estate Finances and Management

Designations:
- Certified Apartment Property Supervisor
- Washington Real Estate License

White space and bullets improve readability.

Professional Experience:

1995-Present   **Senior Asset Manager**   Greengrove Point Properties, Inc.

Quantifies and gives results of achievements.

- Manage marketing and operations programs for over 2,000 units.
- Recruit, train, and hire over 100 employees, maximizing $2M in capital improvements.
- Consult on all EEOC and fair housing issues, minimizing legal consultation costs by $2,000.

1994-1995   **Regional Manager**   Builder Companies of Washington

- Facilitated marketing programs for 10-12 properties throughout Washington.
- Superintended successful lease-up and operation of 23-story luxury hi-rise property in Seattle.
- Directed $2 million renovation of 25-year-old property on coast of Washington.

1992-1994   **District Manager**   Washington Property Management

- Created marketing and operations programs for two properties in Tacoma, WA.
- Facilitated $2 million renovation with lease-up three months ahead of schedule.
- Maintained 98% occupancy in New Construction lease.

Ampersand OK — company name.

1987-1992   **Area Manager**   Benedict, Young, Dalton, & McMillan

Assistant Manager on 1,672-unit property in Seattle, Washington.
- Led company nationally for two years in leasing, averaging over 120 new leases per month.
- Portfolio consisted of 2,000 units and over 100 employees.
- Directed monthly regional sales meetings, initiated energy savings program that accomplished $150,000 work done to 14 properties with profit exceeding $12,000.

Grouping Temporary Jobs
ACCOMPLISHMENT/COMPUTER FRIENDLY

BETH SHELTON

1849 Warner Road, Newark, Delaware 19905   **Phone: (302) 555-6778**
                                                     E-mail: shelton@khl.com

Objective

Position as **Administrative Assistant/Executive Secretary** — using detail-oriented skills and experience accumulated over 9 years

Qualifications

- More than 10 years' secretarial/administrative experience; keyboard speed of 90 wpm
- Proficient in Microsoft Word, WordPerfect, Windows, Lotus, Excel, FileMaker Pro

Accomplishments

- Responded promptly to technical requests from Parker clients (account average: $25,000), advising on hardware and software issues, ensuring client satisfaction

- Supported office operations of 35-bed hospital ward; developed substantial ability to prioritize duties and service large numbers of people in high-pressure environment

- Researched, compiled and prepared crucial data, independently and with little supervision — developing strong self-management skills

- Organized meetings and workshops, arranged travel for conferences averaging 20 executives; as noted by Tom Rogers, corporate vice president: "Beth fits together all the cogs and wheels here; without her, it's chaos."

- Tracked 250 medical admissions, discharges, and transfers on computer

- Resolved issues after hours and on weekends, meeting challenges with commitment

Job History

Combined temporary jobs under one heading to avoid looking like job hopper.

Administrative Assistant and Secretary, Hammond Temporaries, Dover, Del.   1996-Present
Assistant Database Manager, Parker Regional Medical Systems, Newark, Del.   1993-1996
Assistant Office Manager, Hyde Transport Company, Dover, Del.   1991-1993
Secretary to Computing Manager, Range Systems, Newark, Del.   1984-1991

Education

Bachelor of Arts in Business Management, 3.8/4.0 GPA   Awarded 2000
Newark College, Newark, Del.

Seasoned Ace
KEYWORD & LINEAR/COMPUTER FRIENDLY

Objective woven into KeyWord summary.

Griffin T. Stenner

2345 Fremont Blvd.   Santa Fe, NM 87501
(505) 555-0006   Messages taken at (505) 333-8000
E-Mail: griffsten@aol.com

Senior-level sales and distribution management position

12 years' experience in supervisory positions. Sales and distribution experience. Budgeting. Profit & loss responsibility. Customer service. Materials and product management. Employee selection and training. Strategic and tactical planning. Marketing. Facility location. Product training. Labor relations. Manufacturing plant management. Computerized environment and pricing.

Business Experience

Divides jobs by titles, highlighting upward mobility over long period with single employer.

1986-Present DUNCAN TRANSIT COMPANY, Santa Fe, New Mexico
1996-Present   **Director of Aftermarket Business**

Amper-sand OK here — familiar phrase.

Profit & loss responsibility for $40 million aftermarket parts division. Supervise 16 sales and 35 distribution staff for sales, marketing, materials management, customer service, distribution and product management. Serve on Executive Committee for policy making and strategizing.
- Facilitated strategic plan increasing sales 30%, exceeding 25% assets return
- Chaired integrated software system committee
- Edited sales literature and media campaign for $3 million retail expansion
- Sharpened inventory accuracy to 97.5% with new bar code system, significantly reducing manufacturing downtime

1992-1996   **Corporate Distribution Manager**
Managed warehouse, distribution and traffic functions for two locations of more than 10,000 stockkeeping units. Assumed plant responsibility for distribution of product to 860 retail stores weekly.
- Designed and relocated new distribution center on schedule and $200,000 under budget
- Received **Star of the Year** award from employer for product quality and distribution service levels
- Lowered total distribution cost 24%, saving $1.8M over five years

1986-1992   **Account Manager**
Developed first- and second-level distribution and manufacturing accounts in 30 key market areas, while maintaining in excess of 40 existing accounts in eight states. Conducted sales, product, and technical meetings for distributorship managers and sales staff.
- Top company salesperson in 1987, 1988, and 1990
- Increased sales by 220% to $4.4M in two years

Education

Achievement numbers combined for over one year to show high-impact results.

No years given.

Bachelor of Science, Business Administration, University of New Mexico, Santa Fe
Senior Executive Management Course, Santa Fe Community College, New Mexico

Franklin S. Tower

842 Harvest Dr.
Philadelphia, PA 19103
(215) 911-9409
fstower@email.msn.com

Mechanical Engineer

12 years' experience in mechanical engineering with a diverse background in design and engineering contract management.

PROFESSIONAL EXPERIENCE AND ACCOMPLISHMENTS

Mechanical Design
- Designed laboratory expansion for waste treatment plant. Upgraded underground storage tanks to meet EPA standards which also resulted in a 65% increase in treatment and storage efficiency.

- Improved design of fire training pit, including redesign of pump and pipe sizing and oil/water separator selection. Redesign allowed substantial increase in control of flow direction and water pressure.

- Designed recirculation system for waste treatment plant trickling filter which decreased water usage by 18% and filter replacement rate.

- Developed design for electrical contacts for a major electrical connector manufacturer on a contractual basis. New design improved materials usage and improved production time by 5%.

Engineering Contract Management
- Evaluated drafting and engineering sections' performance, quality, and compliance with specified contract, scheduling and ensuring timetables for production. Consistently led teams in finishing projects ahead of schedule.

Converts military jargon into civilian terms.

- Rewrote performance specifications to improve bonus incentive. Eliminated unrelated requirements in bonus program, resulting in 15% increase in worker efficiency.

- Evaluated contractors for compliance with EPA and safety regulations affirming environmental responsibility and decreasing worker downtime due to accidents.

- Implemented priority-setting program that decreased project and production redundancy over a five-year period.

General Management
- Supervised buildings and ground maintenance and repair shops. Duties included review and approval of project schedules, quality inspection of work

(1 of 2)

Franklin S. Tower

in progress and completed work, coordination of requirements between sections, briefing of senior supervisors. Developed rotating maintenance schedule that improved efficiency 20% and eliminated redundant work requests.

- Supervised new office that was created to ease difficulties in closing Air Force Base engineering section. Implemented programs to track location and disposal of supplies and materials resulting in better-than-forecast inventory elimination. Developed and implemented procedures and outplacement programs that ensured meeting the closing deadline and placed 46% of former federal ← *Demonstrates concern for people, not just products.* employees in private sector positions.

- Managed aircraft maintenance and repair branches with 475 employees and 15 shops. Monitored maintenance in progress and briefed senior supervisors on maintenance scheduling. Wrote performance reviews and performed counseling for at-risk personnel, resulting in 12% decrease in worker turn-around.

By not specifying rank: 1. downplays lack of advancement while in military service, and 2. moderates civilian anxiety of military rank.

EMPLOYMENT HISTORY

1988-present, Officer, United States Air Force
5/88-11/88, Mechanical Drafter, Frankish Design Company, Langston, TX

EDUCATION

- Bachelor of Science in Mechanical Engineering, California Polytechnic University, San Luis Obispo, 1988

- Officers Training School, 1990

(2 of 2)

Part VII
The Part of Tens

The 5th Wave   By Rich Tennant

"I see on page 124 of your resume it says you're a concise writer."

In this part . . .

The famous Dummies' *Part of Tens* is treasured for putting information quickly and simply on your table. In this part, you find out how to back up your claims, discover the myths to ignore, uncover great pointers and avoidable blunders, learn how to choose a professional resume writer (not that you'll need one) and receive a detailed checklist you can use to score your own FirstRate resume.

Chapter 22

Ten (x3) Ways to Prove Your Brags

*T*he easy part of resume creation is reading about it in books like this. Now comes the tough part: inventing accomplishments. You'll have to summon up your best creative talents to design workplace successes that are impossible to check. Of course, I'm kidding. But that's what a RezReader will think you've done if your resume alleges wondrous deeds without the support of verifiable evidence.

Highly creative in home arts area; excellent communications skills; more than a decade of experience in writing and publishing; nationally recognized as lecturer and consultant...

And? So? Why should anyone care? What's wrong with this word picture? Answer: The tribute is nice enough, but the description neglects a key FirstRate factor — *measurable good results!*

The FirstRate factor kicks in when you add credibility with certifiable, tangible information.

Quantify your accomplishments when you want to persuade.

For example, suppose a television commercial asserts that Brand X cola is a better drink than Brand Y cola. What a yawn. But when the commercial switches to report a study in which 70 percent of those tested prefer Brand X cola, the boast sounds plausible. Another quick example: Aren't you more impressed by commercials that say, "Nine out of 10 doctors recommend Blue Company aspirin," than those that merely claim, "Blue Company aspirin is the best?"

The message for FirstRate RezWriters is quantify, quantify, quantify! Use these three main quantitative methods to boost the plausibility of your accomplishments: *numbers, percentages,* and *dollar amounts.*

Quantifying the example at the beginning of this chapter, the word picture now moves into the FirstRate class of self-marketing materials. The numbers are for illustrative purposes only, but here's how someone like billionaire celebrity Martha Stewart might do it:

Led my company to a 1999 public stock offering which opened at $18 a share and zoomed to $35. Created Martha Stewart Living, *a home arts magazine with more than $50 million annual ad revenues. Featured in* Martha Stewart Living, *a syndicated television program distributed to more than 150 stations. Author or contributor to 51 home arts books. Give 12 lectures per year at substantial honorariums. Completed $1-million-a-year consulting contract to K mart stores.*

I repeat: quantify, quantify, quantify. Look at the following statements in the three categories of numbers, percentages, and dollar amounts. Fill in the appropriate blanks. You're doing this as an exercise to remind you to quantify your accomplishments and results — anything you're proud of. This numbers game works in virtually any occupation or industry.

Supporting your high performance with numbers, percentages, or dollar amounts takes the sting out of bragging. Regardless of your line of work — a trainer counting 5,000 people instructed, a molecular biology manager sequencing 10 dsRNA genes of reovirus serotype 3, or a fast-food manager noting $3,000 in janitorial supplies saved — don't forget to make your numbers!

Say It with Numbers

1. _____ (#) years of extensive experience in _____
   and _____.

2. Won _____(#) awards for _____
   _____.

3. Trained/Supervised _____ (#) full-time and _____ (#) part-time employees.

4. Recommended by _____
   _____ (a number of notable people) as a
   _____(something good that they said about you)
   for excellent _____(an accomplishment or skill).

5. Supervised a staff of _____(#).

6. Recruited _____ (#) staff members in _____(period of time),
   increasing overall production.

7. Sold _____ (# of products) in _____ (period of time), ranking _____
   (1st, 2nd, 3rd) in sales in a company of _____ (#) employees.

8. Exceeded goals in _____ (#) years/months/days, establishing my
   employer as _____ (number — 1st, 2nd, 3rd) in industry.

9. Missed only _____ (#) days of work out of _____ (#) total.

10. Assisted _____ (#) (executives, supervisors, technical directors,
    _____ others).

Say It with Percentages

1. Excellent (your top proficiency) skills, which resulted in _____ (%) increase/decrease in (sales, revenues, profits, clients, expenses, costs, charges).

2. Recognized as a leader in company, using strong skills to effect a/an (%) increase in team/coworker production.

3. Streamlined _____ (industry procedure), decreasing hours spent on task by _____ (%).

4. Used extensive _____ (several skills) to increase customer/member base by _____ (%).

5. Financed (%) of tuition/education/own business.

6. Graduated within the top _____ (%) of class.

7. Responsible for an estimated _____ (%) of employer's success in _____ (functional area/market).

8. Resolved customer relations issues, increasing customer satisfaction by _____ (%).

9. Eliminated _____ (an industry problem), increasing productivity by _____ (%).

10. Upgraded _____ (an industry tool), resulting in _____ (%) increase in effectiveness.

Say It with Dollar Amounts

1. Supervised entire _____ (a department) staff, decreasing middle management costs by _____($).

2. Purchased computer upgrade for office, saving the company _____ ($) in paid hours.

3. Eliminated the need for _____ (one or several positions in company), decreasing payroll by _____ ($).

4. Averaged _____ ($) in sales per month.

5. Collected _____ ($) in memberships and donations.

6. Supervised the opening/construction of new location, completing task at _____ ($) under projected budget.

7. Designed entire _____ program, which earned _____ ($) in company revenues.

8. Implemented new _____ system, saving _____ ($) daily/weekly/monthly/annually.

9. Reduced cost of _____(substantial service) by developing and implementing a new _____ system at the bargain price of _____ ($).

10. Restructured _____ (organization/system/product) to result in a savings of _____ ($).

Chapter 23

Ten Resume Myths Exposed

*L*ong-cherished notions deserve a second look in times of great change. Here's a brief examination of some popular myths.

The Only-One-Right-Way Myth

Perhaps you've read "inside wire" advice in which an expert insists that two ways exist to prepare resumes — the expert's way and the wrong way. But the experts don't agree. You'd think that after half a century of wrestling with the issues, by now everyone would be painting on the same canvas. Not so — the debates continue with theological intensity.

Squabbles concern topics such as these: Which length is best — one page, two pages, or more? Which format is best — reverse chronological or functional format? Which opening is best — objective or summary?

When I began writing about careers, I was puzzled by the great resume debates. Why were people landing interviews and jobs, despite their breaking various so-called rules of resume writing? Why was I seeing great resumes crash and burn, and trash resumes producing interviews and jobs? Finally, the dawn broke. *There is no one best way.* There are no absolutes in resume writing. There is only the best judgment of advisers, including myself. The reason career experts differ is because the human experience differs. For resumes, the old cliché is true: different strokes for different folks.

The best resume for you is the one that best supports your quest for a job interview. I offer suggestions and guidelines, but have you ever noticed how solutions to problems always seem to work better in books? The message: You may have to experiment a bit before you graduate into the FirstRate crowd.

The Myth of the 90-Minute Resume

Saying that a FirstRate resume can be written in 90 minutes or overnight is like saying Michelangelo could have made better time with a roller. Good work takes effort.

The No-Fun-at-All Myth

You need not always use a straight pitch, nor confine your creative input to a choice between white and ivory stationery. But when you feel compelled to come up with clever ways to catch an employer's eye, be dead sure you know your audience and how the resume will be received by the RezReader. If you apply to a traditional, conservative field such as banking or accounting, stick to the tried and true. Otherwise, your resume will be seen as frivolous.

If you decide to field a quirky resume that shows you put thought into it and didn't just grind it out, deliver it into the hands of hiring managers — not human resource department specialists, who are paid to screen out risky applicants; if you submit fluff stuff, you're risky.

The One-Page-or-Bust Myth

The fallacy that a resume must be kept to one page is a vampire myth: It just won't die and stay dead. Drive a stake through its heart.

The reality is: Your resume should be as long as needed to get your concise message across with zip and punch.

Human resource specialists recommend one pagers because they save reading time. Recognize that you and human resource specialists do not share the same goal. Their goal is to effectively screen applicants as quickly as possible. **Your goal is to present your qualifications as strongly as possible.**

Resume superstar Richard H. Beatty is another person who thinks that doctrinaire demands for one-page resumes shortchange job seekers. Beatty is president of Brandywine Consulting Group in West Chester, Pennsylvania, a corporate outplacement consulting firm. He says that after 30 years as a corporate employment professional, he believes that forcing individuals who have ten or more years of experience to shoehorn it into a single page will cause the "omission of major accomplishments and significant contributions." Beatty says, in such cases, a format of two pages is better.

Digital resumes raise other issues about length. Because your resume remains in databases for long periods of time, you will be considered for more than one job. Suppose you, a registered nurse, submitted a resume to a health facility for a specific job but missed out. Six months later a department manager may telephone the facility's human resources manager: "Sally, can you run a search for an oncology nurse?" If the word "oncology" is on your resume, you'll be considered for the job; if not, you won't. The more information you give, the greater the chances of an electronic hit. While you can accomplish this with an opening summary of KeyWords, somewhere in your resume each KeyWord must be supported by a citation.

My advice: One page for most new graduates, one to two pages for most people, and two to three pages for most senior executives.

The Fibs-Are-Fine Myth

Blowing smoke on your resume — inflating grades, inventing degrees, concocting job titles — is assumed to be risk free because nobody checks, and because the resume is not a legal document. Wrong. Once you lie, you have no easy way out. People do check. Trained interviewers are taught to ask you the same question several ways, spotting inconsistencies. Even if you fib your way into a job, your little lie is a time bomb in your personnel file — tick, tick, tick.

The Typewriter-Will-Do Myth

The difference between computer printouts and typewriter-produced sheets is obvious: The latter leaves the paper lumped with key impressions. In joining the computer crowd, you show yourself to be up-to-date and able to handle office demands for word processing, a serious concern for job seekers over 40.

The ultimate reason why your computer resume is a stand-out and your typewriter resume a throw-out is the finished product: You can make it flawless in a flash, without running to the office supply store to buy a bottle of white-out.

The Resume-Does-It-All Myth

Your resume is only one marketing tool in your job search that can help you get an interview. Once you get the interview, it all depends on you. *You* are what gets you a job — your skills, your savvy, your personality, your attitude.

The Resume-Is-to-Blame Myth

Maybe yes, maybe no. When your resume results in a telephone call from a recruiter, who doesn't issue a come-in-and-see-us invitation, suspect your experience or education. The no-interest response may be an intangible factor discovered in the telephone chat, causing the recruiter to think you're not a good match for the job. Or maybe your resume presents you as a FirstRate star, but your telephone manner doesn't deliver the goods.

If your resume results in interviews, but no offers appear on the horizon, maybe you've oversold yourself in a resume, or maybe you just don't know how to close the offer. Brush up on your interviewing skills. *Job Interviews For Dummies,* Second Edition (IDG Books Worldwide, Inc., by yours truly), can help.

The One-Type Resume Myth

As companies rush to use computers to process applicants (see Chapter 11), it becomes obvious that you may need more than one type of resume. You'll want a *scannable* (computer-friendly) resume heavy with nouns and graphically without frills (see Chapter 12) for computers, a *plain text* version (see Chapter 13) with no embellishments whatsoever for e-mail, and a *formatted* version loaded with action verbs, underlining, graphics and other bells and whistles for human eyes.

I suggest you set up all three types using scannable and plain text versions for electronic transmission and hold the formatted, graphically adorned, verb-rich resume to use when you hand deliver it to the recipient at an interview.

The Always-Expect-an-Answer Myth

In the old, old days before 1975, employers often sent nice, little typed letters to job seekers confirming their resumes were received and declaring the resumes would be held on file in the event that suitable job vacancies occurred. It was a nice, genteel touch. People just assumed they'd get an answer after spending time and postage to apply for a job.

But as human resource departments were cut back in downsizing adventures, the clerical hands to process those gracious notes weren't available. Job seekers didn't understand why employers failed to acknowledge their resumes: *Rude behavior, poor manners, thoughtlessness — why don't they at least say they received what I sent?*

As a result, career advisers, including myself, routinely suggested that job seekers follow-up with a telephone call that began with "Did you receive my resume?" When you don't get a letter or e-mail confirming receipt of your resume, that's still good advice. But, with technology in the picture, a related kind of myth is springing up.

Most automated resume management systems (the kind that intake and store for future retrieval your e-mail or computer-friendly resumes) effortlessly generate automatic responses. These responses basically say "Yes, we got your resume and here's what we're going to do with it ..."

The new myth arises when you get a computer response and think, "Good news, they're seriously considering me." Not so fast. You merely received an impersonal computer message that is cause neither for cheering nor dismay.

What changes when you receive an acknowledgement that your resume has arrived at its intended destination is the content of your follow-up. Unless you want to look like a dim bulb, don't pick up the phone and ask "Did my resume arrive?"

An e-mail follow-up by you is often more practical in today's harried workplace, but there are times when nothing beats the one-on-one voice contact the telephone provides. Regardless of whether you e-mail or telephone, in those cases where you already know they got your resume, find another reason to make contact. Additional information strengthening your candidacy is the most effective approach, but even a simple "Have you made a hiring decision yet?" beats an obvious question that makes you look like you're not paying attention.

Chapter 24

Ten (x3) Great Resume Tips

A FirstRate resume carries you upward and onward because it's faster, smoother, brighter, more focused — like you. Here are hard-hitting points to show what you've got.

Tips for Everyone

✔ **Specifically discuss *teamwork* in job descriptions, with examples and results.** RezReaders love this word. They like *team building,* too. Talk about participating in *tough tasks that help focus teams.* Speak of *trust as being essential to teamwork.* Say that you were *part of a team that succeeded in reaching a unified goal.* The difficulty comes in making clear for which portion of the team's production you can take a bow. You must separate your contribution from the group's. If you don't, you chance being looked upon as one who falsely claims credit for work you did not do. If you find room for hobbies, stick to teamplayer sports such as volleyball, softball, touch football.

✔ **Unless you're headed for a support job where leadership is a liability, give examples of leadership.** Even as organizational structures flatten by the sunlight hour, every team needs a leader. In the same vein, vision and drive are desirable characteristics. What did you originate, initiate, spearhead, or propose? What have coworkers praised about you? What suggestions have employers accepted from you?

✔ **Discuss an upward track record.** Without giving price tags, style yourself as a winner by mentioning that you received raises, promotions, and bonuses.

✔ **Answer the So What question.** This question is hidden and lying in ambush in every RezReader's mind. Forget sticking to the old name-your-previous-responsibilities routine. Every single time you mention a duty or achievement, pretend someone fires back: *So what, who cares, what does it all mean?* Imagining these questions is not pretending — these are RezReader responses.

Don't just relay what you did — spell out the consequences and implications. A medical technologist might say

- *Organize daily work distribution for effective teamwork of 12 lab workers; absorb and solve workload issues from previous shift.*

- *Monitor quality control; identify problems, find solutions; lab insurance rates, related to mistakes, lowered this year by 3 percent.*

- *Perform preventive maintenance on 14 machines on daily basis; reduced repair costs 8 percent over previous year.*

✔ **Showcase anything that you did in the top 5 percent of company performance ratings.** RezReaders are impressed with the cream of the crop.

✔ **Don't apologize on your resume for any weakness that you may observe in your professional self.** Until you can do something about it, like get additional education or experience, don't even think about shortcomings, and they certainly don't belong on your resume. You're an official FirstRater, remember?

✔ **Show how and whom you trained.** RezReaders appreciate the knowledge base suggested by the ability to teach. A smaller company in particular may be run by an entrepreneur whose nightmare is being forced to take time away from running the company to hire and train new people.

✔ **Study the resumes of people in your field.** Seeing how others have handled similar issues is a championship tee-up for writing your own treatment. Libraries have books of resumes for specific career fields. Or look at the thousands of resumes on the Internet.

✔ **If your career history looks like the fall of the Roman Empire, don't try to explain a lifetime of disasters on a resume.** Save your explanations for an interview. Use your friends and acquaintances to help you obtain interviews. Make the resume as brief and as adversity-free as you legitimately can. At the interview, be prepared to justify your moves, without becoming defensive, and be sure to provide good references.

✔ **Ask a business-savvy friend to read your resume before you send it out.** Prepare a list of questions regarding the comprehensiveness of your resume's explanations and job victories for your friend to answer. It's better to know sooner than later if you're rowing with one oar.

Tips for New Graduates

- ✔ **The number one tip for new graduates: Attend resume workshops.**
  Resume workshops are offered at your campus career center or
  vocational-technical school placement office. Whether you're an undergraduate or an alumnus, nothing beats a classroom setting.

- ✔ **Counselors at your school's career service center can help you understand the prerequisites that individual recruiters look for in their specific career fields. Target your resume to the prerequisites.**
  *If you cannot qualify for a prerequisite, try to figure out a compensatory
  benefit you offer.* For example, if your GPA is a little below the prerequisite, use an opening summary to hit hard on knowing the value of hard
  work — especially if you learned that value by holding a series of
  demanding student jobs while working your way through school.

- ✔ **Thicken your work experience by including all unpaid positions —
  internships, special projects, volunteer jobs. List them in chronological order in your *Work Experience* section.** Experience, or lack of it, is
  the biggest obstacle faced by graduates, especially those who are not
  employed before they leave school. Employers who don't cruise cam-
  puses may be especially reluctant to hire newbies; they fear that new
  graduates lack the experience to hit the floor running and become immediately productive. Statements like these are powerful agents on your
  resume:

  - *Sales: Sold $1,200 worth of tickets to college arts festival*

  - *Counseling: Advised 16 freshman students, as peer counselor*

  - *Public Policy Coordination: Coordinator for student petition drive to
    save California Cougar from sports hunting, gaining 2,000 signatures
    in 35 days*

- ✔ **Highlight your work experience that is most relevant to your intended
  future.** If you have more than two years of full-time professional experience, education should be placed at the bottom.

- ✔ **If you use an objective statement, make it clear what objective you
  have in mind.** Don't use a lofty statement of the absurd, like this one:

  - *I'm seeking a challenging position that will allow me to actualize my
    talents in saving the world, with good potential for professional
    growth and pay commensurate with my ability.*

✔ **Don't just identify your education and a laundry list of student jobs — use words that identify the skills you learned or used in school or at work.** "The skill-focused resume wins the [electronic] scanning game!" proclaims the *Journal of Career Planning and Employment,* a publication of the National Association of Colleges and Employers. In a sample resume, the computer found the following list of skills: *clerical, collection, Internet, maintenance, mathematics, property maintenance, quiz, taxation, Windows, Microsoft Word.* A resume-scanning computer can't find what you don't put in your resume. Think of it this way: SIJO — skills in, jobs out.

✔ **Awards, honors, and citations help.** Such items as scholarships, appointments, elections, chairs, and university faculty who hold you in esteem belong in your extracurricular activities or highlights section. Use reverse chronological order.

✔ **Show evidence of dedication and goals.** Many RezReaders perceive a lack of commitment and realistic expectations in recent graduates.

✔ **Include your GPA if it is at least 3.0 or high enough for employer prerequisites.** You can limit your GPA to the courses in your major, if necessary, but make it clear that's what you've done. Do not enclose your resume in a report cover or bulky package or attach school transcripts or letters of recommendation, unless they are requested.

✔ **Delete high school data unless it adds a unique fact to the total impression that you're creating.**

✔ **If an activity reveals skills, accomplishments, results, or the qualifications to support your intended job, include it.**

Tips for Seasoned Aces

✔ **Focus your resume.** For emphasis, I'll repeat that: Focus your resume. Concentrate on highlighting your two most recent or relevant jobs. Do not attempt to give equal attention to each of your past jobs. When your job experience has been diversified, your resume may look like popcorn in the making, a job-hopper tale of unrelated job after unrelated job. Focus and concentrate.

✔ **Strive for the aura of youth through concise, crisp writing.** Your resume ends before the RezReader's chin hits the desk. Avoid dated words such as *people person, self-starter,* and *go-getter.* Instead: *enjoy interacting with people, self-motivating,* and *motivated to succeed.* This is where you get your chance to show off a mastery of 30 Days to a New Vocabulary.

I have an infallible method to determine whether a term is an age give-away: Find a smart 25-year-old and ask, "Do you know what this term means?" If the answer is no, and the term is not a technical term specific to the job you're applying for, replace it.

✔ **Show that you are a tower of strength, that you recover from downturns with few scars.** Give examples of how you solved problems, recovered expenses, and learned to compensate for weaknesses in your working environment. Emphasize how quickly such adjustments occurred. Gray heads who have survived a few fallen skies are valuable assets in difficult times.

✔ **Use buzzwords, KeyWords, and industry terminology.** These words can show your familiarity with important issues in the industry to which you're applying. This tip works across the experience spectrum, but as a seasoned ace, you'll look especially unknowing if you can't talk the talk.

✔ **Demonstrate your political correctness.** This is especially important for positions that have contact with the public. Show that you are familiar with contemporary values by using politically correct terms wherever appropriate. Examples include *multiculturalism, diversity, global community, cross-cultural, mainstream, multiethnic, socioeconomic,* and *people with disabilities* (never *handicapped*). It's an age thing.

✔ **Try shipping your resume over the latest electronic mechanisms — World Wide Web and e-mail.** You'll help dispel any ideas that you're over the hill. See Part III for more on digital resumes.

✔ **Obliterate, annihilate, and liquidate ancient-history dates of your education.** Of course, the absence of dates sends a signal to people who are heavy readers: *This is an old geezer who read a resume book.* But at least it shows that you have sufficient faculties left to play the game. And it beats offering yourself up for sacrifice.

✔ **Assume that your previous job titles will be misunderstood and briefly explain them.** *Marketing manager* may really mean sales, market research, advertising, or all of the above. A regional manager at company A may be a district manager at company B. *Programmer/analyst* is meaningless until the hardware and software are specified.

✔ **Take responsible credit for your previous successes.** Show how you made a difference. Don't go modest on yourself but do go easy on the adjectives. Try to put an appraisal of your worth into someone else's mouth.

✔ **Read through your finished resume in search of anything — from a few words to whole sections — to eliminate or abridge.** For very experienced professionals, sorting out the most powerful resume points can be difficult. It's like being a gifted child — so many choices, and you're good at them all! You know what they say: *The longer the cruise, the older the passengers.*

JUDGMENT CALL

Special delivery: Way-over-the-line gambits

Creative resumes and cover letters are not widely appreciated. But doing something that sets you apart from the great masses of RezWriters can work if you are applying in a creative field, say advertising, marketing, or publicity.

A thoughtful touch may work better to subtly draw attention to yourself. Suppose you research the RezReader and learn of an avid interest in antique cars. If you can find an article on the topic, clip and send it as part of your cover letter, along with your resume. But don't send a book on antique cars — doing so would look like a bribe.

Among the following true stories, the "red shoe man" got the job; the others did not.

On-the-Shoulder Delivery

An in-your-face delivery is what an Ohio job hunter had in mind for his resume. He arrived at the employer's office disguised as a dry-cleaning delivery guy. Slung over his shoulder was a freshly laundered shirt in a see-through plastic bag. Attached to the bag was his resume and a "cover tag" that read: *I'd give the shirt off my back for an interview.*

ABCs of Resumes

A New York advertising agency media buyer smiled when she received a resume and cover letter buried in a box of children's blocks. The blocks spelled: Get Results!

The Red Shoes

A man's red tennis shoe arrived by courier to the Kentucky airline's employment manager. Stuck in the shoe was a resume and a note: *I'd sure like to get my foot in the door.* The ploy worked, and the pilot was interviewed. Within hours after the interview, a second and much smaller tennis

shoe arrived, obviously a child's. This note said: *Thanks for giving my dad the interview!*

High Flyer for Flier

A resume sent to a Kentucky airline human resource manager was attached to a "How to make a paper airplane" kit, trailing a banner that read "*I love to fly.*"

Squeaking Up

An Arizona company received a talking resume. The "press here" button (similar to that found on a talking greeting card), when pressed, caused the imbedded microchip to squeak out the message: *Read me! Read me!* A printed resume was attached.

Nice Try, No Brew

The resume as a miniature beer bottle label is now trite at a Colorado brewery. Ditto the resume as a menu to food companies or a wanted poster to most employers.

References Round-Up

In Illinois, an employment manager was startled to receive a woman's document of references longer than the resume to which it was attached. Each of five pages held three columns of names and addresses — must have been all 72 of her closest friends.

Stay in the Mainstream, Unless . . .

If you have a heavy-duty marketing mind and your approach suits the job you seek, try the resume road less traveled. Otherwise, don't pollute your earnest quest by sending resumes attached to carrier pigeons, or wrapped around a dozen roses, or glued to a chartreuse poster board with a photo of yourself in a bikini. Save your fine imagination for a friend's birthday party.

Chapter 25

Ten (x3) Common Resume Blunders

· ·

In This Chapter

▶ Gaffes anyone can make

▶ Mistakes common to new graduates

▶ Blunders that seasoned aces fall into

· ·

*F*or those who need resume help right this very second, here's a summary of serious resume gaffes to avoid. As in Chapter 24, I've organized the fumbles by groups to which they most apply: anyone, new graduates, and seasoned aces. Although some mistakes occur in one group more than another, it won't hurt you to read every single screwup. It might even help.

Gaffes That Almost Everyone Makes

These are mistakes that anyone can make, regardless of age or experience level.

Excessive vagueness

To keep their options open, many RezWriters mistakenly obscure their intent by stating an objective too broadly, such as "a position in the paper industry." FirstRaters focus and target, as discussed in Chapter 9. FirstRaters who offer a summary of qualifications, rather than an objective, define areas of expertise.

Don't expect an employer to dig through your resume to find out whether your qualifications match the job's requirements.

Poor organization

Advice from a California boss: "If it looks complicated, I lose interest." She loses interest in most resumes, she says, because they're tough to comprehend. Double-check your work for construction and focus. Open with either a summary of your qualifications or an objective statement. Headings should be vivid and distinct from one another. Enter each entry under the appropriate heading; that is, put apples with apples, and oranges with oranges — no fruit salad. You don't want to carry the liability of looking disorganized.

One rule of good organization: **Find a theme and make certain that every item in your resume supports that theme.**

Lack of examples

People who make claims without backing them up with verifiable details are not as credible as those who do back up their claims. Credibility increases with the "storytelling" of solid examples. Rack your reporter's brain for concrete examples of each claim: Ask "Who?" "What?" "When?" "Where?" and "How much?" Weave a convincing tale.

Missing achievements

The missing achievements gaffe is related to the storytelling concept: You must give results. Without results — measured in some way (numbers, percentages, dollar amounts) — that show how you successfully reached high points in your work efforts, your workplace victories will sound as though you made them up.

Irrelevant information

Why tell the RezReader more than the RezReader wants to know? Chapter 7 discusses the obese resume; basically, skip personal information if it doesn't add to the image you're trying to convey. You're selling your professional hours, not your entire life. While you're on litter patrol, delete nontransferable skills and duties and bypass references.

Typos and grammatical oversights

Even the sharpest eyes miss mistakes, so proofread for errors in five steps.

1. **Spell- and grammar-check on the computer.** That's a good start, but don't stop there. Spelling and grammar checkers won't find words that aren't there, ones inadvertently left out. Check the punctuation and grammar: A period often looks like a comma, a *he* like a *she,* and an extra gawky space is often overlooked; a computer won't catch these errors. Furthermore, checkers will approve spellings that represent the wrong word, as this comical but true example:

As indicted, I have over five years of analyzing investments.

---

2. **Slow down.** Use a ruler to read the entire document aloud, line by line. Speed kills FirstRate resumes.

3. **Read backward, from the bottom up.** Start at the lower-right-hand corner, reading backward from the bottom to the top, word by word. You may be a little goofy when you're finished, but, as you are not reading for content, you're likely to spot word warts and other blemishes.

4. **Get a second opinion.** Beg a hawkeyed word mechanic to proof your resume yet one more time. If neither of you can spell a word or find it in a dictionary (I've never understood how you can look up a word you can't spell), change words.

5. **Read for content.** Do one more read-through, this time for clarity. To illustrate how words can trip over themselves, smile at these misspoken signs discovered by travelers in England:

   - *In a Laundromat:* "Automatic washing machines. Please remove all your clothes when the light goes out."

   - *In a dry cleaner's store:* "Anyone leaving their garments here for more than 30 days will be disposed of."

   - *In a conference room:* "For anyone who has children and doesn't know it, there is a day care center on the first floor."

   - *In a rural pasture:* "Quicksand. Any person passing this point will be drowned. By order of the District Council."

   - *In a safari park:* "Elephants Please Stay In Your Car."

Not checking small details

A number of "little" mistakes cause big rejections. By itself, no single, small flaw is deadly (unless you're applying to be a proofreader). The trouble comes when you add several together on the same resume, collectively zeroing out your chances. A few examples:

- ✔ In a job history, unless you worked for well-known companies, briefly tell the RezReader what the company was in business for. What product does the company make, or what services does it provide?

- ✔ A weak opening produces disinterest.

- ✔ Using telephone numbers answered by small children or by people who say, "She no longer works here," doesn't help your search.

- ✔ Highly unusual paper may make you look "too different." Die-cut, oddly shaped, colored paper and fancy binders raise the question of why, if you're such a hot candidate, you need a graphic designer to package you. High-gloss presentations are wasted on electronic resumes — job computers have no taste. Or maybe they do.

An exception to the statement that no one small thing ends your chances is a handwritten update or correction in the margin of your resume. This horrible mistake makes you look lazy and, by itself, is likely to be disqualifying.

Information overload

Many RezWriters forget that *resume* literally means *summary* — to sum up. Their documents suffer from terminal length. Don't let wordiness wreck your resume. Start with a highly selective choice of content and then streamline each item. For example, the statement "Performed managerial functions and delivered employee training" slims down to "Management and training."

Admittedly, it's hard to boil down a lifetime to a page or two or three. Mark Twain said that it took him only five minutes to write a 30-minute speech, but 30 minutes to write a five-minute speech.

Imitating a flat organization

Try to portray yourself as having an upwardly mobile track record even if you've held lateral jobs for years. Mention raises (do not specify amounts) and increasing responsibilities, even if your title never changed. It's human nature for RezReaders to prefer people who seem to be doing better and better over those who are same-o, same-o.

Failing to list all appropriate KeyWords

Because writing digital resumes is a new bag of tricks to most people, legions of RezWriters do not list every single KeyWord describing their fitness for specific jobs. See Chapter 13 for more information on identifying KeyWords. New ones are created all the time — so pay attention.

Gaffes Common to New Graduates

New graduates and job rookies are more likely to make these mistakes.

Not meeting image standards

If you present your resume personalized with little printing errors, such as off-centered or crooked placement, ink blotches, or flaws in the paper itself, you flunk. Chapter 10 tells you how to avoid looking like an amateur.

Aiming too high too soon

An imperfect understanding of the world off campus may cause you to indicate in a job objective that the job you're seeking is over your head. You'll be dismissed as naive if you write such aims as becoming "an operations manager in a well-established organization." *Manager* isn't quite the word for an entry-level person, although graduates with several years of experience leading up to a managerial position could swing it. *Well-established organization* may exile you not only from dynamic start-up companies but cause a perception that you expect a lot — perhaps more than an employer can deliver.

Overcompensating with gimmicks

Don't tart up your resume to cover barren qualifications. Avoid using exotically original language, such as the "eyelinered genius," a term used by a business graduate applying for an entry-level marketing position in the cosmetics industry. The term may be colorful, but charm communicates better in the interview.

Making employers guess

Employers hate it when they are asked to decipher your intent. Merely presenting your declared major and transcript excerpts is not enough to kick off a wowser job search. Either add an objective to your resume or add a skills summary directed at a specific career field. Show potential employers that you've thought about your next move.

Leveling the experience field

Your resume is no place to give every job equal billing. Many rookie resumes are little more than rote listings of previous jobs — subpoena server, TV satellite dish sales representative, waiter, landscape helper, and computer coach, for example. Separate your jobs into an A list and a B list. The A list contains the jobs that relate to what you want to do next, even if you have to stretch them to make a connection. Briefly mention jobs on the B list in a section called *Other Experience* or *Other Jobs*.

Stopping with bare bones

Some rookies look at a sheet of paper and then at their embarrassing, bedraggled collection of instant-rice jobs in their paid-experience stew. Desperate to get *anything* on paper, they settle for name, rank, and serial number (employer, job title, and dates of employment).

The solution, says one of my favorite resume authorities, Yana Parker, is to pull in *all* experience, including volunteer and part-time gigs. Sit, think, think some more, and pull in all relevant skills pointing in the direction in which you hope to thumb a ride.

Hiding hot information

Data entombed is data forgotten. RezReaders remember best the information you give first in a resume, not the data smushed in the middle. Decide what your selling points are and pack that punch up front. Ask three friends to read your resume and quickly tell you what they remember about it.

Highlighting the immaterial

Featuring the wrong skills and knowledge attached to each job is an error that many first-time RezWriters make. Suppose you want to be a multimedia producer, and one of your work experience citations is your three years of effort for campus student theatrical productions. You painted scenery, sold tickets, and designed sets. It's the experience in designing sets that helps qualify you for multimedia producer, not painting scenery or selling tickets. Costume yourself in the skills that will help an employer imagine you playing a role in the sought-after work setting.

Ignoring employers' needs

Even the smartest rookies, who may have survived research challenges as rigorous as uncovering the body language of ancient French cave dwellers, make this mistake. They forget to find out what employers want from new hires. In addition to following the standard research techniques mentioned in Chapter 3, if you can find former or present employees willing to share company culture information *from the inside,* go to the head of the FirstRate class.

Writing boastfully

Appearing to be too arrogant about your talents can cause RezReaders to question your ability to learn as the junior member on the team. As one recent graduate says, "It's hard to work in a team structure when you're omniscient." Even when you're just trying to compensate for your inexperience, avoid terminology that comes across as contrived or blatantly self-important. If you're not sure, ask older friends to describe the kind of person they think your resume describes.

Gaffes Common to Seasoned Aces

When you've a long job history, you're more likely to need updates on the following issues.

Using old resume standards

Many seasoned aces, still working on last decade's calendar, have an outdated concept of what a resume should be. An ace office neighbor recently expressed surprise when I told him to leave out his personal information, which once was standard fare on resumes. "Oh, I thought personal information was supposed to humanize you," the ace said. Busy RezReaders and job computers don't care that you are a par golfer or play tennis; this kind of personal bonding information comes out at the interview.

Sell performance!

Revealing age negatively

Don't blurt out your age. Your mind-set should be: Start with ageless — you can always move to senior. Do not put old education first on your resume (unless you are a professional educator). Avoid listing jobs with dates older than 10 or 15 years. If you must include dusty jobs, de-emphasize the dates or omit them, as noted in Chapter 17. You can summarize old jobs under a heading of "Prior to 20—" and avoid being too specific. Alternatively, you can include all jobs under functional headings. Try not to describe older jobs in detail.

Using words of the past

When you are changing job fields, it's a gigantic error to use jargon from your earlier jobs. Former members of the armed services, in particular, must be alert to militaryspeak that leaves civilian recruiters puzzled. *WESTPAC, O-700,* and *cammies* mean virtually nothing to civilian employers. Write in civilianese. The same warning holds true for anyone who formerly worked in an industry that uses jargon not commonly understood by others. Substitute the jargon with translations or equivalents.

Choosing the wrong focus

Choosing the wrong focus is a problem shared with new graduates who have a string of jobs in their background and fail to choose those that best address the hoped-for next job. Try this approach: Use the worksheets in Chapters 8 and 9 to draft an encyclopedic master resume. The number of pages doesn't matter — you'll never use it in its entirety. Each time that you're tailoring a resume for a specific job opening, review your master resume and choose those jobs most directly related to your new goal.

Lacking a summary

Because of the extensiveness of your experience, your resume may be unwieldy without a summary. Usually, it is superfluous to use both an objective and a summary, but exceptions occur. Suppose you're fed up living as a city slicker and want to move to a small town where agribusiness is dominant. Your objective may take only one line — "Wish to work as internal auditor in the farm equipment industry." Follow that statement with a one- or two-paragraph summary of why you are qualified. Think of a summary as a salesperson's hook. It describes some of your special skills, your familiarity with the target industry, and your top achievements. For examples of summaries, see Chapter 9 and the sample resumes in Part VI.

A guide: **If your objective and summary are two ways of saying the same thing, dispense with one of them.**

Appearing low-tech

Seasoned aces who do not have computers still type resumes; others with computers have old-fashioned dot matrix printers. Their resumes are often stopped at the door. RezReaders like crisp, attractive layouts that only a computer and laser printer can create. Trade a dinner for resume services from a friend, use a computer free at a library, rent a computer by the hour at a copy center, or pay a professional to do your resume.

Moanin' and groanin'

The stress of job hunting at midlife and older tempts many seasoned aces to reveal professional troubles on their resumes. *Big mistake.* Unless you were forced out in a downsizing, skip reasons why you left. When you must explain them in the interview, take the high road and stay positive.

Not considering delivery questions

You've done a real FirstRate resume and dropped it in the mail. That may be a shortsighted move.

If you have already contacted a RezReader who is interested and if the job is important to you, consider delivering your resume by hand or by courier service or use the modern means described in Part III.

When should your resume arrive? Mondays are busy days, and Fridays are termination days; try for arrival on Tuesday, Wednesday, or Thursday.

If you send your resume to a hiring manager, send a duplicate to the human resource department. Note this effort in your cover letter to the hiring manager, which means that not only is the human resource specialist not treated disrespectfully, but the hiring manager gets to keep your resume as a constant reminder of you instead of having to send it "down to HR."

Not following up

Job seekers who fail to follow up after sending out their resumes stop short of their goals. Always telephone within a few days, making certain that your resume arrived. Ask whether your resume was received and what happened to it. Was your resume scanned into a database? Were you a match for an open position? Was your resume passed on to a hiring manager?

If the answer is "Yes, you're in the database," expect to receive written confirmation within a couple of weeks. (If your resume wasn't received, send another resume and start the cycle again.)

Once your resume is in the database, don't bother calling back the human resource department — you're automatically considered for all open job requisitions. If your resume was passed on to a departmental hiring manager and you can pry loose the manager's name, try calling that manager early in the morning or late in the day.

If the company does not scan resumes into a database, tactics change. Some very smart career advisers suggest calling every ten days until you're told that you'll be arrested if you call again. (You probably won't get the job, either.)

But busy employers insist that, unless you're in a field such as sales and need to demonstrate persistence, call two weeks later and then no more than once every six weeks. Their argument: An excessive number of telephone calls brands you as a nuisance. Instead, try sending interesting short letters, faxes, or e-mail with additional facts about your qualifications, or ideas to solve a problem you know the company is facing, or just to express your continuing interest in working for them.

Not correcting mistakes

The time to correct a mistake is before your gaffe sends your resume to the isolation ward. The causes of mistakes are: I didn't know it was wrong . . . I didn't think it was important . . . I didn't care enough to find out.

Chapter 26

Ten Tips for Choosing Professional Resume Help

· ·

In This Chapter

▶ Selecting a personal resume pro

▶ Looking over online resume builders

· ·

*T*o use a professional resume writer or not? That is the question.

No! "I don't recommend professional resume services. I say it's best to write your own. Interviewers have certain expectations from the resume and if professional resume writers create a false professional image, it can result in an immediate clash with the interviewer's expectations of the person. A barrier rises between the parties because the interviewers feel they have been fooled and the person has wasted their time," wrote a college counselor on *JobPlace,* an Internet discussion site for counseling professionals.

Yes! Another counselor in the same discussion responded: "Seldom would I recommend that job seekers write their own resumes, regardless of their intelligence or writing ability. They lack objectivity and often spin their wheels trying to focus on the wrong things, either over-reacting or under-reacting to their experiences."

These two opinions differ because effectively packaging yourself on paper is not a naturally acquired ability, but a skill you purposely set out to learn. Years ago I was lukewarm to the idea of hiring someone to write your resume. But I've come around to a different position on the issue. While I still urge you to organize your own material to prime your mind for job interviews, the riptide of ruthlessness in today's job market makes it imperative that individuals think of new ways to win. A good resume pro can help.

Using a Resume Pro

In an age of personalization — personal financial advisers, personal trainers, personal tax preparers, personal lifestyle coaches — why not a personal resume pro? Prime candidates for resume services are first-time resume writers, people with a checkerboard history, and people who haven't thought about resumes in years. Follow these tips to choose a personal resume pro wisely.

Resume firm or clerical service

Many *clerical services* do a nice job of word processing your resume for a fair price of $50 or more. A clerical service is a good option if that's all you need.

Most people need more, and clerical services are in a different business than *professional resume firms.* Clerical services sell clerical processes. Resume firms sell specialized knowledge in fluently verbalizing what you want to do and the evidence that proves you can do it.

A resume pro knows a great deal about the business of marketing you to employers, has the latest trends and buzzwords on tap, and coaches you through old potholes in your history. The best pros know how to do digital as well as paper resumes. Writing resumes can cause anxiety in some people who, lacking confidence in their writing ability, fear the document lacks quality. Resume pros recognize this form of risk-avoidance and hold your hand through anxious times. That's not surprising.

Resume writing is a kind of poetry — the art of using high-impact words with spitfire sales power — and few of us are poets.

The seeds of your anxiety also promise a stressful harvest because a resume forces you to see yourself as you actually are. You may face yourself for the first time and be dismayed to learn you have not gone as far in life as planned, or you may discover distressing ability gaps. In short, you are faced with the thought: *This is who I am, this is the best I can make of what I've done in my past, and this is the basis on which I must build a future.* To calm such anxiety, you can hire a resume pro who knows how to use words that sell you with a flourish — boosting the confidence you need to move your job search forward.

Signs of reliability

Once you've decided to use a resume professional, how can you find a good one?

1. **One of the two best ways to choose a resume pro is following the recommendation of a satisfied customer.**

2. **The other best way is asking for a referral from a local career center consultant, recruiter, employment agency consultant, outplacement consultant, or copy shop manager.**

   If you're being laid off, inquire within your corporate human resource department. These people often know who is doing the best work.

The fact that a resume firm has been in business for a long time and has done thousands of resumes is no guarantee of competence — but it's a sign that some customers must like what they do and have spread the word. The acceptance of major credit cards is another indicator of stability. Check with the local Better Business Bureau for the number of unresolved complaints; if the number is more than a couple, move on. Merely asking the firm for its interview success rate wastes time — how can the rate be proven?

Free initial consultation

Request a free, brief, get-acquainted meeting. A telephone encounter serves the purpose, but you may prefer a face-to-face session. Speak not to the boss or a sales representative, but to the writer. The same firm can have good and poor writers. Ask the writer what general strategy will be used to deal with your specific problems. If you don't hear a responsible answer, keep looking.

A responsible answer does not imply discussion of the specifics of how your resume will be handled. Much like people shop retail stores to look at the merchandise and then order from a discount catalog, people shop professional resume services to pick writers' brains and then write their own resumes. Resume pros caught on to this move and developed laryngitis. Moreover, it is irresponsible for a resume pro to go into detail about how your resume will be handled until more is known about you. You want to know the general approach — the kinds of strategies discussed in this book.

 Another tip-off is the technology issue. Ask prospective resume writers: *Do you know how to prepare and send resumes by e-mail? Do you send them in text or attachments (see Part IV)? Do you know how to add lots of KeyWords to make resumes computer friendly?* Positive responses suggest the professional is on the leading edge of technology and, by inference, on the leading edge of the employment industry.

Dependence on forms

Most resume pros ask you to fill out a lengthy form with details — much as new patients do in a doctor's office. (FirstRaters can substitute the worksheets in Chapter 8.) That's a good start, but it's far from enough. Eliminate the firms that don't offer dialogue with the writer. The resume pro should interview you to discover your unique experience and strengths. You and the resume pro are colleagues, sharing a task.

The problem with form dependency is you may merely get back your own language prettied up in a glitzy format. That's not what you want a resume pro to do for you.

The cost issue

Prices vary by locale, but expect to pay between $15 and $500 for a core resume. Never pay by the page — longer isn't better. Find out the rate for branching out from a core resume to create a targeted resume specifically for an individual employer or occupation. Perhaps you'll want to target in several directions, requiring several resumes — can you get a fleet price? What is the charge for minor alterations? What is the charge for an update two years later? What is the cost for extra copies?

Speaking of copies, don't be swayed by an offer of, say, 100 copies for a discount price. Even if it seems like a bargain, you may want to make changes long before your inventory is gone.

Beware of a resume professional who gives lifetime free updating — it's unrealistic to expect quality work when the professional isn't being paid.

Serving alumni is a trend sweeping across the country in college and university career services. Most of these services offer some form of resume writing assistance free or at a low cost.

Samples

If you make a site visit, ask the resume pro to show you samples of the writer's resumes. Look not only at content, but at production values. Hire a resume pro who has invested in state-of-the-art technology: a good computer and a laser printer. The resume pro doesn't need showy graphics programs or 30 typefaces with 300 fonts. Nor does the resume pro need a high-end copier — copy shops are plentiful. You are judging the quality of content, layout, word processing, paper, and printing.

Taking aim

For maximum impact, target each resume you send out to a specific employer or career field. Do it either by customizing your resume or by using a core resume in tandem with a targeted cover letter.

Make sure your resume pro understands this concept. You need a resume that has "you" written all over it — *your* theme, *your* focus, and *your* measurable achievements — all matched to a career field you want. Skip over those who sell the same cookie-cutter papers over and over.

Avoid resume pros who offer assembly-line presentations, virtually indistinguishable from thousands of others created by the service. Ignore resume pros who plug your information into a fill-in-the-blanks standard form, garnished with prefab statements. Double ignore those who try to cover the sameness of their work by printing them out on 11-inch x 17-inch parchment paper and folding them into a pretentious brief. Employers use these resumes for kindling.

Also, be careful of the pro who caters to you instead of to your target audience. A heavyweight resume pro warned me that some resume services cater to their customers, not their customers' customers — with fancy brochures, excessive color, and whimsical paper.

Your industry and its jargon

Even the most talented resume pros may not understand your industry and its language. Why should a resume pro learn a career field on your nickel? (This issue is especially pertinent in technical fields.) The obvious question is direct — *How many resumes have you written for the construction (or another) industry?*

If the pro is a neophyte in your industry, try bartering instruction in your field for a price break. Or find a resume pro who already knows your field.

About certification

The *Professional Association of Resume Writers* (www.parw.com) is a for-profit organization. The organization was the first in the resume-writing industry to certify professionals who meet the required criteria of experience and examination. Those who become certified are allowed to use the title Certified Professional Resume Writer (CPRW) after their names. The association maintains a membership directory on its Web site from which you can choose a member to construct your resume. Now that distance communication opportunities are available, you can easily work with any resume writer, regardless of location.

The *National Resume Writers' Association* (nrwa.com) is a not-for-profit organization. It started as a spinoff of the above organization but is now totally independent. Many professional resume writers maintain memberships in both organizations. Those who become certified through this group are allowed to use the title Nationally Certified Resume Writer (NCRW) after their names. Certification must be renewed every three years. Visit the organization's Web site to locate members who are well qualified to write your resume.

Must you hire a certified resume writer to get a masterful work? The many changes in personal marketing today — online and computer-friendly resumes, electronic profiles, portfolios, computerized interviewing — suggest that someone interested enough to strive for professional recognition is a cut above and could serve you well.

But that likelihood doesn't mean end of story. A number of noncertified resume writers are excellent professionals as well. For instance, Yana Parker, the unofficial queen of resumes (`www.damngood.com`) doesn't belong to either organization. In my book, Yana Parker is the world's best resume writer — a mentor from whom I learned a great deal.

Using Online Resume Builders

I no longer get questions asking which resume-creating software is the best on the market, presumably because too many free programs are available on the Net.

On the theory that you get what you pay for, you may be wondering how good are the resume builders offered online at virtually all substantial Web sites? (See Chapter 14.) Not great, but not bad.

The online resume builders can be very useful with one Big If:

If you remember to think for yourself and not assume the technology will bring to light your most marketable qualities.

The automated resume builders are designed to benefit the recruiting side of the employment industry, not the job seeking side. So if you use a free resume builder as your chief template offline as well as online, be alert to making amendments as needed. Here's a couple of examples: If the template calls for a section on references, delete it. If you prefer to use a skills summary, lose the job objective section if it calls for much more than a position title.

Poor Resumes Are No Bargain

Appreciate the hidden costs of a poor resume: A hack job can cost you good job interviews. When the finished product is in your hands, you should be able to say:

- ✔ This is a FirstRate resume — it makes me look great! It looks great!

- ✔ This resume doesn't leave out any skills that are targeted to the jobs I'm after.

- ✔ I like reading my resume; it won't put the RezReader to sleep.

Chapter 27

Your Ten-Point (Or More) Resume Checklist

In This Chapter

▶ Making sure you have a FirstRate paper resume

▶ Making sure you have a FirstRate digital resume

*B*efore going public, rate your resume. Check the box in front of each item only when your resume meets FirstRate standards. The point value for the specific resume factor is printed below each box.

Some jobs are best scouted in traditional ways; others rely on technological prowess. What follows is an attempt to bridge the familiar paper trails and the new technology tracks. Here is a scoring key:

✔ The highest total you can reach for a paper resume is 240 points. In traditional job search, 240 points meets the FirstRate standard.

✔ The highest total you can reach for a digital (e-mail, scannable) resume is 290 points, what you need to achieve FirstRate rank.

✔ The highest total you can reach for a resume that goes both ways — paper and digital — is 300 points, which is a FirstRate winner.

Format

☐ Correct format for your situation; for example, reverse chronological when staying in same field or functional when changing fields.

20 pts.[1]

Focus

☐ Overall impression: You appear focused, not desperate to take anything.

10 pts.

☐ Says what you want to do, proves you have qualifications to do the work.

10 pts.

☐ Has theme — targeted to specific occupation or career field.

10 pts.

☐ Opens with job objective (job title preferred) or related skills summary; leads from strength — opens with strongest sell statement.

10 pts.

☐ E-mail resume: Strong resume title of 50 characters or less (Sales rep/12 yrs exp/printing/San Diego) grabs attention.

10 pts.

Achievements and Skills

☐ Your skills relate to the skills needed to do the target job or career field; try to match skill for skill; express in powerful, selling words.

10 pts.

☐ For each skill, cite at least one achievement.

10 pts.

☐ For each achievement, measure by numbers, percentages, or dollar amounts; quantify any statement you can.

10 pts.

☐ Speak of results, not just responsibilities.

10 pts.

Length

☐ RezRookies: 1 or 2 pages; RezAces: 2 or 3 pages.

10 pts.

Appearance

☐ Paper resumes: White or eggshell paper. Open layout: white space, minimum 1-inch margins best, headings, bullets — RezReader does not have to dig through crowded, unreadable blocks of text.

10 pts.

☐ Digital resumes: Unless employer requests otherwise, resume is included in a single unified document in plain text (ASCII) following a cover note. If resume is offered in attachment (Word document, for example), it is an additional presentation noted in the cover message. (ASCII).

20 pts.[2]

☐ Digital resume substitutes: On a job Web site, the electronic profile (a standard Web-generated form, rather than your self-created resume) is filled out according to instructions posted on the site. But caution was exercised in providing data (like salary history/requirements) that may hamper favorable pay negotiation.

10 pts.

☐ Digital resumes: Familiar, scannable typefaces; no handwritten updates.

10 pts.

☐ Digital resumes: Each line of text no longer than 65 characters.

10 pts.

Contents

☐ Gaps in employment handled with FirstRate care, including filling in with unpaid work.

20 pts.[3]

☐ Contains KeyWords (nouns) — especially on digital resumes.

20 pts.[4]

☐ Contains GoodWords (action verbs) — especially on paper resumes.

10 pts.

☐ Special problems handled with FirstRate care.

10 pts.

☐ Features education and training if related to target job.

10 pts.

☐ Groups irrelevant jobs/long-ago jobs/part-time/temporary jobs briefly or eliminates them.

10 pts.

☐ Translates acronyms, technical jargon, or military lingo into English when necessary.

10 pts.

☐ Contains no unnecessary elements — eliminates the word "resume" at top, references, "references available" statement, photos, and designs for noncreative career areas.

10 pts.

Proofreading

☐ No typos, no grammar disasters — you and others have read it.
20 pts.[5]

Comments

---

[1]   20 points for selecting the most favorable format for your situation.

[2]   20 points for conforming to computer technology; resumes that do not conform are dumped in an e-mail and electronic compost heap. Their fate is worse than rejection — they are never seen by human eyes.

[3]   20 points for good gap management. Gaps, a growing problem in today's economy, can be disqualifying.

[4]   20 points for KeyWords that permit a computer search to retrieve you. Without matching KeyWords, your resume rots in electronic limbo.

[5]   20 points for clean copy. Typos are hot buttons to many employers — two goofs, and you're gone.

Give Yourself an Award for Accomplishment

I certainly enjoyed sharing these tips and pointers with you. Perhaps we'll meet again in my other two books, *Cover Letters For Dummies,* 2nd Edition, and *Job Interviews For Dummies,* 2nd Edition.

And now, you've come to the end of these pages. I hope you found in them the strategies and techniques that will bring you ever better jobs — exciting jobs! — throughout your lifetime.

Already you've earned an award for accomplishment by taking in the personal-marketing ideas offered here. So here's a "ribbon" you can cut out and pin on as a reminder that you now write FirstRate resumes. Color it blue.

— Joyce Lain Kennedy
Resumes For Dummies, 3rd Edition
Published by IDG Books Worldwide, Inc.

Index

● ●

• *D* •

IDG BOOKS WORLDWIDE BOOK REGISTRATION

Register This Book and Win!

We want to hear from you!

Visit **http://my2cents.dummies.com** to register this book and tell us how you liked it!

- ✔ Get entered in our monthly prize giveaway.
- ✔ Give us feedback about this book — tell us what you like best, what you like least, or maybe what you'd like to ask the author and us to change!
- ✔ Let us know any other *For Dummies®* topics that interest you.

Your feedback helps us determine what books to publish, tells us what coverage to add as we revise our books, and lets us know whether we're meeting your needs as a *For Dummies* reader. You're our most valuable resource, and what you have to say is important to us!

Not on the Web yet? It's easy to get started with *Dummies 101®: The Internet For Windows® 98* or *The Internet For Dummies®* at local retailers everywhere.

Or let us know what you think by sending us a letter at the following address:

For Dummies Book Registration
Dummies Press
10475 Crosspoint Blvd.
Indianapolis, IN 46256

...FOR DUMMIES ™

BESTSELLING BOOK SERIES